To Be Loved

Ain't Gonna Be Denied

By

Ronald D. Steele

Copyright © 2022 Ronald D. Steele

All Rights Reserved

ISBN: 979-8-9877565-1-5

Table of Contents

Part I i

  Big Risks, Small Gains i

  Chapter I 1

    Sheriff Road: Lost and Turned Out 1

    Forging Bonds: A Tapestry of the Tribe 9

    Spingarn High School's Enigmatic Allure 15

    Young and Angry Find Sanctuary in Melodies 19

    Surviving Gunshots at Home on The Wall 24

    Longing for Love: in the Beauty of an Angelic Majorette 27

    With a Little Scissors & Syrup – I got a Job 29

    Yearning to Get Away: Learning to Drive 31

    The Awakening: The MLK Uprising 33

    Need to Get Away: My First Car 35

    My Car is Stolen: I Know Who the Thief Is 37

  Chapter II 39

    The Boy That Turns Men into Slaves 39

    First Gov't Office Job: Mental Hospital 43

The Bully: Not in My Neighborhood 49

Downtown Stores Belonged to Us 53

Malcolm X: Woke 61

The Black Awareness Organization: Anger II 64

Some Had to Die 67

Chapter III 69

Finished School and Prepared for What? 69

Buy a Gun, Steal a Car and Rob a Bank 72

30 Day Notice to Buy Home or Move 76

Pat: What's Love Got to do With It? 78

Chapter IV 87

Things Ain't What They Used to Be 87

Wake Up Everybody: Activist or What 91

Breaking Barriers, Making Progress 93

Father: Ngina Steele 100

Inmate 110

Chapter V 115

No Place to Be Somebody 115

February 23, 1972 149

Chapter VI 153

On Target: The Judge 153

Chapter VII 183

All the Way Down to Get Up 183

The Court Responds to My Letters 196

Back on the Block 203

No Longer at Ease 212

Confronting the Past 215

Positive Thinking as Remedy? 236

Chapter VIII 248

Confronting the Past: Unveiling Trauma 248

Rebounding 271

From Ex-Con to College Student? 282

Fear and Intimidation Constants 292

In Search of Love: Roberta 312

Kwanza 314

Fallback Career in Retail/Sales 316

A Father's Need to Know 318

On Holiday: Back to Prison? 320

Facing 15 Years in Prison, Again 324

Suing the MPD 326

Promotion Offer: In the Suburbs 334

Love & Tragedy 340

Holiday at Take It Easy Ranch 343

Working for the Government, Again 346

The Green Sheet 351

Chapter IX 359

Love of Self: Ain't Gonna Be Denied 359

Ngina, My Daughter 369

Racism at Work 371

New Style Best Friends 378

Controlling Destiny 381

Relationships' Emotional Challenges 385

The Green Sheet: Managing Editor 389

Who's Who Among Students 394

Chapter X 399

The African American Writers Guild 399

Public Affairs Specialist 403

MPD Brutality Suit Won 405

Oakcrest Towers: Tennis Community Meetup 412

Aminata 416

Suing Employer for Discrimination 424

Writers' Guild President.. 429

Tennis Alchemy 438

HHS Discrimination Complaint Settled 446

U.S. Mint: Internet Project Manager 447

The Trauma 452

Dedication

This memoir is dedicated

to parents who aim to

make their children feel loved.

You grow the nation; and

You rock the world.

Preface

In the pulsating heart of the Nation's capital, amidst the whirlwind of change from the 1950s to the 1980s, emerges a story of resilience, redemption, and transformation. "To Be Loved" is a coming-of-age memoir that navigates the labyrinthine alleys of Northeast Washington, D.C., as a lone soul forges his path through the smoldering crucible of life.

The tapestry of my childhood in the bustling streets of Washington is painted with the hues of longing and desire, where my heart sought the love that was missing from the hearth of home. Like a moth drawn to the flame, I spiraled into the seductive embrace of the streets, finding solace and success in their dark corners, aiming to master every challenge I embraced, including crime.

As a teenager, I metamorphosed into a petty hustler, haunting downtown patrons with phantom heists and stealing treasures from glittering department stores. Alas, fate had other plans, and at the tender age of 19, I found myself shackled by a 15-year prison sentence for a crime the victim said I did not commit!

Imprisoned on the precipice of despair and contemplating the abyss of suicide, I discovered salvation within countless books' pages.

Like a phoenix rising from the ashes, I transformed my life, forged goals, and charted a new course that led me out of the iron bars within 18 months of the 15-year-sentence. With unwavering determination, I used the stigma of an ex-convict as a ticket to the hallowed halls of higher education, where I earned a B.A. in communications and recognition as a Who's Who Among Students at American Universities and Colleges.

My journey led me through the corridors of power, where I served the administration of seven Presidential Cabinet Secretaries, and into the realm of words, where additionally, I flourished as a freelance writer and president of The African American Writers Guild. I stood defiant against the torrential storms of socio-economic challenges, from the tumultuous tides of family, race, and history to the swirling vortex of politics, and found a way to minimize the scars of past trauma and rise above the mire.

With "To Be Loved," I hope my story will ignite a spark within others to seize destiny's reins and control their destiny. Let not the opinions of anyone cast a shadow upon your true self; you have the power to define yourself. Embrace that power, and you unleash your limitless potential. Remember, it's not the beginning of the game that defines us, but the strength and grace with which we reach the finish line.

Part I
Big Risks, Small Gains

"To be loved to be loved

Oh what a feeling

To be loved..."

Excerpted from "To Be Loved," Berry Gordy, Jr., Gwendolyn Gordy Fuqua and Tyran Carlo

To Be Loved

Chapter I

Sheriff Road: Lost and Turned Out

The most important things that I had learned, by age 15, was that I had to fight for respect, and if I wanted anything in life, it was up to me to get it; nobody was gonna give my poor ass anything; and I wasn't gonna be denied anything, either.

Love was the one prize that I couldn't win through force or cunning, and everything else seemed to bear a price tag that grew heavier with each passing year. When my desires outstripped my meager means, I resolved to acquire them by any means necessary, walking the razor's edge between right and wrong. By then, I had been trained to see authority as people who would rarely enable my ambition but only tell me why I couldn't have what I wanted.

My unyielding attitude, fueled by the fires of ambition and circumstance, led me to prison at age 19 years old; even though the victim declared my innocence. But even in the cold embrace of a prison cell, I discovered the resilience to write my way to freedom. Within 18 months, I emerged from prison, driven with ambition, I used what was supposed to have been proverbial yolk around my neck, my ex-con status, as a key to unlock the doors of higher education.

In only five years, I defied the odds and shattered the chains of expectation, graduating from the University of the District of Columbia with a

Sheriff Road: Lost and Turned Out

B.A. in communications. I stood proudly among the Who's Who Among Students at American Universities and Colleges, carving my path into the middle class.

In hindsight, it seems I was always destined to be a writer, a calling born from the painful echoes of my upbringing. As I grew older, by extension, I became acutely sensitive to the injustices and imbalances that plagues society. I searched relentlessly for the reasons behind them, determined to mend the broken world around me and rescue myself.

My journey from the unforgiving streets to the hallowed halls of a university was a testament to the transformative power of self-determination and the unyielding belief in one's potential. As a public affairs specialist, writer, and photographer, I wielded my pen and camera like mighty swords, cutting through the darkness of ignorance and illuminating knowledge and injustice.

More about that later, for at 15, I plunged into the swirling cauldron of another hood: Deanwood, Northeast, Washington, D.C. It was the summer of 1967, a time of change and upheaval when my Mama embraced her dreams and rose from the ashes of welfare dependence with the grace of a phoenix.

She completed cosmetology training at an adult school, earning her license and renting a booth in a beauty salon on Georgia Avenue, NW. Her newfound independence as a self-employed beautician brought fresh air to our lives, lifting us from the clutches of poverty for the first time in nine long years since my father's passing at age 36.

Our family of eight siblings migrated from a cramped two-bedroom

To Be Loved

house in far northeast D.C. to a grand, ancient fortress of stone and brick in Deanwood, a three-bedroom haven that would shelter us from the life's storms. Our new community was a mere ten blocks from our old neighborhood, a stone's throw from the Division Avenue that intersected with Sheriff Road as part of my Afro newspaper route three years prior.

The U4 Sheriff Road Metro bus line traced a winding path to its terminus at Eastern Avenue, the District Line that separated the District from Maryland. There, a vibrant corner teemed with life and energy, pulsating with the comings and goings of local pedestrians.

Across the dividing line of Eastern Avenue, Sheriff Road led to Fairmont Heights and Chapel Oaks, MD. This bustling corner served as the community's business district, a colorful tapestry of shops and services that included Jock's Liquor, Dr. Robinson's medical office, Ince Texaco, The Laundry, Shabazz Dry Cleaners, Mr. Cobb's Delicatessen, and Al Frank beauty salon. A three-foot brick wall bore witness to our laughter and conversations as we perched upon it, soaking in the sights and sounds of our ever-changing lives in this corner of the world.

Sheriff Road was a mosaic of semi-detached brick homes and modest four-and eight-unit apartment buildings. Our new home, the largest we had ever had, meant that Frank, my mother's friend, joined our family, and for the first time, the girls and boys each had their own rooms – a taste of luxury we had never experienced.

No longer limited to a small backyard, we embraced the entire

Sheriff Road: Lost and Turned Out

community as our "playground." The neighborhood became my home, my haven in a world filled with the opportunity to be accepted and perhaps even loved.

I enrolled in the newly-built Roper Junior (now Ronald Brown College Preparatory) High School, eager to escape the violence and horrors that haunted the halls of Kelly Miller Junior High in Lincoln Heights. But even as I stepped through the doors of Roper in Deanwood, the anticipation of relief turned to trepidation as the specter of fear reared its head once more on the first day of school.

In the first week of school, chaos erupted in the cafeteria like wildfire as students gang-jumped Mr. Davidson, the beloved gym teacher. It was a scene of unparalleled anarchy, one that left me reeling and questioning the very fabric of my reality. I had never seen anything like it, not even at Kelly Miller, where the suffocating presence of Lincoln Heights gangs cast a dark shadow over the school.

Kenilworth Projects' gangs rivaled their Lincoln Heights counterparts, and the violence had escalated to a new level – targeting a teacher, of all people! As Mr. Davidson crumpled to the floor, a boy snatched a chair, and slammed the helpless teacher. The Kenilworth boys, their point made, scattered like leaves on the wind, leaving behind in their wake shock and fear.

Rumors circulated like toxic fumes, whispers that Mr. Davidson had begun carrying a gun, a desperate measure to protect himself from the students he was tasked with teaching. The reputation of Kenilworth Projects' guys was so menacing and destructive that even the police dared not tread on their territory.

To Be Loved

Roper's welcome was a baptism by fire, an unnerving introduction to a place where the angriest, most disruptive, and most intimidating students ruled like tyrants. Born from the ashes of shattered homes and scarred souls, these kids sought solace in the school – a refuge where they could unleash their pent-up rage. Anger simmered beneath the surface; a dormant volcano ready to erupt.

In this unforgiving world, survival hinged on the delicate balance of asserting one's presence while avoiding the crosshairs of gang or community rivalries. To remain invisible, to fade into the shadows, was a precarious dance, and on occasion a fine line that determined whether one would become a victim or escape unscathed.

I discovered an unlikely comrade in Ronald Matthews at school, amidst the swirling chaos of man impoverished and disillusioned youth. He was an island of vitality and purity in a sea of lost souls, a lighthouse accompanying me through the storms of adolescence. Like me, he wielded a fearless determination when chasing his dreams, leaping into the unknown in a world that taught us to tiptoe with trepidation.

I once fancied myself a prodigy, yet the courses I pursued were less about cultivating my intellect and more about traversing the path of least resistance. In the ninth grade, I enrolled in a typing class, enticed by its illusory simplicity and, above all, the tantalizing prospect of a homework-free course. The allure was akin to a siren's song, irresistible and beguiling.

In stark contrast, my English class felt like navigating the treacherous

Sheriff Road: Lost and Turned Out

labyrinth of a sunken ship. Mr. Valley, our teacher, resembled a gaunt, wiry man with the unsettling aura of a praying mantis. Beneath his seemingly innocuous facade lurked a tormented, depraved soul. Hushed voices echoed through the corridors, sharing tales of sordid after-school encounters in Mr. Valley's apartment, where desperate students bartered their dignity for improved grades or pocket change. Like a cunning spider, he wove a tangled web of manipulation and deceit, trapping his students in a vortex of darkness and humiliation.

One fateful day, Ronald and I lingered after school, our conversation meandering like a lazy river in the summer sun. As we strolled past a home economics classroom, the irresistible scent of a freshly baked cake wafted through the air, wrapping its seductive tendrils around our senses. Through the doorway, I spotted the teacher's large brown leather purse, deserted atop a desk. A nefarious spark ignited in our minds, and we transformed, plotting to snatch the prize without arousing the vigilant shepherd's suspicion.

Mrs. Johnson, the teacher, had just wrapped up a cooking class, and I swiftly concocted a plan. I would distract her with idle chatter while Ronald stealthily swiped the purse. He agreed, his eyes gleaming with opportunity.

"Whew, that sure smells good! What is it?" I inquired, feigning curiosity.

"It's a German chocolate cake. I'm baking it for a class. The class made the cake. I'm just baking it since it takes so long."

"Boy, that smells good! Maybe I should take a home economics class," I remarked, at a time when only women were attracted to the course, and while

To Be Loved

keeping a watchful eye on Ronald as he slid the purse from its perch.

"Well, I think I'm gonna look into it," I continued, "You may see me sooner than you think."

"Well, you would be most welcomed in my class, young man," the teacher replied, basking in the unexpected adoration.

With the swiftness of shadows, Ronald and I slipped away, our hearts pounding like tribal drums, only to find ourselves face-to-face with the principal, Mr. Greene, as we emerged from a nearby stairwell. Trapped, we froze like deer caught in the blinding glare of oncoming headlights.

Unbeknownst to us, the teacher had noticed her missing purse almost as soon as we left her classroom. She had alerted the principal, who ordered all doors locked as they marched towards her classroom. Cornered in his office like villains, Mr. Greene demanded we reveal the puppet master behind the heist or face expulsion; we were both expelled.

The home economics teacher expressed her disappointment in us, mourning the lost opportunity for me to join her class. She lectured us on the perilous gambit, explaining that her credit cards could have plunged us into a legal abyss. Had we not been apprehended, she would have summoned the police, and we might have been branded with criminal records. I thought, 'Credit cards?' We had no idea what were credit cards. I craved cash; I would have discarded the rest of her purse like trash.

Mama meted out a severe punishment, and I knew I had earned it. At 15,

Sheriff Road: Lost and Turned Out

I was tumbling down a slippery slope, blissfully ignorant of the tempest I'd become. Having no clue as to the reasons for my behavior. But the storm had yet to reach its peak. Once caught in a downward spiral, the descent continues until you find the strength to slam on the brakes—if you have any.

I became acquainted with the local boys within weeks of my family's move to Sheriff Road. I had shared the first grade with David Williams years prior. David resided at the junction of Sheriff Road and Dix Street with his erudite twin sisters, an older brother who oscillated between hostility and indifference, and a father who was a playful, nurturing presence in our lives.

United with my newfound comrades, we ventured through the labyrinthine alleyways of our adolescence, searching for a way to rise above our circumstances. But, like a ship caught in a whirlpool, we were steadily pulled deeper into the darkness. With each passing day, our path grew more treacherous, our futures more uncertain, and our dreams, although we thought they were getting closer, in fact, were becoming more distant.

In those formative years we learned life's most valuable lessons: that friendship can anchor you in the most turbulent of seas, that courage can be found in the unlikeliest of places, and that, sometimes, you need to risk it all to find your way home.

To Be Loved

Forging Bonds: A Tapestry of the Tribe

On a frosty evening, Nutbush from Kenilworth ventured to Sheriff Road to visit his beloved Helen Lee, flanked by four friends. They settled in The Laundry, and since I wasn't ready to go home, I lingered, captivated by guys engaging in a risky game with a cigarette. They pummeled the person left clutching the smoldering butt when the flame fell to the ground.

Nutbush beckoned me to take his puff, guaranteeing he'd bear the brunt if I faltered. It felt like an initiation into their Kenilworth fraternity. Fortunately, another lost, but individuals from Kenilworth, Clay Terrace, East Capitol Street, Deanwood, and other districts began to convene at the crossroads of Sheriff Road and Eastern Avenue.

Our motley crew swelled to around 20, each hailing from a smaller faction within a larger community. The Kenilworth crew, including Gilbert, Smooth, Nutbush, and Tiger, flaunted their sartorial splendor. The Grant Street squad, like the Smiths, were brawlers but lacked a keen fashion sense. The Clay Terrace collective, featuring Jake and Roach, both stylish and enterprising.

I began to attract a crew of my own, enlisting Robert for his serenity and Tyson for his cunning thievery. Their loyalty evoked memories of my childhood companions, John and Gary Henry. Our crew gravitated closer to the Kenilworth ensemble than the others.

Sly was our fashion maestro, his sole purpose being to look impeccable. His style lent an air of resourcefulness to our crew. We were like the musical

Forging Bonds: A Tapestry of the Tribe

sensation The Temptations alternating as the front man depending on the situation.

Smooth exuded calm and composure, never entangling in brawls. Tiger, conversely, was a firebrand, never hesitating to confront adversaries. Gilbert, towering above us, symbolized might but lacked an affinity for hustling or combat. Tyson's forte, like Sly's, was his social prowess, while Robert maintained a quiet and reticent demeanor.

One day, as I saddled on the wall in front of the beauty salon, soaking in the neighborhood's vibrant pulse, Robert appeared beside me. We instantly connected, and his cool demeanor and sharp attire commanded respect. Though not a hustler, Robert was an exceptional listener and evolved into my closest confidant. Living nearby, we'd commence our daily adolescent rendezvous on the wall. Life was a constant whirlwind, and everything was a hustle.

What enthralled us about risk-taking was that, generally, adhering to the rules seemed insipid. And compliance reaped no rewards. When someone defied conventions, we deemed them ingenious and audacious. Naturally, as youngsters, we reveled in it! We idolized "crazy" individuals. It was a badge of honor to be deemed crazy enough to risk everything to have or do what you want. Crazy!

David's father embodied this craziness. One night, he whisked his son and a few friends on a breakneck ride along the I-295N highway in his 1960 Ford Galaxy 500 convertible. He accelerated as though the devil himself pursued us. The crisp night air caressed our faces, and our adrenaline surged. Suddenly, Mr.

To Be Loved

Williams slammed the emergency brake, sending the car into a wild 180-degree swerve. The car screeched to a halt, facing the distant, oncoming traffic. Shocked, we fell silent. The approaching vehicles rapidly closed the gap.

Mr. Williams sprang into action, executing another U-turn in the right direction, and we sped away. Our collective silence shattered abruptly, dissolving into laughter. Our uncontrollable spin seemed like the punchline to a ghastly joke. The exhilarating "near-death" experience left us all buzzing as cars whizzed by. We were now certain that Mr. Williams was indeed one crazy dude.

David frequented a dusty basketball court behind an apartment building on Division Avenue near his abode. We'd shoot hoops in the evening and sometimes into the night.

However, boxing held a special place in my heart. I only partook in other sports for their social currency. After a round or two of basketball, I'd stroll down to Sheriff Road to mingle with the boys. The game's dust and grime clung to my hair and clothes, often necessitating a trip home to freshen up before rejoining the fray. I rarely wanted to go home, except to eat and sleep. It dawned on me that I didn't particularly appreciate getting dirty, too. So, I suspected my time with David would be wanning.

Mama never mastered the art of driving, so Frank and one or more of my siblings would pick her up from work daily. The journey to fetch Mama was a family affair, akin to visiting my eldest brother Mitchell at Lorton Youth Center, except in that case, the ride felt interminable. Upon arriving at Lorton, we'd endure

Forging Bonds: A Tapestry of the Tribe

multiple checkpoints and prolonged waiting to see him. Finally, catching a glimpse of Mitchell made all the effort worthwhile.

Mitchell didn't move to Sheriff Road with the family. He had briefly returned home while we resided on 58th Street but was caught again. This time, he was charged with burglarizing a teacher's home in Clay Terrace. Convicted, Mitchell was sentenced to 18 months. By now, I understood his modus operandi. Mitchell was hustling and paying the price for getting caught.

On other occasions, I'd have Mr. Cobb's Delicatessen's pinball machine nearly levitating to the amusement of onlookers. I reveled in the machine's rhythm. The timing and sounds it produced thrilled me. The cacophony of accumulating points, fused with the pinball machine's flickering lights. I'm convinced I adored the experience because it sounded like a success symphony.

A week before my anticipated ninth-grade graduation, I strolled through the school's parking lot, chatting with a buddy while puffing on a cigarette, when someone bellowed from behind.

"Mr. Steele! You're out of here!" A furious voice exclaimed. The wavy-haired Mr. Coward, the student counselor, and disciplinarian, admonished, "We don't tolerate kids smoking on school grounds!"

I extinguished the cigarette and trailed him back into the building to his office. Consequently, I was expelled. It signified that I likely wouldn't graduate and might fail the ninth grade due to this expulsion. Worse still, it spelled another harrowing thrashing at home with a vinyl-coated clothesline, extension cords,

To Be Loved

belts, or braided switches.

I returned to Roper a week later to collect my report card. The school year had concluded, and I was certain I had failed the grade. It was a haunting echo of the fourth-grade incident that led to my expulsion one-day shy of the school year's end. I would run away from home rather than accept another whipping from my mother in the absence any love.

"What's your name?" The office secretary inquired.

"Ronald Steele," I replied.

She scanned the graduate record and declared, "Congratulations. I will fetch your diploma and report card."

I had triumphed! The secretary handed me my diploma! My joy could rival any graduate's. I shook hands with everyone in the office and bid farewell to Roper Jr. High School as a student for the last time.

Upon returning home, I announced, "Mama, I passed!" hoping for some form of affirmation from my mother.

"Put it on the table. I'll look at it later," Mama responded, preoccupied with styling my sister's hair.

Despite the lack of immediate celebration, I relished my achievement. With my diploma, I embraced the future, ready for whatever adventures awaited. Little did I know my life would continue to be a thrilling roller coaster ride filled with camaraderie, risk, and the pursuit of "love." And as I stepped out of the familiar confines of Roper Jr. High School, I carried with me the friendships,

Forging Bonds: A Tapestry of the Tribe

lessons, and experiences that would shape the person I was to become.

To Be Loved

Spingarn High School's Enigmatic Allure

In the autumn twilight, the silhouette of Joel L. Spingarn High School, alma mater of NBA greats Elgin Baylor and Dave Bing, cast a long shadow from the hill at 24th Street and Benning Road, NE. It stood sentinel, shadowed by Phelps Vocational High School, Brown Jr. High School, and Charles Young Elementary School, with the historic Langston Golf Course all but invisible across 24th Street.

One day, I found myself wandering into Phelps Vocational, drawn by curiosity and the hope of seeing Robert, who was studying barbering there. As I drawn to an auto mechanics lab, the gears of time seemed to grind to a halt. A full-size, transparent, plastic engine model from 1957 captivated me as the instructor demonstrated its inner. Although I marveled at the ingenuity, I couldn't help but feel a pang of sadness, realizing that the technology had been outdated by a decade.

This moment of revelation mirrored my experience at Spingarn, where our education was supplemented by the past, like forgotten relics left behind by a bygone era. English books from the 1950s and Kelly Miller Junior High School inkwell desks whispered a tale of feigned progress.

The excitement of a new school year, with its social whirlwind, fashionable attire, and anticipation of forging new friendships, quickly faded into the monotonous grind of daily attendance. I found solace in the tactile pleasure of new textbooks, pencils, pens, and notebook paper. But even these small joys paled

Spingarn High School's Enigmatic Allure

compared to the magnetic allure of Wiggins Hamburgers Carry Out and Rip's Pool Room, nestled across the street on Benning Road.

These establishments teemed with the hustle and bustle of teenage life. Girls flocked to Wiggins for juicy hamburgers, crispy French fries, and the rhythmic melodies of a jukebox playing the latest records. The boys, naturally, were drawn to the girls and the chance to share a soda and a smile. Meanwhile, Rip's Pool Room was the stomping ground for the neighborhood's hustlers, who strutted like peacocks adorned in alpaca sweaters, gabardine slacks, and diamond rings. They commanded attention as they arrived, driving their gleaming Cadillac Eldorados and Lincoln Mark IIIs, embodying new money and untamed ambition.

Eager to immerse myself in this glamorous world, I'd sneak away during lunch hour to shoot pool with the up-and-coming players. As a kid, I had learned to shoot pool at the recreation center, shooting flat rings into the pockets. I made the transition from kid pool to adult pool seamlessly. No one had taught me adult pool. The challenge and individual skill required in pool were akin to boxing, with its solitary requirements, and it was easy to fall in love with the game. Victory or defeat determined who would pay for the time on the table, further fueling my desire to excel at the game. I had learned amid the drama that I could excel at anything I put my mind to.

The bittersweet taste of reality struck when we learned that Hank Summer, my former next-door neighbor from 58th Street, had gone Missing in Action (MIA) and was presumed dead in Vietnam. A heavy sadness weighed on

To Be Loved

me as I mourned the loss of a young life, barely 18 or 19 years old, and the devastation faced by his family. Yet, amidst the sorrow, I couldn't help but feel a grim sense of relief that his prediction of my demise by age 18 had been proven false. He had done all of the things right, and he was gone before I.

The Vietnam War left an indelible mark on everyone. The survivors returned home with haunted, bloodshot eyes and a shattered sense of self; forever scarred by the horrors they had witnessed. The once-proud soldiers now faced a cold, unfeeling society ill-equipped to provide civilian re-entry support, especially for Black veterans. Responsibility, unemployment, nightmares, and heroin welcomed them home.

Stories of harrowing encounters with the devil in Vietnam poured forth from the lips of these fractured men. Tales of deception and betrayal swirled like a malevolent fogas. They recounted how the same children who sold them cigarettes by day would transform into deadly assailants under cover of darkness. The relentless persistence of the Viet Cong, who seemed to multiply and outwit the Americans at every turn, serving to underscore the futility of the conflict.

Back home, the nation was in upheaval as demonstrations against the war and the insidious roots of discrimination spread like wildfire, fueled by a demand for change. Turmoil reigned as society grappled with the aftershocks of this tremendous upheaval. But amid the chaos and uncertainty, a flicker of hope and promise burned, struggling to illuminate the darkness that enveloped the nation.

Spingarn High School's Enigmatic Allure

The tides of national change were swirling around us. As we navigated the turbulent waters of adolescence and the shifting landscape of our world, I clung to the hope that we, too, could rise above our circumstances and find our own path to success. In Spingarn halls and the streets that surrounded it, we learned valuable lessons that would stay with us long after we left the shelter of the school's walls.

As we pursued our dreams and aspirations, we were shaped by the events around us, the experiences that tested our resolve, and the people who left indelible impressions on our hearts. Within this crucible, we forged our identities, emerging stronger and more resilient, ready to face the challenges ahead in our journey through life, or so we had hoped.

To Be Loved

Young and Angry Find Sanctuary in Melodies

In the intricate tapestry of life, our crew was a cluster of frayed threads, a motley collection of teenagers, mostly boys, who had been estranged from our families and spurned by our parents for one reason or another. As we navigated the labyrinth of adolescence, we hid the feelings that gnawed at our self-esteem, burying them deep within our souls. We were like secret agents, disguising our emotions, always on the lookout for potential threats. But, like water seeping through a dam, these feelings would inevitably escape their confinement, seeking an outlet in the most unexpected places.

Music was a sanctuary, a hidden realm where we could express our emotions without exposing our vulnerabilities. A melody was like a secret handshake, allowing us to communicate our pain and longing without betraying our true emotion. When a song came out that resonated with our hearts, we would use the third person to talk about it, deflecting attention from our own emotions. "Oh, man! That record, right there -- that's baddd, man! I like the part that goes..." Or we'd sing the verse or chorus repeatedly, our voices merging with the lyrics like rivers flowing into an ocean, soothing some unspoken ache within our hearts. It was as if these songs were keys to unlocking Pandora's Box of emotions that festered within us, a balm to soothe the scars left by our parents' rejection and or abuse, scars that manifested in other, more dangerous ways.

One day, as my crew and I strolled up Sheriff Road, a man stumbled into our path, reeking of alcohol and defeat. In a swift, unexpected movement, Smooth

Young and Angry Find Sanctuary in Melodies

unleashed a punch that toppled the drunken man like a felled tree. The rest of the crew pounced on him, following through with their own blows, a tempest of fists and fury. I alone stood back, a silent observer, wondering what drove Smooth, among the most benevolent guys among us, to lash out at this helpless figure. Was he striking at the specter of his father or some phantom embodiment of authority? Was he punishing the image of the absentee father for his abandonment? Or was he retaliating against the memory of a childhood marred by whippings and other forms of violence? The truth remained as elusive as a shadow dancing in the twilight, an enigma that would haunt me for years.

On another occasion, we were on a bus, returning from a party at Tyson's father's house, his sanctuary from the fractured world of divorce. Denise, Valerie, and Sylvia were with us, regaling us with tales of the lecherous man who had flashed them before we got on the bus. We laughed, assuring them that we would mete out justice, exacting vengeance for their honor. When we stepped from the bus at the end of the Sheriff Road line, the man followed suit, unwittingly stepping into our court of justice.

With his towering 6'5" frame and nearly 200 pounds of force Gilbert, struck like a thunderbolt, knocking the man to the ground. We swarmed him like bees on honey, vindicating our girlfriends by stripping him of his dignity, wallet, watch, and rings, leaving him battered, clad only in his long johns. As we fled the scene, laughter echoing through the night, I couldn't help but feel a pang of guilt.

To Be Loved

I took no pleasure in the violence, but the stolen watch on my wrist felt like a badge of honor, a token of the camaraderie I needed.

Our crew was a band of misfits, each of us a wayward ship tossed by the stormy seas of life, searching for a safe harbor in the storm. We clung to one another like driftwood, hoping to find solace in our shared despair. Like the frayed threads of an old quilt, our families, were unraveling at the seams. Our parents, unable or unwilling to provide the love and nurturing we craved, left us to seek comfort in the streets, wherever we could find it.

It was a world where vulnerability was seen as weakness, and emotions were like open wounds, hidden from view, festering beneath the surface. We found solace in the melodies of our favorite songs, the lyrics giving voice to the love and longing that lay buried in our hearts. Like a balm to our wounded souls, music offered us refuge from the often-bitter reality of our lives.

The songs that blared from the radio made us feel like love was all we needed. With the risks, neglect, and abuse that enveloped our young lives, the songs were mainly about the pursuit of love; which made the longing for love all the more urgent, although we had no path to love; no training in it. And, Black artists were corralled to love songs, just as Black people were redlined into ghettos.

You're "All I Need To Get By, Higher and Higher, When a Man Loves a Woman; I Was Made To Love Her; My Cherie Amour, Ain't No Mountain High Enough, My Girl, Tracks of My Tears, La La Means I Love You, Get Ready, I

Young and Angry Find Sanctuary in Melodies

Could Never Love Another, What Becomes Of The Broken Hearted, I Wish It Would Rain" and on and on. Wasn't more going on in our community?

I learned about love through the songs. Little did I know that the soothing melodies set us up, intoxicating us to become brokenhearted, expecting so much from love, although we would receive so little, nothing like the songs had led us to believe. And the anger and resentment that simmered beneath the surface of our young hearts would not be contained. It burst forth in sudden and unexpected acts of violence, like the strike of a serpent, lashing out at the world that had forsaken us. It was a desperate protest, a futile attempt to assert control in a world that seemed determined to ignore or deny us.

Our troubled lives played out against the backdrop of the streets, It was a world where the strong preyed upon the weak, and the weak banded together for protection. But there was no honor among thieves, and betrayal was an ever-present threat, lurking in the shadows like a thief in the night.

And yet, amid life's challenges, there were moments of joy and camaraderie, fleeting glimpses of innocence and wonder. We laughed and joked, teased and flirted, oblivious to the ticking time bomb within each of us, searching for the right moment to explode.

But the sands of time were slipping through our fingers, and the day of reckoning was drawing near. As we stood on the precipice of early adulthood, our choices would determine our fate, for better or worse. Would we succumb to the

To Be Loved

neglect that threatened to consume us, or find the strength to break free from the chains that bound us to our past?

The answer would lie within each of us, hidden deep within the depths of our souls. The path to redemption was treacherous and uncertain, fraught with danger and despair. But there was hope, a glimmer of light in the darkness, a chance to rise above the pain and suffering that had defined our lives.

For in the crucible of our struggles, we would forge a new destiny born from the ashes of hampered dreams. And in the process, some of us would learn the true meaning of strength, resilience, and the indomitable spirit of the human heart.

Surviving Gunshots at Home on The Wall

One evening, Robert and I sat on the wall, talking and watching people go about their business. I told Robert that I wouldn't mind becoming a bus driver someday, as it seemed like a good job where you could get paid well and meet people.

As we talked, Lester, a middle-aged man who cleaned Al Frank's Beauty Parlor and lived in the back, came out for air. He was an intelligent but troubled man who kept to himself. I tried to make him smile with a comment about the visitors to his home, the beauty parlor, but he abruptly walked back into the salon. Robert sensed something was off and urged me to leave. We started running, and suddenly, we heard what sounded like firecrackers behind us – Lester was firing a gun at us. The shooting stopped when we reached the 51st Street corner, out of breath and in shock. We never considered calling the police, which was against the hood code. Looking back, it was likely a blank gun.

Another time, we were sitting on the wall late at night when a man living in the house next to the wall burst out of his front door, firing a gun. We immediately ran, hiding behind store entryways and eventually seeking refuge at Ince's gas station. We narrowly escaped getting shot, we thought, which was both terrifying and thrilling.

Puzzled and adrenaline-pumping, I asked Robert what the incident was about. He reminded me that the man had previously told us to stop making noise

To Be Loved

under his bedroom window, and apparently, he meant it. It was likely another blank gun. We got the message. We agreed to be much quieter from then on, at night, not wanting to provoke any further incidents.

Brother Sibley, the manager of Shabazz Cleaners, was a middle-aged fine dresser, who occasionally spoke to us about unlocking our potential by joining the Nation of Islam. A rare adult figure who looked us in the eyes and treated us teenagers with genuine care, he was always respectful. Yet, his talks were laced with the refrain, "The Honorable Elijah Muhammad teaches us..." which, to me, rang like a discordant note in a symphony.

Please don't misunderstand me; I admired the way the Muslims carried themselves, with an air of clarity, intelligence, and focus. They abstained from smoking, drinking, and pork, and their ladies wore modest dresses. But their mantra hinted at a uniformity and rigidity I couldn't embrace, like trying to squeeze myself into a mold that didn't quite fit. At 16, relinquishing my fun and committing to a mission felt daunting. Their views on non-Muslims also unsettled me. Like a bird soaring through the sky, I longed for freedom and originality that I feared would be caged within the confines of a doctrine.

One day, at the wall, Tyson showed up with a motor scooter. Eager to try it, I hopped on and we sped down the sidewalk, with him on the back, feeling like the kings of the road. As we approached the corner of 51st Street, with the wind whispering in my ears, suddenly, a police cruiser materialized behind us, flashing its searchlight and patrol lights. Our hearts raced in fear, and I turned the

Surviving Gunshots at Home on The Wall

throttle, launching us into a high-stakes chase that felt like a scene from an action movie.

Despite the odds, I was determined to outmaneuver the cruiser, drawing upon memories of my go-cart as a kid racing down Eads Street Hill. With Tyson clinging to me, we sped around the corner at breakneck speed, praying that no vehicles would emerge from the dark bend. But I had rather face the wrath of a hospital bed than the cold walls of a police precinct, I reasoned.

Luck smiled as we rounded the corner without incident, completing a wide arc through an open, debris-strewn lot. After hitting a bump that sent us airborne, we landed on our feet, sprinting. Tyson and I split up, each disappearing into the dark.

Stealthily, I slipped home, changed clothes, and emerged to join the crowd of spectators, Tyson among them, to watch the police take control of the stolen bike. We exchanged a knowing high-five, having cheated fate once more in a thrilling game of cat and mouse.

To Be Loved

Longing for Love: in the Beauty of an Angelic Majorette

I thought I was in love with a girl living one block over on Just Street. She had black hair and was fairly light-skinned. She reminded me of all the beautiful ladies of Disney lore: Sleeping Beauty, Snow White, Cinderella, etc. She was a majorette at Spingarn. She looked angelic. I wanted her so bad I could barely swallow around her. What could I say to her? How do you nurture a relationship beyond the basics? I had never learned how to love. I was so bad. She was so good. I wanted the most beautiful girl to see something positive in me; to validate me. I would see her at `school and go into a daze, almost. I saw her in a classroom once and stared through the door pane, being late for my class, watching her until she noticed me, and then I would leave. Weird! If I looked at her long enough, I thought she might see me and be impressed with the depth of my love for her, which I imagined my eyes had reflected, if not my face. Or, I thought, if I stared at her long enough, I might think of what to say to her. I never thought I could be scaring her with this funny behavior. All I could think of was how angelic she looked. But that wasn't enough! I couldn't offer to take her home and meet my family. Similarly, I couldn't imagine her wanting to take me home to meet her family. They would probably ask me many questions.

Later, I heard she was having a relationship with Thomas. Thomas was a dwarf nerd. Smart, even athletic, but he wasn't good-looking, didn't dress as fly

Longing for Love: in the Beauty of an Angelic Majorette

as me, didn't have a crew, and didn't have style. I knew she would have been better off with me. I looked at Thomas with envy briefly. Then, I admired him because even though I didn't understand it, he had the least to offer her. Yet, he mustered the courage to approach the baddest babe and succeeded with her.

Sharon Smalls, whom I considered too young, was a nice girl. She was neat, a little cherubic. She would be in the walkway of her apartment building, not far from the wall. Occasionally, she would sit on the wall before all my boys would come up there. Or else, she would assemble in front of her apartment building door with other young cuties. I'd catch her staring at me occasionally, or I would see her girlfriends and her looking at me. And they would snicker the way girls do when one of them likes you.

To Be Loved

With a Little Scissors & Syrup – I got a Job

At the age of 15, I stood in front of the mirror with hair clippers, ready to take the plunge. My brother, Mitchell, had taught me the art of cutting hair, and ever since, this skill has served me well, saving both time and money.

One Sunday evening, Mitchell took it upon himself to show me how to find a job, flipping through the Yellow Pages like an explorer navigating a treasure map. His persistence led us to the Ascot Restaurant, a Greek establishment next to the Warner Theater. Mitchell, ever the prankster, crafted a fake mustache from hair clippings and syrup to make me appear older for the job interview. Mitchell, was the closest person I had to a father figure; he had a way with my mother: she never punished him for anything he did. So, I trusted him in saying that we would fool a prospective employer into thinking I was 18.

Wearing my newfound disguise, I ventured into the restaurant to meet Mr. Lukas, the owner. He probably admired the audacity of a young teenager trying to pass for an 18-year-old to get a job. He hired me immediately, and I quickly began my foray into the work.

My new colleagues were a mix of Black kitchen staff and Greek or Persian wait staff, most of whom were college students. I quickly learned the ins and outs of dishwashing, stacking, and shuttling dishes between floors. My syrupy mustache eventually melted in the kitchen heat, prompting smirks from my co-workers, who pretended not to notice.

I worked hard, earning $1.25 per hour, with occasional tips from the wait

With a Little Scissors & Syrup – I got a Job

staff. With my first paycheck, I bought a portable radio record player and a handful of 45s, excitedly embracing the new age of portable technology and yearning to hear more songs about love.

In time, I spent my hard-earned money on H Street, N.E., one of D.C.'s primary shopping districts for Black people. The fashionable clothes and accessories drew us in like bees to nectar. The combination of white store owners and black clientele created a bustling commercial hub.

During this time, Rod, a friend of Mitchell's, began visiting our house to see my older sister, Yvonne. An introverted homebody, Yvonne fell for the first guy who showed interest in her; Rod, the charismatic lead singer of the local doo-wop singing group. Their unexpected romance blossomed, providing a comforting presence in the often absence of our brother, Mitchell, who was away often serving time.

Meanwhile, I was eager to learn how to drive, as I was approaching age 16. I paid Rod and another friend, Thomas, to teach me to drive. They would take me to the D.C. Stadium parking lot when there were no events and I would drive all over. Behind the wheel, I discovered a newfound sense of freedom and independence.

To Be Loved

Yearning to Get Away: Learning to Drive

I was so desperate for that driver's license that I felt that I would do anything to pass the test. But my hard work paid off, when the day came, and I passed on the first try. It felt like I had hit a jackpot. Now, with the open road beckoning, I could finally escape the limits of my neighborhood.

The world was tumultuous in the background of these seemingly ordinary teenage milestones. Dr. Martin Luther King Jr. was a constant presence on TV and in newspapers, but to adolescents, he felt like a leader for the older generation. We admired his courage, but his nonviolent approach seemed like strategy for loosing. Instead, we were drawn to the fiery passion of the Black Panthers, Stokely Carmichael, H. Rap Brown, etc. King's message of love and forgiveness in the face of mob and police assaults was difficult for teenagers to digest. We couldn't imagine living by those principles in our neighborhood, even less the nation.

The era was marked by protest marches, campus demonstrations, and the ever-present specter of the Vietnam War. Muhammad Ali, "The Greatest," was barred from boxing for refusing to enlist, and the Black Panthers faced violent persecution from the U.S. Government. Amid this turmoil, Stokely Carmichael's call for "Black Power" became a rallying cry, and James Brown's "Say It Loud, I'm Black, and I'm Proud" echoed in our hearts.

On April 4, 1968, the world changed. The Rev. Martin Luther King Jr. was assassinated in Memphis, Tennessee, and the shockwave reverberated

Yearning to Get Away: Learning to Drive

throughout the nation, including our community. I was at Harold's house when the news broke, and we immediately gathered on Sheriff Road to discuss the unthinkable. Anger and sorrow filled the streets, and calls for revenge echoed among many.

In the following days, H Street was set afire, consumed by the fury of a community whose leader offered non-violent activism and was assassinated at age 39. The Government didn't protect him. But The National Guard was called in to protect businesses, and the once-vibrant shopping district was reduced to a charred husk. It would never fully recover. For 60 years, the ghostly remains serve as a reminder to the pain and loss that had engulfed our nation and community.

Though the media would later claim that the Black community was the real loser in the destruction of H Street, it was the Jewish store owners who had exploited us with high prices and unfair employment practices who genuinely suffered. They had to shut down and find another community to exploit. We took our dollars elsewhere, moving to F Street, N.W., downtown Washington, D.C., and the suburbs.

Much like the open road I had longed for the road to adulthood, was paved with challenges and triumphs, set against a nation in turmoil. As I navigated my way through the streets and the tumultuous times, I understood that the journey was not just about the destination but the lessons learned and the bonds formed along the way.

To Be Loved

The Awakening: The MLK Uprising

The following day business strip in our community ablaze with chaos, a wave of raging anger, frustration. Sly and I wandered like lost souls through the storm, drawn to the wreckage of the Grant Street shopping area by the hypnotic whirl of police cruisers' lights. The shattered storefronts lay before us like broken dreams, a testament to the boiling outrage that had finally erupted. It was as if a dam had burst, and we were caught in the flood.

With the adrenaline coursing through our veins, we ventured into a battered dry cleaner, determined to claim some cathartic release for ourselves. But before we could take hold of anything, we were met with the cold bite of reality – the voice of a police, threatening to kill us.

We surrendered, as directed; our hands raised high as the officers closed in. Shackled and subdued, we were crammed into the back of the cruiser on the floor and driven through the streets of burning buildings to the 14th Precinct Police Station. We were warned to keep our heads down, but we couldn't resist the temptation to sneak a peek at the devastation outside.

At the precinct, we were herded into overcrowded offices, a sea of battered and bruised Black men overcrowded with standing room only. It was a chilling reminder of the control whites had over our lives. Eventually, Sly and I were released without charge and returned to our families like chastened children.

The Awakening: The MLK Uprising

But the experience left a mark on us, a sense of camaraderie forged in the city's fires and across the nation.

The following months brought more upheaval as Mitchell, returned home. His mischievous ways resumed, and I found myself caught in the crossfire of his schemes. While at home one evening, Mitchell sent my sisters, Carlean and Paulette, after me in the basement of our home and to beat me up for his amusement. I defended myself, and Paulette ended up with a black eye. My mother's wrath was swift, but, Mitchell evaded punishment.

My relationship with Mitchell was shifting, and the awe I once felt for him was beginning to fade as I was finding my way. The world had changed, and I had grown in his absence. No longer was I the little brother hoping to be shown the ropes; now, I could teach him a thing or two. Our bond, once so strong, felt more like a distant memory, a connection frayed by time and circumstance.

And so, we walked separate paths, Mitchell returning to his old haunts in our former neighborhood while I navigated the new world before me. We remained bound by blood, but also, a testament to the trials and tribulations that had shaped us both.

To Be Loved

Need to Get Away: My First Car

A man in my neighborhood was selling a Black 1956 Buick Roadmaster, with no reverse, for $70, which was more than a week's pay for me. I bought that car. We didn't need auto insurance then, and gasoline was less than $.35 per gallon. However, not having a reverse meant I had to park the car on a hill against the curb where no other vehicle could park ahead of me.

One day, a budding auto mechanic, David, pulled up beside me on Grant Street (now Nannie Helen Burroughs Avenue) in his 1957 Ford Galaxy, headed east towards 46th Street, N.E. We both had a few people in our cars hollering and greeting each other. But then David yelled, "Can that muthaf**ka run? Let's race these muthaf**kas."

"Alright! Let's go!" I said before asking, "Where to?"

"The stoplight," he said. I looked up ahead to the 49th and Grant Street intersection.

"Let's go!" I exclaimed, and we both pressed our pedal. My big, '56 Buick Roadmaster roared, inching ahead of David's '57 Ford Galaxy with the long fishtail. Everybody in our cars was screaming us on, "Get him, get him, beat that muthaf**ka!"

I was beating David by two or three cars. I couldn't believe it! He was turning that '57 Ford into a racer, or it sure looked like one. Now, he was losing as we were approaching the light. Time flew. We were there; my '56 had made its point to David. I had won the race and began to slow down for the red light

Need to Get Away: My First Car

ahead. David continued to accelerate, zooming past and entering the red-lighted intersection and swerving to and fro around the other cars before hitting his brakes and fishtailing recklessly out of danger. Then, David revved up and continued onward.

"Damn!" I exclaimed. "That was close!" I couldn't believe it.
Robert said, "Did you see that muthaf**ka, man? Damn!"

"He almost took all of them to heaven just to win a car race," I allowed. "He's one crazy muthaf**ka, just like his Daddy!"

To Be Loved

My Car is Stolen: I Know Who the Thief Is

A few weeks after buying the car, I was about to go to school when I noticed my Buick was missing. I called the police and filed a report. I put the word out among my crew that my car had been stolen. Upon my investigation, it had been crashed into a lamppost A neighbor spotted it on Division Avenue. I checked it out. My car wasn't there. But an auto crash had nearly broken the lamppost into. It meant that someone must have hit it pretty hard and heavy. I talked with the neighbors to see what I could find from any witnesses to the car crash. One neighbor told me that when she heard the crash and went to her window, she noticed guys jumping out of the crashed black car and into a blue car with a white top. That car sounded familiar. Rod's car?

"Was it a Plymouth?" I asked. "I don't know what kind of car it was. But they backed away up the hill, over Division Avenue to Jay Street, and then sped off over the hill toward Sheriff Road."

"Thanks," I said, a little crushed at the prospects. Rod came by our house in his white-on-blue 1968 Plymouth Fury that evening. I knew that had I asked him directly, that loyalty would lead him into denial. So, I took another route.

"Damn, Rod," I said, half-jokingly, "Mitchell told me about that goddamn accident ya'll had with my car last night."

My Car is Stolen: I Know Who the Thief Is

"Ya'll? Mitchell was driving your car, not ya'll."

Damn! I thought to myself, that's all I needed to hear. Mitchell had stolen my car as I slept and was probably racing it and crashed.

"Yeah, well, he pretty much totaled my car."

"Yeah, I know," Rod said.

When I saw Mitchell, I told him I knew he had stolen my car the night before and wrecked it.

"How did you know?" Mitchell asked.

"I played a trick on Rod. He told me!"

"I'll get you another car, don't worry; I'll get you another one. When I get my next job, I want you to go down to Uptown Used Cars and pick out anything you want on the lot."

Needless to say, I believed him again and immediately started to look at the loss as a gain. Yet, it would never materialize. Mitchell would never be home long enough before entering another cycle of crime, conviction, and serving time.

To Be Loved

Chapter II

The Boy That Turns Men into Slaves

As I sat on the ancient stone wall, its rough surface prickling my thighs, the sun dipped low in the sky, painting the horizon in hues of pink and orange. The breeze carried the scent of lilacs and the distant hum of life as Thomas' car crawled down Sheriff Road like a prowling cat. I raised my hand in a languid wave, and his car eased to a stop beside me. The window rolled down, revealing his grinning face.

"What's going on?" he asked, his voice infused with the energy of youth.

"Not much," I replied, my words echoing the serenity of the dying day.

His eyes sparkled with mischief as he beckoned me closer. "Get in; I got something for you."

Curiosity piqued, I slid into the leather car seat, the scent of age and memories enveloping me. "Whatcha got?" I asked as we cruised down Sherriff Road.

With a flourish, Thomas revealed a small gelatine capsule from his pocket. "Here, snort that."

"What do you mean, snort it?"

"Sniff the cherry up your nose," he explained, pointing to the tiny mound. "It's a 'Doogie,' heroin, go 'head."

"Heroin, huh," I murmured, the word tasting bitter and sweet. I took a

The Boy That Turns Men into Slaves

cautious sniff, an act of trust and adventure.

"Dope!"

The word reverberated through my soul like a struck gong, its power undeniable. I had heard whispers of it before – a dangerous, manly, risky, thrilling substance. It couldn't be harmful if Thomas, my brother's friend, was offering it. I believed wouldn't do anything to hurt me.

The white powder seemed innocuous, causing no sting or discomfort. As we rode through Sherriff Road, chatting as old friends from childhood, a lightheaded euphoria washed over me. I felt like I was floating, untethered from reality, wrapped in a warm blanket of mellowness and relaxation. I craved the nod, the sensation of everything feeling good as if I were basking in a sunbeam of pure contentment. My words came out as a hushed whisper, "Man, this is some good stuff."

But the allure of heroin, its siren song of relaxation and bliss, was also its most insidious downfall. It lured us in, then shackled us to its chains, dragging us into oblivion. Before heroin, a simple 40 oz., Colt 45 Malt Liquor and a bag of Bon Ton potato chips were enough to transport us to paradise. But now, we were trapped, mesmerized by a mirage of happiness as we surrendered to the drug's thrall.

The tumultuous 1960s had ignited a firestorm of freedom, breaking down barriers of discrimination and igniting the flames of excess in the form of everything, including sex and drugs. It seemed as if everyone, from the hippies to

To Be Loved

the socialites, was indulging in some form of escape. Concerts were awash with clouds of reefer smoke, while at parties, people snorted lines of cocaine through crisp dollar bills, seeking status and pleasure in equal measure. And the music – oh, the music – seemed to stretch on for eternity, the very notes infused with the spirit of rebellion and intoxication.

Yet, amidst the cacophony of hedonism, some artists dared to stand against the tide, creating masterpieces like the Dramatics' "The Devil is Dope," James Brown's "King Heroin," Curtis Mayfield's "Freddie's Dead," and The Temptations' "Cloud Nine." These were desperate calls to reason, cries of warning meant to pierce the fog of addiction. But it seemed as if the voices of these artists were drowned out by the thunderous beats of temptation and escape.

And then, like a U.S. Government conspiracy, drugs appeared everywhere, surging like a tsunami in response to the rebellions and demonstrations for freedom. There were substances for every taste, every budget: Mr. Magic, a hallucinogen; Quaaludes; Mescaline; and countless others. Cocaine, with its $3 price tag, was too steep for most; its fleeting high was a mere shadow compared to the longer-lasting heroin.

Heroin, this insidious beast with several names – "doogie," "boy," "scag," "smack" – devoured us whole, stripping men of their dignity and reducing them to mere shadows of their former selves. It tore through our crew like a ravenous wildfire, consuming almost everyone in its path.

Sly, who always sought the adoration of the boys, became a dealer, the

The Boy That Turns Men into Slaves

pied piper of our descent into darkness. He was 'the man,' the one everyone sought for their next hit, their next fleeting moment of ecstasy and escape.

Our friends became hollow shells; their once-sparkling eyes were now glazed and vacant as they nodded in public, scratching phantom itches, jaws slack, their words tumbling out in hushed tones and whispers like words were an interruption of their high.

And so, heroin claimed many of us, transforming our lives into a desperate dance of addiction, crime, and absent-mindedness. We traded our dreams, our futures for the siren song of the snort or the needle, urging folks to do almost anything for the dragon of oblivion. In this new world, getting high was no longer a choice – it had become a way of life, an all-consuming hunger that swallowed many of us whole, leaving them adrift in a sea of darkness, clinging to the wreckage of what we once were.

To Be Loved

First Gov't Office Job: Mental Hospital

As the school year ended, I discovered a summer jobs program and eagerly applied. Soon, I was working at St. Elizabeths, a federal hospital nestled in the heart of poor, Black Southeast Washington, called Congress Heights. A sprawling complex, with its century-old red-brick buildings and expansive grounds, treated mentally ill individuals from all corners of the nation. In 1968, I worked in the Procurement Section; our office was next to the bustling laundry compound.

St. Elizabeths was a self-sufficient microcosm, a village teeming with life and activity. The 326-acre campus encompassed over 120 buildings, straddling both sides of Nichols (now Dr. Martin Luther King) Avenue in Congress Heights.

The workers from the laundry often cast curious glances my way. Clad in overalls and laboring alongside patients, they battled the stifling summer heat while I enjoyed the crisp air conditioning in my stylish street clothes – the only summer worker with an office job. My first foray into a professional environment felt strange and foreign. The workers were predominantly middle-aged white men, except Mrs. Ford, the secretary, and myself. By a twist of fate, Mrs. Ford lived just up the hill from Sherriff Road, on Just Street.

"Since you live so close to me, you can ride to work with me, okay, honey?" she offered warmly, like a dear friend or relative.

"Okay, thanks," I replied, grateful for her kindness.

First Gov't Office Job: Mental Hospital

My supervisor, Mr. Smith, was a man in his early 60s with weathered skin, grey hair, and piercing green eyes. A chain smoker, he tasked me with filing requisitions by number. Growing up on a steady diet of television shows featuring white characters, I observed my new colleagues with wonder and fascination. They appeared polite, sterile, and distant – a far cry from the funny, warm, personable people I had encountered on the TV screen.

Despite their courteous demeanor, white people rarely socialized with Black people, as if they were hesitant to disturb us or draw attention to themselves, except when assigning work.

Whenever I completed a task, I'd approach Mr. Smith for more. "Mr. Smith, I'm done. Is there anything else I can do?"

He would rise from his chair, put a reassuring hand on my shoulder, and lead me back to my area. "Damn, you work so fast; you keep me busy trying to keep you busy," he'd say with a chuckle.

During lunch breaks, I'd venture outside to mingle with the laundry workers. It felt like coming out for air, a refreshing change among other young Black men. I'd seek out someone I felt a connection with, and soon enough, I'd befriend the entire group, each of us sharing a common bond in this miniature world.

Jericho, a boisterous laundry worker with a cap perpetually cocked on the side of his head, instantly stood out among the guys. His infectious laughter and playful banter drew people in, and he took a liking to me.

To Be Loved

One sunlit afternoon, as I made my way to move Mrs. Ford's car to the upper-level parking lot, Jericho called out, his voice laced with intrigue, "I got something; I want to turn you on. You ever had any scag?" Astonished, I replied, "Yeah, you got some? Don't be jiving me."

"Want some?"

"Man, you better turn me on; what is wrong with you?" I demanded, excitement building in my chest.

"I'm selling the shit," he confessed with a grin. "Yeah, that's right, I'm the man, muthafucka!"

As we strolled toward the parking lot, I hesitated, "But I ain't trying to cop now."

Undeterred, he insisted, "I'm a turn your muthafucking ass on. You ain't got to pay me for it."

He produced the heroin, and I inhaled it greedily. "Thanks a lot, Jericho," I said, our palms slapping together in camaraderie before I moved on to Mrs. Ford's car.

As I turned the ignition, the high washed over me like a tidal wave. 'Wow, is that some good shit or what?' The world seemed to dissolve into a calm, mellow haze. Struggling to regain my senses, I murmured, 'Take the car up on the upper lot and get the fuck back to work.'

I slipped the car into reverse, intoxicated by the euphoria of the heroin. As I pressed the accelerator, the car careened into a wall, shattering my high and replacing it with a rush of cold, unadulterated fear. I exited the car, surveying the broken taillight and dented back fender. Jericho, in the distance, threw up his

First Gov't Office Job: Mental Hospital

hands in disbelief before disappearing into the laundry.

I parked the car and went to tell Mrs. Ford what I had done. "I don't know, the car just went out of control," I stammered, my voice trembling. "I'm sorry."

"You don't know what happened?" She asked, her tone gentle yet firm. "That's okay, don't worry."

On our ride home, Mrs. Ford chastised me for my irresponsibility and requested that I pay her insurance deductible – a hundred dollars, nearly two weeks' wages. No one but Jericho ever knew I was drugged.

St. Elizabeths was a macabre spectacle. Patients with varying degrees of mental illness roamed the grounds, displaying bizarre behavior. One black patient, who claimed to be Abraham Lincoln one day and Thomas Jefferson or George Washington the next, was a source of constant amusement for the workers. Others, like the Alaskan native who worked in the laundry, would hurl racial slurs when taunted, only to be met with laughter and more teasing.

Almost all patients smoked hand-rolled "Bull Run" cigarettes, taking their time to meticulously craft each one as if it were a lifeline. The ritual seemed to breathe meaning into their fractured lives.

With the money I earned at St. Elizabeths, I bought a 1957 Mercury Monterey, its light green exterior gleaming like a jewel. The car I purchased for $200, appeared in mint condition. As I drove through the neighborhood, heads turned, and I couldn't help but beam with pride.

To Be Loved

I had planned that my friends and I would ride together in my new car, the radio blasting hits like "Little Green Apples" by O.C. Smith or Archie Bell and The Drells' summer anthem, "I Just Can't Stop Dancing." I was ecstatic to have a means of escape and independence, the wind waffling through over my face as I cruised down the streets.

When I first showed off my gleaming new ride to my crew—Robert, Tyson, Tiger, Gilbert, Sly, Smooth, and Nutbush—I felt a surge of accomplishment. My beloved automobile would transport us to wherever our hearts desired.

Washing my car meticulously, I reveled in the warm sun reflecting off its polished surface. The world felt alive with possibility as I tuned in to the songs that filled the air. *"God didn't make little green apples, and it don't rain in Indianapolis in the summertime,"* O.C. Smith sang, his voice like a comforting embrace.

In those moments, I felt invincible, as if I could accomplish anything I put my mind to accomplish. There was a certain satisfaction in knowing I had earned this slice of freedom, this tangible symbol of my hard work. The music, the laughter, and the camaraderie of my friends filled my heart and soul, drowning out any lingering doubts or fears.

For a brief, shining moment, I was content with the world and my place in it. Little did I know life had more lessons in store for me, but for now, I enjoyed the ride, fueled by the music, the friendships, and the dreams of an even brighter

First Gov't Office Job: Mental Hospital

future.

*****

To Be Loved

The Bully: Not in My Neighborhood

The night was alive with laughter and music, and the air was thick with anticipation as we gathered for a party. Jake, notorious for his antics, appeared and tossed a handful of coins into the air. They rained down on the dance floor, glinting like fallen stars as people scrambled to claim their share of the unexpected bounty. The next day, we discovered that Cobb's store had been burglarized. I knew it was Jake. Anger bubbled inside me like a volcano on the verge of eruption. We had welcomed him into our community, and he had betrayed us by stealing from one of our own. It wasn't right, and I couldn't shake the feeling that the more time I spent around him, the more inevitable a confrontation would become.

Jake's presence was like a storm cloud threatening to burst on one of Roper Junior High School recreation's roller-skating nights. As he skated alongside me, he forcefully shoved me, clearly trying to provoke a reaction. I tried to ignore it, but couldn't hold back when he did it again. "Come on, man, you got a problem?!" I yelled, knowing that this would likely lead to a physical altercation.

"What you say, muthaf**ka? You talking to me?" Jake retorted, his voice daring a challenge. The crowd around us stopped skating, sensing the drama, and gathered in anticipation.

As we removed our skates, my heart pounded like a war drum, echoing the fierce battle that was about to take place. We stepped outside, the crowd in tow, and began exchanging blows. I fought against the fear coursing through my

The Bully: Not in My Neighborhood

veins, knowing that Jake was the worst kind of opponent; he had no respect for the codes of conduct that governed our conflicts. We wore each other down with jabs and blocks, our breaths coming in ragged gasps, until someone finally stepped in to break up the fight.

Walking home that night, accompanied by my friends and sporting a black eye, I reflected on the events that had transpired. When I arrived home, Mitchell commented, "They were supposed to have carried Jake's ass off that playground for blackening your eye. Did he have a black eye?"

"No," I replied, feeling a strange sense of satisfaction despite the bruising. I had shown Jake that I could—and would—fight, and I knew he would never bother me again.

Soon, Mitchell found himself entangled in the drug scene, and the allure of heroin began to consume his life. The pedestrian underpass beneath Benning Road, a once innocent underground passage, had transformed into a drug-shooting gallery.

"You want to sell this shit?" Mitchell asked me one evening.

"Sure," I responded, enticed by the promise of extra money and a seemingly endless supply of heroin. My brother handed me 20 gelatin capsules of the potent white powder, and I took them to school, eager to spread the word.

Our lives revolved more and more around getting high. We would snort the Doogie or scag in basements or cars, out of view, losing ourselves in music and the blissful haze of oblivion. A friend introduced me to a young couple who

To Be Loved

lived on the corner of Jay and 51st Streets. With their relaxed demeaner, they welcomed us into their home, where we would indulge in our self-medication, listening to the soulful melodies of Isaac Hayes.

Hayes' music captured the essence of love and heartache, stirring emotions within us that resonated with our own experiences. Hayes' bold, daring appearance, shirtless, bald headed and embodied the perfect blend of vulnerability and masculinity. As we listened to his album, we would lose ourselves in the rich tapestry of sound, letting the music and heroin wash over us and transport us to another world.

One fateful evening, as I returned home, a man leaped out from behind a hedge, his face contorted with anger and desperation. He brandished a revolver and demanded, "Stick up; give me the drugs and the money!" Terrified, I handed everything over, catching a glimpse of the thief's face in the darkness. I recognized him from Fairmont Heights, the community down the hill on the Maryland side of Eastern Avenue. I vowed that if I ever saw him again, I would have to exact revenge. That was the street code. But at that moment, I also realized that this might have been a blessing in disguise; selling drugs was not my thing.

I confided in Mitchell about the incident. In his bedroom, and he said, "Don't worry about it. Look, I want to show you why we haven't seen much profit." With that, he revealed that he had been using the profit to fuel his addiction.

He pulled out a belt and a hypodermic needle, demonstrating his steps to

The Bully: Not in My Neighborhood

prepare the dose and inject himself. His face relaxed, and his eyes shone with the unmistakable glow of euphoria. As he pushed the plunger. I couldn't help but want to experience that same feeling.

He cleaned the needle, prepared another dose, and said, "Give me your arm." As he spoke, he warned me of the power of addiction, and Mitchell said that I had a strong constitution and could resist falling into the same trap. He assured me the high would be like nothing I had ever experienced.

I offered my arm without fear, and as the needle pierced my skin, I felt the rush of the most incredible high. As the radio played and James Brown's voice filled the room, I knew I had to share this moment with someone. "I Feel Good!" James Brown sang, and in that instant, I was propelled into bliss.

"I did it," I declared as if I had just completed a rite of passage. I had injected heroin, which accelerated and intensified the high compared to snorting the white powder. But little did I know that the path I had chosen would be filled with ever more darkness and despair, forever altering the course of my life.

To Be Loved

Downtown Stores Belonged to Us

In the bustling downtown D.C. of the 1800s, department stores and other institutions excluded and exploited Black customers. So, my friends and I devised clever ways to compromise these stores. We would buy one shopping bag for a quarter but take two, using one to prop the other open and disguise its emptiness. With calculated moves, we would visit the clothing section and discreetly steal stylish items. I even managed to pull off a daring shoe heist, but it didn't come without risks.

One day, while attempting to escape with stolen shoes, a salesman chased me, shouting for the police to stop me. I managed to outsmart him and evade capture, but the shoes were too small and uncomfortable. Despite this, I wore them as a symbol of my triumph.

In another incident, I concealed a stolen wool, double-breasted coat in my shopping bag, and a store employee approached us. With defiance, I stood my ground, refusing to reveal the contents of my bag and threatening legal action. We managed to walk away unscathed, heading to another store for more boosting.

Our success led to requests from neighborhood friends for specific items before our downtown excursions.

It probably annoyed Mama that she would see me looking so fly and not have bought me any of my clothing. But, I guess she knew I was determined to have what I wanted, and now that I was older, I wasn't gonna be denied. I had on-and-off jobs and I would always use that as an alibi. Besides, I would slip the

Downtown Stores Belonged to Us

clothes out gradually. Shoes, one week; a coat the next, etc.

"If you keep it up, you're gonna get caught." She would warn me.

"I ain't doing nothing to get caught about," I declared. I didn't care what Mama thought anymore since I didn't feel she ever cared about how what I thought.

Meanwhile, my friend Smooth had joined a downtown crew specializing in pickpocketing. They would dress impeccably, blending in with white passengers on the bus, and discreetly steal from inside their purses. Smooth shared his stories with us, creating an atmosphere of fascination and danger.

Once in Lansburgh's on 7th Street, N.W., down from Hecht's, next to Kann's, I had rolled a double-breasted wool, coat into my shopping bag, thrown it over my shoulder, and was headed for the door when a store police, we called a "floor walker," eased up from behind. He watched Tyson and I and followed us to the door. We kept walking. He called out to us, "What you got in the bag?"

I said, "None of your goddamn business what's in my bag." For emphasis, I turned to him and looked him in the eye and said, "If you touch my bag, I'ma sue Lansburgh's and you!"

"You think you're one of those smart asses, huh!" he said.

"Nope, you think all we do is steal stuff. Well, if you didn't see me steal nothing you got no reason to suspect. You touch my bag, I'm gonna have my parents sue. I'ma own Lansburgh's and your ass' gonna be fired," I bluffed as I pushed the door open and exited the store. Tyson and I never looked back. I

To Be Loved

imagined the floorwalker staring at us as we walked out of his grasp, and then looking for others. We went on our way to another store.

"How did you know that shit, Ronald," Tyson demanded. "Damn, I was scared as shit, man. You bluffed the shit out of him."

"No, I knew what I was talking about, that's all," I replied. "They can't think you stole something. They've got to see you do it. If they search you and you don't have anything you can sue their ass."

"For what?"

"Fuck if I know!!!" I said, "Let's go to Woodies."

Tyson and I went downtown to hustle at Kresge 5¢-10¢-25¢ store, 11 and G Streets, N.W. Tyson looked at wallets. I said, no. He dropped them in the bag anyway. A floorwalker pulled up beside us and asked, "Will you two come with me?' That meant going into the back offices of the store; him calling the police; they calling our parents; me getting my ass whipped.

"Do you have the money to pay for these wallets," the overweight light-skinned brother asked.

That was a different approach, I thought.

Tyson said, "No."

I said, "If we could get the money would you allow us to pay for them?"

The floorwalker looked in our bag and found clothes from Bruce Hunt Men's Shop and he threatened to call them and have them bust us, too.

"No, no, I got a cousin who lives not far from here," I pleaded. "Let us

Downtown Stores Belonged to Us

go visit her and I'll bring the money back to pay for the wallets."

"Okay. But, the stash stays here!"

We were obliged.

Once outside, Tyson asked, "Who you know downtown, Ronald?"

"Nobody. I figured, if we could get out of that store, we can make ten dollars somewhere."

"Damn, right, shoot, 'whatchu' say!"

"But, Tyson, you have got to listen to me when I make calls, man. I said, 'fuck them wallets.' But you went ahead, anyway."

"You're right, Ronald"

"Yeah, I know I'm right. You got to get right!"

"Yeah, you're right; I can dig it."

We went to McDonald's at the corner of 14th and New York Avenue, across the street from the Town Theater, which was near the Greyhound Bus Station which was across the street from the Trailways Bus Station. So, the McDonald's was a busy one. A white woman and man sat talking. We sat down near her. I nodded to Tyson and he sat beside me. Her back was to me. I stuck one hand under the other shoulder and slipped her purse down the counter to Tyson. Tyson left. Then, I followed.

No problem. We got about $50 and some diamond rings, went back to Kresge's, paid for the wallets, listened to the floorwalker's warnings, and left to go home.

To Be Loved

"What if we didn't get any money, man?" Tyson said with a big cheesy grin.

"I don't know, I said. "I didn't think about us not getting any money."

Tyson laughed and said, "You crazy!" And laughed some more.

As our boosting continued, the neighborhood fell prey to the ravages of heroin addiction. My closest friend Robert became addicted, and witnessing his decline and that of others deeply troubled me. I used heroin occasionally but refused to let it consume me. The experience of feeling nauseous and the foul taste it left in my mouth were reminders of its destructive power.

It was a tragic sight to witness friends and acquaintances falling prey to its ravages, their lives consumed by the drug's destructive allure. Yet, amidst the darkness that enveloped our community, I was determined to forge a different path for myself.

Once, I rode up to New York with Gilbert to hang out with his cousin who was also into scag. After several trips to New York, Gilbert had learned that heroin was more potent there than in D.C. Gilbert went usually to visit family, but he wanted to cop some of that good 'ol New York heroin, too. We drove to a little apartment to cop some scag, where Gilbert was allowed to use an eyedropper syringe to shoot it. Except, when the high rushed Gilbert, he fell back in his chair, and passed out. Usually, when guys OD'd (overdosed), they were abandoned or dumped somewhere else to deflect police attention. I grabbed Gilbert, slapped him awake, picked his big ass up and took him outside into the fresh open air,

Downtown Stores Belonged to Us

where I ran him all over Brooklyn to work off the high. He lived to joke about it later. But, years later, at about age 30, unable to shake the past, Gilbert, while out with Tiger, would OD again and die in 1982. It is believed that Tiger may have been able to save Gilbert, but he probably panicked to save his own ass and abandoned Gilbert The crew attended Gilbert's wake, discussed what happened with Tiger but we could neither fix what broke down or call Gilbert back. Sadly, we let it go, knowing we would surely miss big Gilbert.

Meanwhile, I continued to use heroin sparingly, wary of its power and determined not to let it consume me. The allure of the drug was always present, but I resisted its seductive pull, reminding myself of my strength and resilience. I couldn't help but feel relief that I had managed to avoid the same fate as my friends.

In the neighborhood, the drug problem escalated. An old apartment building, on Jay Street, which had once house families, had been transformed into a drug rehab center where methadone, a synthetic substitute for heroin, was dispensed. However, even within the walls of the so-called center, addiction persisted. The methadone pills were often sold on the street, perpetuating the cycle of dependency and feeding the ever-growing demand for drugs.

Witnessing the devastating impact of addiction on my community, I felt a deep sense of responsibility. I couldn't save everyone, but I was determined to help those who were willing to change. One by one, I reached out to those still teetering

To Be Loved

on the edge, sharing my experiences and encouraging them to seek a different path.

I organized another meeting, this time at David's place. The atmosphere was heavy with both apprehension and hope. As I looked into the faces of my friends, I saw a reflection of my journey, a reminder of the potential we all had. I spoke from the heart, reminding them of the good times we had shared and the vibrant individuals they once were.

"We're better than this?" I pleaded, my voice filled with desperation and determination. "We deserve more than a life consumed by drugs. It's not too late to change, to reclaim our dreams and our futures."

Some listened intently, their eyes filled with a flicker of hope. Others shifted uncomfortably, their addiction holding them tightly in its grasp. David interrupted, apologizing for his sudden need to depart, triggering the others approaching the door. Despite my efforts, the power of addiction was stronger than any words I could offer.

I watched them go, a mix of sadness and determination welling up inside me. I couldn't save them all, and I couldn't give up on them either. I vowed to continue fighting, to be a beacon of hope and support for those ready to break free from addiction.

Days turned into weeks, and weeks turned into months. The struggle against addiction persisted, and I found solace in knowing I had remained

Downtown Stores Belonged to Us

steadfast in my resolve. I continued to surround myself with a small circle of trusted friends who shared my commitment to a better life.

As time passed, some of my friends did break free of addiction. It wasn't an easy journey, and the scars of their past remained, but they found the strength within themselves to overcome their demons. Together, we supported one another, celebrating each victory and offering solace in moments of weakness.

While the shadows of addiction, crime, prison and even death still loomed over many, we became beacons of resilience and hope. We knew the fight wasn't over, but we were determined to create a better future that wasn't defined by the destructive power of drugs.

Through it all, I held onto the belief that we were more than our struggles. We were individuals with dreams, aspirations, and the potential for greatness. And as long as we continued to fight, there was always hope for a brighter tomorrow.

.

To Be Loved

Malcolm X: Woke

Spingarn High School 1969 brought an unexpected opportunity for me to explore literature that would reshape my life. Mrs. Lynch, my white English teacher, assigned two books: "Catcher in the Rye" by J.D. Salinger and "The Autobiography of Malcolm X" by Alex Haley. Though initially hesitant, I delved into Malcolm X's autobiography with fervor.

Malcolm X's powerful narrative immediately captured my attention. I connected with his experiences of racism, poverty, and violence that had shaped him into a hustler. His conversion to Islam while in prison marked a turning point, awakening his consciousness and inspiring him to fight against white supremacy.

Reading Malcolm X's words, I realized the deliberate erasure of Black history and culture from our education system. Our African ancestors, who had invented civilization, were kidnapped, enslaved, and stripped of their heritage. Instead, we were force-fed a distorted history which cemented the twin destructive notions of white supremacy and Black inferiority.

This revelation fuelled my anger and awoke a desire for change. I recognized the power of education and knowledge in reclaiming our dignity and challenging the oppressive systems that marginalized us. Malcolm X's call to declare our unalienable rights resonated deeply with me, pushing me to question the stereotypes imposed upon us.

The weight of Malcolm X's words and my newfound awareness prompted me to share my insights with my friends. I became a source of

Malcolm X: Woke

information, passionately discussing our history that had been denied to us. At Spingarn, to reclaim knowledge of a stolen and repressed history, a small group of students formed The Black Awareness Organization, embracing the ideals of our rich and hidden history, black nationalism and fighting for political, social, and economic empowerment.

As I immersed myself in literature and conversations about Black history, I discovered the remarkable contributions our recent ancestors had made to the development of the United States. From inventions to scientific advancements, our legacy was a great deal more extensive than what had been taught in schools. The deliberate omission of our history only reinforced the perception that we didn't matter in this country, which harbored all manner of stereotypes and hatred towards Black people.

Recognizing the need for change, I vowed to teach my future children their history at an early age. I understood that self-esteem and a positive self-image were essential for progress, counteracting an oppression that had conditioned African Americans to mimic white culture to be accepted.

Determined to prove that I was more than the derogatory stereotypes, I pursued knowledge and sought to uplift my community. I reclaimed my identity and embraced symbols of Black pride, from wearing Afros and Dashikis to exchanging raised, clenched fists as a sign of solidarity.

Yet, despite my accomplishments and intelligence, I knew that many white people would always view me as a "Nigga." Racism and white supremacy

To Be Loved

persisted, fuelled by the guilt that to acknowledge their inhumanity to Black people also would be tantamount to admitting that white America harbors a false sense of their history and notions of superiority.

Nevertheless, armed with knowledge, history, and a sense of purpose, I pressed on. Malcolm X's autobiography ignited a fire, compelling me to want to fight for justice, uplift my people, and challenge the oppressive systems that sought to define and diminish us.

The Black Awareness Organization: Anger II

The Black Awareness Organization approached Spingarn's principal, "Doc" [Dr. Purvis] Williams, to demand that the school refer to the student body as Black rather than Negro.

Doc Williams was a distinguished looking older man. Pecan brown complexion, he wore gold-rimmed glasses, and stylish, baggy, double-breast, gabardine suits. He always seemed to wear a mild-mannered smile. He demonstrated that he was in control of the school by walking the halls and showing us he was comfortable with us, busting a crap game, chastising us about drinking sodas. "Does your mother know you drink sodas at school?" he would ask, half-jokingly.

Doc Williams told us, "I understand what you young men are doing, but the word 'Negro' has a proud heritage, too, and I am completely satisfied with it! Excuse me," and he walked away.

We stood there in the hall, dumbfounded as to what to do next. We thought that the idea of referring to Negroes as Black had meaning and was relevant and the school officials were waiting for someone to suggest it. Well, we did. But it fell on deaf ears. What do we do next?

My passion for reading and sharing knowledge with my friends grew amid these struggles. Friends nicknamed me "Preacher" as I fervently imparted my newfound insights. Fueled by anger and a desire for retaliation, I began

To Be Loved

targeting white people with a vengeance. I rationalized that if we were to rob anyone, it should be those who had amassed wealth through robbing us. Downtown became our hunting ground, where we would confront and threaten or assault white individuals, and take their money.

One encounter at McDonald's on New York Avenue involved us staging a fake stick-up, instilling fear in a European tourist who had never been warned about what American oppression does to fellow Americans. Another time, we stumbled upon a white man brandishing a large revolver in a park, prompting us to swiftly turn and flee, laughter echoing in our wake.

The presidential inauguration parade of Richard Nixon and Spiro T. Agnew presented an enticing opportunity for hustlers. As wealthy white people flocked to witness the event, we planned to exploit their distraction. Rather than drawing attention to ourselves, I decided to wait until the excitement peaked during the motorcade's passing. Amid the chaos, I deftly pickpocketed a woman's purse, securing $90 before heading home.

After a night of hustling, we sought solace and entertainment at Lowe's Palace Theatre, where we honed our tactics for free entry. One of us would distract the manager and request to use the restroom, slipping out to unlock the side exit for the rest of the crew. In the darkness, we'd swiftly find seats and enjoy a movie. On one occasion, we watched "100 Rifles," witnessing Jim Brown, a black all-time great former NFL running back, turned actor engage in a love scene with the famous, sexy white actress Raquel Welch. It was supposed to represent societal

The Black Awareness Organization: Anger II

change, but for Black Americans, nothing had truly changed.

As the 11th grade drew to a close, my academic performance remained average; I aimed not to fail rather than strive for excellence. Curious about my final grade in history, I attempted to bluff my way into a satisfactory result by threatening to sue my teacher if she had planned to give me an F for the course. Well, she called my bluff and flunked me. It left me stunned, unsure if I had failed the class or if my comment had provoked the failing grade.

During a brief stint at Eastern High School's summer program, an older brother donning a dashiki, barged into the classroom and denounced our white teacher for perpetuating white supremacy and neglecting to teach our natural history. He tore up her textbook, symbolically rejecting the biased narrative. While the teacher acknowledged the brother's commitment to black liberation, she obtained another copy of the book and continued teaching U.S. History.

Amidst the turmoil and confrontations, my thirst for knowledge and the awakening of my consciousness continued. The struggle for racial equality burned within the nation and me, propelling me to strive to challenge the status quo and seek the truth buried beneath layers of oppression and neglect.

To Be Loved

Some Had to Die

Despite his comfortable lifestyle and nice clothes, Charles tried to fit in with the tough crowd. However, it was clear he wasn't cut out for the dangerous hustling life. Tragically, he attempted to rob a gas station and was shot and killed at 15. His death left a somber atmosphere, and everyone who mourned the loss of his young life.

Attending Charles' funeral and the subsequent gathering, I observed the absence of sorrow among the guys. Instead, there were jokes and laughter, masking their pain and avoiding the shame of vulnerability. It struck me as cold-hearted, and I couldn't help but feel an emptiness with this lack of public empathy.

A few weeks later, Roach, who had transformed from a cheerful kid to a member of the Clay Terrace crew, met a similar fate. He was stabbed to death over a dispute involving a girl he had danced with at a party. His untimely death saddened the entire neighborhood, too, as we were teenagers living amid war conditions.

Knowing that revenge killings were likely to follow, I had a strong desire to intervene and convince the brothers in Clay Terrace to forgive Roach's killer. I wanted to emphasize that justice would be served through the legal system. However, I hesitated, unsure if they would even listen to me or if my efforts would have any impact. I felt trapped by the hood's mentality of an eye for an eye.

Nevertheless, I began to realize the power of words. I observed how others listened to me when I shared our history and engaged in debates. I saw that

Some Had to Die

individuals who were skilled with words were respected and admired. This realization motivated me to study vocabulary and etymology, aiming to strengthen my language skills and gain the power to influence others.

At home, my attempts to convey the greatness of our history to my siblings were often dismissed or tolerated. Eventually, I stopped trying to talk to them about it. However, I noticed that people outside my family paid attention when I discussed the books. This intensified my interest, and desire to change my ways for the better. However, I struggled to find the right path forward and continued engaging the future with all that I knew: the past.

To Be Loved

Chapter III

Finished School and Prepared for What?

After completing summer school in 1969, I returned to work at St. E Hospital. My job was to assist an older man who lived near me in the janitorial supply section. He was a gray-haired gentleman and a father of two grown children who rarely visited him and his wife. Unfortunately, he struggled with alcoholism. Every day, he would carefully drive us to work in his 1963 Chevrolet Impala, stopping at Jock's Liquors to purchase a half pint of Seagram's Gin. He would meet his buddy, and they would drink it without ice or a chaser before he would resume driving us to work. At lunchtime, they would have another half pint and a third one on the way home after work. I couldn't help but wonder what could push a man to drink such bitter stuff three times a day, like they were meals. His generation also lived the deprived, harsh life of segregation in the land of plenty. They were punished for succeeding or failing. They were largely war veterans, rarely rewarded in civilian life, unless an action benefited a white person. They worked hard, endured humiliation at work, beat their wives and children, drank liquor to self-medicate, smoked cigarettes and died relatively young and broke and with little to no retirement. When he was sober, he appeared withdrawn and in great anguish.

At St. E, I worked alongside the delivery man, unloading trucks and making deliveries to various buildings on the hospital campus. The patients ranged from

Finished School and Prepared for What?

psychotic to sedate, worn down by the medications administered by the hospital. They would often be half-dressed, with food remains or drool around their mouths and with their arms curled around their heads. The patients crowded at the door, and when the delivery man shook his keys, they would back up and retreat, their arms still curled over their heads, a disturbing sight.

One day, I struck up a conversation with a young male patient. I asked him why was he in the hospital. He replied, "I know I ain't crazy, but I keep getting in trouble." Curious, I inquired about the type of trouble he faced. He mentioned fights and other issues. I couldn't help but relate to his struggles, wondering if I, too, might be crazy. He wanted to show me something and asked me to follow him. We went to an underground tunnel with railroad tracks running through it. The darkness made me uneasy, and I decided to leave. However, before I could go, he grabbed my arm. I reacted defensively, ready to knock the patient's block off, when he said he had a girl patient who would meet him there to have sex with her, and suggested I could also have sex with her. Disgusted, I walked away, refusing to engage in such an exploitative, unseemly encounter. On another occasion, I conversed with another patient who appeared to be sane. I asked how he ended up in the hospital. He told me that he and his accomplices had recently robbed a bank and were driving down the highway when the police pulled them over for a routine check. When the police discovered the money they had stolen, he claimed to have gone crazy. These encounters with mentally ill patients left me with curiosity, compassion, and a sense of unease. It reminded me of the diverse

To Be Loved

range of experiences and struggles that people faced, and it made me question the line between sanity and insanity.

Buy a Gun, Steal a Car and Rob a Bank

Buy a Gun, Steal a Car and Rob a Bank

In 1970, along with desegregation, our music was liberated, too. Black music began address the scope of our lives. There were still great love songs. But artist like Curtis Mayfield began to address social predicament of our lives. Mayfield first solo album, titled "Curtis," captivated me. As a former leader of the Impressions, Mayfield's smooth falsetto had always resonated with me, his songs serving as a musical extension of Martin Luther King Jr.'s message. His earlier works, like "We're A Winner" and "Move On Up," were subtle, stroking of the listeners' consciousness. However, "Curtis" showcased a more direct and deliberate approach. The album featured powerful tracks like "Miss Black America" and explored the depths of our culture, reinforcing our pride. Mayfield, along with Marvin Gaye and Stevie Wonder, were guiding lights to my emerging consciousness. I found solace and inspiration in their lyrics, wearing out their albums as I listened and absorbed their messages over and again.

Carrying a gun became a symbol of power and control for me. Knowing that I could stop anyone in their tracks gave me a sense of empowerment, In the hood, owning a firearm meant carrying it, and carrying it meant eventually using it. I obtained a .22 caliber revolver and began carrying it with me, especially to parties, as a testament to my newfound authority.

We caught a cab to Tyson's apartment with a different plan— sticking up the cab driver. While we waited in the cab as collateral, Tyson was supposed to go inside

To Be Loved

the building and return with the .22, ready to carry out the heist. However, time passed, and Tyson hadn't returned. Impatient, I stormed out of the cab, determined to find out what was taking him so long. I instructed the others to wait as I ventured inside.

To my surprise, I discovered that Tyson had chickened out. Frustrated, I snatched the gun from him and returned to the cab, ready to take matters into my own hands. Reaching into the passenger side, I announced, "This is a stickup!" The cab driver's response was a mixture of shock and fear as he pressed the accelerator, attempting to escape. In a desperate attempt to deter him, I fired a shot into the dashboard, hoping to scare him into driving off. We raced through the alley and across the playground until we reached the safety of Sheriff Road and the familiar refuge of the wall.

The allure of bank robberies captured my attention as I watched daring heists unfold on TV. The thought of pulling off such a feat and gaining a reputation among my crew excited me. I contemplated robbing the St. Elizabeth Hospital's Credit Union and discussed the plan with Robert, who surprisingly found it appealing. Armed with a sawed-off shotgun, we scoped out the credit union, confident that we could control the situation with our weapon. We had a getaway route planned through the Barry Farms Public housing projects, adjacent to major thoroughfares.

However, our plans quickly crumbled when a security cruiser stopped us during our reconnaissance mission. Someone had noticed us and alerted the hospital

Buy a Gun, Steal a Car and Rob a Bank

police. Faced with questioning, I improvised a story about returning for a job but changing my mind due to not wanting to work with mentally ill people, anymore. I managed to convince the officer by showing him my ID, but Robert didn't have his, putting us at risk of being searched and arrested for possession of a firearm. Thankfully, I interjected, stating that he was only 17 and didn't require ID. The officer warned us to leave and drove off, leaving us both relieved and amused by our close call.

The failed robbery attempt became a topic of laughter among my crew when we gathered later that night at the wall. Smooth, with a snicker, prodded me about the rumors he had heard. I reluctantly admitted our intentions and recounted the encounter with the cop. Robert praised my quick thinking, grateful that I had averted a potential disaster. In the end, we laughed, recognizing the absurdity of our failed heist and the risks we had unknowingly taken, but we learned our lesson after being bruised a few more times...

Robert, praised my quick thinking, grateful that I had averted a disaster. Amidst the laughter and camaraderie, I couldn't help but reflect on the dangerous path we had almost embarked upon. It was a humbling moment, a stark reminder of the consequences that awaited those who succumbed to the allure of crime and the false promises of reputation and wealth.

With the failed attempt robbery and the brush with the law behind us, I made a silent vow to myself. I would let go of these reckless fantasies and seek a different path that aligned with the messages of empowerment and unity I had found in the

To Be Loved

history books and the music of Curtis Mayfield and other influential artists. It was time to redefine my priorities and pursue a future that would make a positive impact, rather than chasing fleeting notions of power and acclaim, but before that....

A moment of recklessness led me to try stealing a car. There was a Chevrolet Corvair parked in front of my neighbor's house. I possessed a "knockout key," a tool to start many GM cars. I entered the Corvair, inserting the key into the ignition to test it. To my surprise and horror, the car lurched forward towards the street. Panicked, I quickly exited the vehicle. As I would find out, the car belonged to one of my mother's hair salon customers; my mother was doing her hair. My sister spotted me and told my mother, who told me to wait upstairs until the customer left.

I hid behind a wall, intending to avoid punishment. As my mother passed, I seized the opportunity and ran downstairs and out of the house, determined not to face another whipping, the second time in my life. I sought refuge at Stretch's house, a family friend from childhood, and stayed there for several days. Eventually, I returned home with Mitchell, confident he had informed Mama of my whereabouts. Surprisingly, Mama said nothing more about the incident and never whipped me again. Mitchell had indeed saved me from the wrath of my mother.

30 Day Notice to Buy Home or Move

With the uncertainty of our future and the impending move from Sheriff Road, I couldn't help but feel a mixture of excitement and trepidation. As our time in the big stone house came to an end, my family relocated to Seat Pleasant, a community that held both familiar memories and the promise of new beginnings. It was a place where I had once been caught after stealing "Johnny's" bike, and where Mama worked as a part-time domestic for white families. Seat Pleasant was undergoing a significant transformation, transitioning from a majority White community to a primarily Black one. Leaving Sheriff Road behind, we embarked on this new chapter without saying goodbye, the remnants of our former neighborhood slowly fading.

Frank drove the truck carefully. He was very near-sighted and wouldn't wear the bifocals he needed for near-normal vision. I couldn't imagine how he saw his way as he drove us to our new community.

We rode along Carmony Hill Drive down the hill as we passed what I believed was the essence a beautiful girl. She had a big afro and high cheekbones; wow, she was beautiful. I was in love; I dreamed. She wore a sleeveless, form-fitting mini on her petite frame perfectly. She had thick eyebrows, a caramel brown complexion,

To Be Loved

pearly white teeth, and complete, flawlessly shaped lips that smiled when I waved at her.

I was stunned as she walked on. I watched her until I couldn't see her anymore. Then, we rode up the hill of modest ramblers and cape cod-styled homes until we reached 4308, our new home.

Our Sheriff Road house was big-time compared to this little wood frame rambler. It had a huge front picture window. My family housing choices had moved on up, then slid back. I scanned the whole neighborhood and went to check out our new home.

This house had three small bedrooms: one for Mama and Frank, one for the girls, and one for the boys. In addition, we had an eat-in kitchen and a separate, small living room.

I went back out to help unload the truck. I noticed that beautiful, petite girl with the 'fro,' again, coming up Peacock Street, our street. I got excited; it was like I was supposed to meet her. She passed and went into the house directly across from me.

Pat: What's Love Got to do With It?

Pat: What's Love Got to do With It?

Her name was Pat. Intrigued by her enchanting allure, I often stole glances at her from the window, admiring her as she sat on her porch, lost in the pages of a book. It was as if fate had brought us together, and I couldn't ignore the pull I felt toward her. With my sister Paulette as the catalyst, I mustered the courage to approach Pat and introduce myself, hopeful that we could have a connection.

As we walked up Peacock Street, our conversation unfolded, revealing shared interests in history, the Black struggle, and our demand for equality. I found solace and inspiration in Pat, like the music that had always been my refuge. Pat became my confidant, my muse, and my lover. Our love blossomed on the hill overlooking Carmony Elementary School, a sanctuary where we sought solace under the stars. On that hill our passion ignited, and making love intertwined with the melodies of Diana Ross and the Whispers, urging a symphony of emotions.

Our relationship deepened and Pat invited me to visit her at her brother's apartment, where his dual life as a carpenter and a drug dealer lay bare before us. Amidst the hidden weapons and stashes of drugs, our love intensified, fueled by the moment and the pulsating beats from the radio. It was an exploration of desires and a merging of souls that left an indelible mark on our hearts. In the embrace of Pat's love, I discovered not only the ecstasy of physical connection but also a profound understanding of the strength and depths of love. Our journey together,

To Be Loved

walking hand in hand through the challenges and triumphs of life, held the promise of transformation and growth. And as the melodies of our love story continued to play, I was grateful for the refuge she provided. In a world that often seemed uncertain and overwhelming, I finally got the finest girl around; I mattered!!!

***

As graduation from high school approached, I eagerly prepared for the momentous occasion. Mama bought me the green and gold cap and gown set, and I made arrangements for the prom, including renting a tuxedo. I couldn't help but feel a surge of excitement at the thought of attending the prom with Pat, someone unknown to the students at Spingarn High School.

However, Pat's response to my invitation puzzled me. Unlike most 11th-grade girls who would be thrilled to attend a senior prom, Pat seemed reluctant. It was unlike her usual character, and I couldn't understand her reservations. As we walked past Danny's house on Peacock Street, I wondered if she wanted him to see her with her new love. There was a sense of jealousy within me as I realized she had been keeping secrets from me, particularly about Danny. Marvin Gaye's "I Heard It Through the Grapevine" played in my mind, highlighting the doubts and uncertainties that clouded our relationship.

On prom day, J.C., a friend of Mitchell's and Biscuit's brother, offered to chauffeur us to the prom in his '69 Plymouth Roadrunner. It was supposed to be an exciting night, a final celebration with all our high school friends, marking the

Pat: What's Love Got to do With It?

end of an era. But Pat's lack of enthusiasm dampened my spirits. The evening unfolded without any memorable moments, overshadowed by the subdued atmosphere between us.

It was a bittersweet experience, as the excitement of graduation and the prom clashed with the underlying tension in my relationship with Pat. The significance of these milestones was marred by unspoken concerns and a growing sense of unease. Little did I know that these events were merely the precursor to the challenges and obstacles that awaited me. Graduation day arrived, and I found myself in a predicament.

After an incident during graduation practice led to my expulsion from the ceremony, I didn't have the nerve to tell Mama what had happened. So, we rode the bus together in silence, making our way to Spingarn High School. The gym was filled with graduates adorned in green and golden, surrounded by friends and family eagerly awaiting the commencement ceremony.

As nametags were distributed, I seized an opportunity to take the place of a male-named graduate who didn't respond. I hastily wrote my name on the card and stood in line with the rest of the graduates, praying I wouldn't be caught. The ceremony commenced, and with each passing moment, my heart raced. It was my turn to walk across the stage. the announcer proudly called my name. Filled with triumph, I strode across the stage; my pride mushrooming into relief. After the ceremony, I joined Mama in the auditorium, sharing our mutual pride. We journeyed back home, carrying the weight of that momentous day.

To Be Loved

Following graduation, I embarked on a job hunt. However, the people who used to be on the receiving end of my criminal tactics now held the reins of employment. Their questions about experience, marital status, and veteran status reminded me of the limitations imposed on an 18-year-old seeking work.

Amidst this employment search, my attention returned to Pat. I couldn't help but feel possessive of her, even questioning her interactions with other men. Pat's presence in my life was undeniable, and the thought of anyone else desiring her as much as I did seem incomprehensible.

One day, while sitting beneath the shade of a tree in Pat's yard, Iris, Pat's sister, shared some photos with me. My curiosity got the better of me, and I attempted to snatch the wallet from Iris's hands. In the process, pictures fell out onto the table, revealing a photo of Pat and Iris at a bar with two guys. The realization hit me like a ton of bricks—I hadn't considered that Pat would go out to bars with men. Naturally, she shifted the blame onto Iris, her sister, and I declared that I didn't want her going out with her sister again.

When the opportunity arose for Pat and Iris to go out again, my anger flared. I called out to Pat, expressing my disappointment and reminding her of our previous conversation. Despite her pleas to go to a movie, I stood firm, stating that if she left, our relationship would be over. As she hurriedly joined her sister, walking away from me, I was choked of anger and heartbreak; I didn't matter, I thought, not even to Pat.

Pat: What's Love Got to do With It?

The following day, still upset with Pat, I found solace in the music playing on my stereo. Two motorcycles pulled up before Pat's house. The riders went inside, and moments later, Pat emerged. Crossing the street, she approached me and said, "I want to talk to you when I come back." Although still upset, I agreed to wait, hoping for an explanation that would alleviate my anger.

Pat explained that she was going out with her cousins from Detroit, who were taking them for a ride. I watched Pat and her sister hop onto the back of each motorcycle, and speed away into the night. Left standing there, my anger and confusion lingered, now uncertain, again of what my future with her or anything else.

I was still out there when Reggie, Pat's older brother, walked casually up Peacock Street, eating a snack.

"Hey, Reggie, why didn't you tell me you had cousins from Detroit?" I said jokingly.

"Shee-it; I ain't got no cousins in Detroit!"

"Pat said--" "I think you were hoodwinked. I don't know who they were, but they weren't my cousins."

"Come on over to the house," Reggie said. Pat and I had been dating for a little over a month. "I'm staying out here until they return," I said, traumatized. I loved her madly, maybe too much. Does she see my weakness? Is that why she does this to me? Or does she not care? She's gone out again, lying in my face and standing me up. It's always somebody with wheels; maybe I need some wheels,

To Be Loved

yet, I can't even get a job. So now I don't care how much I loved her; the dream is over. I was shattered; Pat introduced me to a pain I had never known, a heart in shambles.

I sat with Reggie, rapping about the times and listening to records. A new group, "The Jackson 5", popped up on the scene with a string of hits. By no means were they the Temptations. The Jackson 5 kept coming up with hits, like the Temptations. The latest, "I Want You Back," "A.B.C.," "The Love You Save," and "I'll Be There" were playing on the radio.

It was about midnight; we heard motorcycles approaching. They were arriving.

Pat, riding on the back of the motorcycle, wore the dude's helmet.

"What is this?" I demanded.

"Oh, nothing!" she snapped angrily and got off the bike.

"Pat!" her mother called out from the door. "Come on in here, girl!"

"I'm coming," she responded. And, as if I wasn't even standing there, she handed the driver his helmet and marched past me, up the stairs, and into her house.

I stood there staring at the guy who had taken my girl on a bike ride. I wanted to fuck him up but had no reason: he hadn't kidnapped her; Pat voluntarily went out with the guys, a pattern I found hard to comprehend.

I couldn't sleep that night. First thing in the morning, I gathered all of Pat's souvenirs, including photos, letters, and cards, and I called her and met her

Pat: What's Love Got to do With It?

outside to give them back to her. I was hurt like never before. What I thought was deliverance, in terms of females, turned out to be devastation by her indiscretion. I told her it was over. I didn't want to see her again; even that hurt. It was my pride speaking. My heart was entangled in a mesh of mixed feelings. She didn't put up a fight. She turned and walked back to her house.

***

My summer job was over a few weeks later, and Pat returned to school. It would be 30 painful days before Pat, and I got back together. It didn't take much for us to return to our routine of walking to the hill or making love in her basement.

***

When all my efforts to get a permanent job seemed lost, I got another summer youth job through the Neighborhood Youth Corps and went to work at Andrew Air Force Base as a stock clerk. I worked in the supply warehouse, assisting soldiers in stocking the inventory of airplane parts. They kept me on the fringe, not learning anything that would help my future job prospects.

Pat and I discussed having sex. I said, "You are using birth control pills, aren't you?"

"Yeah. Sure."

"Yeah, because I don't want to have any children now. Shit, I don't know what I'm going

to do with my life, let alone with a child's life, too."

84

To Be Loved

Weeks later, Paulette, pregnant with her first child, exclaimed that Pat was pregnant, too.

"Pat," I said, "You told me you were using birth control."

"I was!" she said, "But, I stopped," as she looked away pensively.

"You stopped?! Listen, I don't want to have children now. I have no idea what I will do with myself, let alone a family with kids!

How many months are you?" "I'm not sure --"

'Not sure.' What the fuck was this? The first thing girls usually found out when it was confirmed that they were pregnant was how many months. But she didn't know.

"The doctor says I'm due in July," which would have made her one month pregnant in November.

I naively thought guys had babies who wanted them. I didn't know it would happen to me unless I wanted it, too. So, I did nothing to prevent a baby except tell Pat I wasn't prepared to have a child.

Without consulting the guys, teenage females elected to become pregnant at epidemic proportions. The 1960s and early 1970s liberation movements ushered in social change. Pregnant teenagers, formerly ostracized or sent away when they became pregnant, were now openly accepted.

I was afraid for my future. Here I was, fresh out of high school, unable to find a job, and I had to prepare for another life to devote myself to caring for.

Pat: What's Love Got to do With It?

Now, because Pat was pregnant I was attached permanently to Pat; I didn't believe we would stay together for the rest of our lives.

I dreaded becoming a parent before I knew early adulthood or myself or had a chance to choose parenthood. It chose me, and I didn't like that feeling.

Occasionally, when I'd see one of the fellows, I would talk about the pregnancy. They'd tell me I'd better get ready to buy stuff. The baby will need about $500 worth of things to come home. Yikes!!! I didn't have $500; diapers, blankets, clothes, a stroller, a bassinet, a crib, etc. Damn!

First, I fell in love with the most beautiful girl, only to be led to believe that she was promiscuous. Then, after we barely recouped from a breakup, I learn that she is pregnant. My life was way out of control. Early adulthood had turned me upside down. If this was the big payback for all the wrong, I had ever done, it would have been enough, yet there was still worse to come. I had thought about no longer doing crime because, at age 18, you'd pay with prison time. But, to stop behaviors that had become a lifestyle proved to be more than a notion. Fear gripped me as I grappled with the uncertainty of my future. Fresh out of high school and unable to secure stable employment, the prospect of becoming a parent seemed daunting. The social liberation movements of the 1960s led to a shift in attitudes toward females, including teenage pregnancy. Still, it brought anxiety and a feeling of being trapped.

To Be Loved

Chapter IV

Things Ain't What They Used to Be

In January 1971, I landed a job at the U.S. General Accounting Office, but my typing skills were not needed as black employees were limited to menial roles. Fueled by my growing racial consciousness, I yearned to expose the truth to everyone and especially to Black people. I believed the Civil Rights Movement would bring about change, but discrimination persisted.

Working in the mailroom, I observed the stark racial divide within the office building. The lowest floors housed primarily Black employees, while the upper floors were occupied predominantly by white employees. It infuriated me to see how blatantly white people kept black individuals confined to lower-status positions and limited opportunities. And, if Black workers didn't act like they were privileged to be employed in offices with whites, they were considered troublemakers with an attitude problem.

Suppressing my anger became a necessity. White colleagues didn't overtly express their dislike for me based on race, but their subtle reactions revealed their true feelings. I had to adopt a friendly demeanor and play along to maintain peace.

While delivering mail on the seventh floor, a white supervisor praised my attitude and offered me a position there. It seemed like a promotion, but in reality, it only granted me the "privilege" of working closely with white

Things Ain't What They Used to Be

colleagues. I accepted the offer, bidding farewell to my fellow mailroom workers, and feeling like I was "moving on up," already.

I shared a workspace on the seventh floor with two older black employees. Observing their subservient behavior when called upon, I confronted John about his apparent loss of dignity whenever white people called him. He confessed that it was too late for him to change, he had kids in college, but it didn't have to be that way for me. Determined not to break down like him, I resolved to maintain my self-respect.

Outside of work, I occasionally engaged in petty theft with my hustling buddy, Tyson. We stole cars, temporarily enjoying the illusion of having our own vehicle. When Mitchell came home briefly on prison work release, he asked me to give him a ride back to the halfway house in a car Tyson and I had stolen. Mitchell returns to home this last time, setting in motion a chain of events that would eventually engulf me.

One day, when I responded to the buzzer, the secretary met me in the hall and asked me to buy the Comptroller a cup of coffee and a pack of chewing gum. She looked grand-motherly, her blue eyes contrasted against the wrinkle, pale skin and white hair. She looked so comfortable, like she had been in the building all of her life.

"Mam, I'm sorry. But that's personal. I will not run personal errands for the Comptroller or anybody else," I said, looking into her eyes.

"Mr. Steele, we'll talk about this later!"

To Be Loved

I returned to the station and saw Mr. Perkins, his eyes lowered, in passing me on the way. I was disgusted. Next, they'll be asking me to go make coffee for the Comptroller. I ain't got to do that old shit even if Mr. Perkins and Ms. Hall always had. Times have changed.

Before long, I was called into the office of the lady who introduced me to the key people in the office.

"That's not why I came up here," I said, seated in front of her large wooden desk.

"What did you come up here for, Mr. Steele?" she asked sternly.

"For a better opportunity."

"What's a better opportunity?"

"I don't know, but I know it ain't running personal errands."

"Maybe you don't fit up here."

"Maybe *not!*"

"Thank you, Mr. Steele," she said icily. I took that to mean I should pack up and move back to the mailroom. Later in the day, my feeling was confirmed. I was told to report to the mailroom on Monday.

I went back to the mailroom feeling like a warrior. I had stood up to the system. Upon my return to the mailroom, I was applauded by the other workers. The only difference in working upstairs and working in the mailroom, I thought was, in the mailroom I didn't have the arrogance of white supremacy rubbed in my face.

Things Ain't What They Used to Be

The comptroller's driver, a coconut-brown complexioned natty, gray-haired man used to hang out with the light-skinned mailroom supervisor.

I told the chauffeur, "One day, Black people are going to get tired of oppression and take over this country."

"And do what?" the chauffeur snickered, "Run the country! Shee-it. Negroes can't run nothing," he said with the rapt authority of a professor. "Better be glad whites are in control-"

"Where's your faith in your own people?" I declared, knowing well the Uncle Tom had sold out, probably many, many years ago.

He reached in his pocket and pulled out some dollar bills and said, "These, here, are my peoples. And Negroes ain't making none of these."

In the face of adversity and laughter from those who doubted us, I held on to the hope of a better future.

To Be Loved

Wake Up Everybody: Activist or What

The GAO Black Caucus, named for the newly emerging U.S. Congressional Black Caucus, was a small, loosely organized group that set about integrating the employee union to obtain representation in battles against discrimination. I immediately joined the GAO Black Caucus. I was ready for the next stage of awareness: converting anger to fuel activism against discrimination. It was time to learn from mistakes and the Movement, a time to stand up to white supremacy. Almost everybody seemed touched by Black activism and inspired to fight and resist... It was an honorable service.

Once, we had a showdown in a white union official's office. As we mulled about in his office, he stopped working. He looked like he was suppressing rage. I stepped forward with my fearless attitude and said, "Who do you think you are to deny Black people membership in the union when they can support it and give as much to it as any group? Why shouldn't we be afforded the same opportunities you have always enjoyed?"

He stared above the rims of his glasses and said nothing. The crowd applauded me. At subsequent meetings we attended, I volunteered to chair the grievance committee. I collected employees' grievance letters for subsequent action. Most of the grievances were of employees who had earned a college degree or better, with over 35 years of experience, some of whom had trained whites to become their supervisors. Yet, the Black employees were never promoted above a GS-5 grade on a pay scale that went up to a GS-15.

Wake Up Everybody: Activist or What

The GAO Black Caucus considered a class action Equal Employment Opportunity lawsuit.

EEO was represented by a smooth, young brother in his 30s. He seemed different than the other Blacks. He seemed untouched by discrimination. His easy smile and "pearly whites" suggested he'd never had less than a good life. He appeared sharp and relaxed, and approachable. He was a GS-11, an almost unheard-of GS grade for a Black employee in 1971. I had never seen a brother so comfortable and stylish in those mostly white government plantation corridors. I wanted to say, "Hey Brother, you're badddd! How do I get to be like you?"

Then, I thought, 'To be that sophisticated in your 30s or any age, you must have been groomed for it from childhood – loving, caring parents, family, good diction, private schools, college, etc.; I thought I had missed out on those kinds of opportunities.

To Be Loved

Breaking Barriers, Making Progress

I became active in the GAO Black Caucus. I met many people and assured them we'd do something about discrimination there. Our leader was Mr. Otha Miller, whose career epitomized the Caucus struggle. Having earned a B.A., Mr. Miller worked at the GAO for 32 years but was not promoted beyond a GS-4.

I became more vocal, and I was encouraged to speak at meetings. A 'Civil Rights Activist;' had a special meaning to me; it would give me a purposeful life.

The Black Caucus matched me with a sister, Patricia Bell. We became the Caucus delegates to civil rights organizations like the Washington Urban League, The Black United Front, and the NAACP. The GAO Black Caucus asked Patricia and me to represent it at a dinner hosted by the Congressional Black Caucus. Wow, what a privilege!

Pat and I walked up North Capitol Street, past the Government Printing Office, towards the grand old Post Office near Union Station. Then, as if prompted by my thoughts, Marvin Gaye's melodic voice from a parked car's radio sang "What's Going On," and defined the moment and time.

Marvin Gaye had recently completed a five-year hiatus following the death of his female duet partner, Tammie Terrell. We were on the heels of a social revolution with political assassinations, environmental pushes, a national uptick in teenage pregnancies, and the Vietnam War. Marvin Gaye asked, "What's

Breaking Barriers, Making Progress

Going On?" Are we losing control? Can we take it anymore? Do we realize what's happening? Marvin Gaye, in a groove, made us reflect on our fast-changing society. The album featured him on the cover standing in the rain -- that's how I felt; that album mirrored my consciousness.

I was in awe of the stature of the Congressional Black Caucus dinner, attended by Congressmen Charles Diggs (D. -Mich.), a pioneering legislator who co-founded the CBC and served as Congress' expert on Africa. I also saw the D.C. Delegate, the Rev. Walter Fauntroy, one of the late Dr. Martin Luther King's lieutenants, and others. Patricia and I had dinner together, smiling graciously and chatting with others about our efforts at the GAO.

***

The GAO Black Caucus had demonstrated against discrimination in front of the GAO. One major demonstration was at the U.S. Civil Service Commission at 19th & E Streets, N.W. Mr. Robert "Bob" White, president of the National Alliance of Postal and Federal Employees, the largest black-led union, hosted the march. He stood before the crowd of thousands of protestors and gave remarks to thunderous applause. Then, off the cuff, he asked me to speak, and I blurted out, "We are tired of discrimination, and we are not taking it anymore! It is time for us to demand to be treated equally," to more applause.

***

Due to my activism, this guy, a mailroom driver at GAO and an alcoholic, used to tell everybody that I was studying to become a lawyer. And he

To Be Loved

would also tell me privately, "You better watch yourself; something bad is gonna happen to you."

"What do you mean?" I asked, not really concerned. What could happen worse than what I have been through to get there?

"Just watch yourself, 'Sonny.'"

I thought he projected the fear all blacks felt about activism and the consequences Blacks faced when fighting for their rights. Unfortunately, his fear was rooted in fact this time; when Blacks stand up, the system comes after them.

***

Tyson, my former hustling partner, was wandering and couldn't get anchored. I brought him to my house and trained him to take the civil service exam for a clerk typist position in the federal government. He passed it the first time around. When a job in my office became available, I recommended Tyson. The office hired him. I felt proud that I could help make a difference in a friend's life. But, it was a sentimental, reckless move.

But, Tyson hadn't broken with the past. Neither had I. When he got on the job, he began stealing personal property from offices. I thought whites certainly were robbing us with minimum wages and discrimination; we were supposed to rob them every chance we got.

Once, while delivering mail, we discovered the building's vending machine serviceman's office, where he kept his supplies and cash. During office hours, we burglarized his office, took bags of coins, and hid them in the bottom basket of my mail cart. Then, we eased the bags out of the building in boxes and split the money, about $150 in coins.

Other times, we'd be in the credit union lines on payday, selling coats and hats we had stolen out of offices of people who lived a life of luxurious indifference while we suffered from their exploitation and oppression.

In May 1971, Tyson told me about a purse he took. It had only $3 in it. "Tyson, take it back," I warned him. It wasn't worth the suspicion it would put on my mail route. Take it back, take it back!"

He agreed. Later, a secretary called the office and asked that I go to an office for a "pick-up." When I arrived, she handed me a holey government envelope containing a white envelope of change and dollar bills. The secretary asked me to deliver it to another office. Something didn't feel right. After I had delivered the envelope and returned to the mailroom, Tyson was gone. However, two white officials were there.

"Mr. Steele," my supervisor called me. "Mr. Steele."

"Yes."

"These gentlemen are here from personnel. They need you to go to personnel with them."

The white guys said nothing as we walked to an office in personnel. Once there, they left me alone for a while. Another official came in.

"Mr. Steele, there's been a theft, and you're implicated!"

They had set up the purse that Tyson had stolen. Tyson confessed and

To Be Loved

told them he had told me about it, and I hadn't reported the theft to officials. They had called the police.

We were fired, charged with petty larceny, handcuffed, and walked through the building before everyone who saw me as a GAO Black Caucus civil rights activist to a squad car waiting outside. Once at the precinct, in exchange for us admitting other thefts in the building and resigning our jobs, they dropped all charges and released us. I surmised that Tyson had told them everything -- It was a plant to get rid of me. I was too clever; Tyson wasn't, and he took me down. I realized what the man on the job was talking about when he predicted something terrible would happen to me!

I had not learned to value my life. I should have seen the larger picture and protected my goal, to become a civil rights activist. The anger at oppression, and my lack of preparation, had blinded my vision and judgment. I had made commitment of intention to never commit another crime. That 'ol drunk on my job knew that when I became visible as an activist, the enemies would want to know who I was and come after me. If I had known, I wouldn't have made it so easy for them; we are fish fighting whales. Ants may tie up an elephant, but they must have ad much more intelligent defense than I did.

Damn. The civil rights "lawyer," who promised so much hope and who exhibited so much courage, was a common thief, the people would say. They could now say that my activism was a cover. I hoped I would never see anybody from the GAO again. I had let them down. I did see Patricia again, years later, at a demonstration downtown. I felt ashamed, and I avoided her.

I was out of a job, and more importantly, my brief civil rights career was over.

What's Going On?

Mr. Miller and the GAO Caucus, on behalf of 600 workers, were awarded, 10 years later, $4.2 in damages for being "passed over for promotion after promotion because they were black."

***

The FBI was coming around looking for Mitchell. He was robbing again, too. The threat of prison never seemed to faze him. He was one confident crazy brother.

Mitchell, blowing cigar smoke in my face, awakened me one night. He had a wild story about some hotel heist that he, Too Tall, Fats, and a girl had pulled off. He had a handful of money.

On another night, Mitchell awakened me, and again, he told me of his exploits. This time he told me where they split the money.

"I got a lot of foreign money and threw that shit in a dump."

"A dump, what dump?"

"Right at the apartment."

The following day, I went to the dump at the apartment complex on Sheriff Road in Landover, Md., to recover the foreign money. Sure enough, after rummaging through the trash bin, I found it. I remembered a foreign money

To Be Loved

exchange on 14th Street, N.W., and New York Avenue, N.W. I took the money there and exchanged it for $125. I finally got compensation from Mitchell for the $90 he swindled from me years ago, though he still owed me for stealing and crashing my car.

These tumultuous events underscored my challenges and the personal struggles I faced in my early adulthood. Love, betrayal, unemployment, and the consequences of my actions left me feeling lost and ill-equipped to navigate life's difficulties.

Yet, the fight for equality and justice persisted, even in the face of personal setbacks. The lessons I learned from these experiences would shape my future, reminding me of the importance of perseverance, self-reflection, and the need to balancing anger with strategic action.

Father: Ngina Steele

Pat and I began to argue frequently after she became pregnant. I felt misled about her not taking birth control. Pat was getting close to graduating from high school and wanted a kid, like so many teenage females during and since that time.

I came into the house on June 7, and Paulette, who had recently given birth to Paula, her baby girl, asked, "Haven't you heard?"

"Heard what?"

"You're a father, man! Pat had a baby girl!"

Maybe now that the baby was here and I was a father, my mother or Frank would say, "Let's talk." However, there was only chilling silence. Communication was difficult, at best, between my mother and me. I came home and wanted to talk to Mama about Pat. I began with, "Mama, I love Pat."

Mama was looking at a newspaper and wouldn't look up. I was trying to outgrow our old relationship, and she wasn't ready. On another occasion, I blurted out: "Mama, I want to marry Patricia. Would you sign for me?"

She looked at me from the table and said, "If you don't get out of here!" All the times I had ever gone to my mother with matters of the heart, it was me crying out for her love. She would almost always dismiss me. I guess my missteps and misdeeds had trained her view of me.

Patricia and I had agreed that the baby would have an African name. She

To Be Loved

would name the baby if it's a girl; I would name him if a boy. I went to Prince George's Hospital to see Pat soon after Paulette's announcement. The health chart listed my daughter with her mother's maiden name. I said, "Look, if she is my child, I want her to have my last name; you change it, or I'm leaving now."

Pat called a nurse in and made the change.

The nurse, a black woman, read Ngina's name on the chart and said, "Ya'll are not going to name your child that name, are you? Before continuing: "They'll pick on her in school!" We ignored her as Pat filled out the request form.

Ngina had a much lighter complexion than both Pat and me. She had greenish, gray eyes. Immediately, I wondered if Ngina was mine, then who was her father -- the guy on the motorcycle? That's why Pat knew she was pregnant but not how many months; then she claimed the baby would be born in July, projecting that the pregnancy occurred when we reunited in September. In September, Pat was one month to come to a full term in June, which meant she got pregnant in August, I thought. Pat understood we were not going together in August for 30 days, so she claimed Ngina was born a month early. Pat was trying to hide something.

However, once Ngina came home, I tried to fit the role of a father; my father was no teacher. I had to learn on the job. The females in my family weren't hearing any doubts about whether Ngina was mine. The uncertainties raised many questions and haunted me. When I would try to talk about them with Pat, she'd only answer, "I don't know."

Father: Ngina Steele

I hated that phrase. Her use of "I don't know" was her way of avoiding accountability or responsibility.

***

On June 26, 1971, 19 days after Ngina was born, Pat and I had an argument, and I stormed home. In the street, Mitchell pulled up with his gangster crew in their 1969 orange Firebird. They were hanging out, celebrating their latest heist. I told him I was going through some changes with my girl, and he said, "You want to hang out with us?"

That night we hung out, got high and went to sleep. The next day, we had planned to go horseback riding out on Route 301 South, the main north/south thoroughfare before I-95 replaced it as the main interstate highway. It was a southern Maryland motel corridor for interstate travelers. By the time we had gotten there, the horse stable had closed. So, Mitchell and Too Tall drove on down 301-S.

"This motel looks good," Mitchell said at about 10:30 p.m. as we pulled into La Plata Motel's horseshoe-shaped driveway.

He pulled out a sawed-off shotgun and told me to "get behind the wheel!" That wasn't exactly my plan for that evening. I knew Mitchell would always protect me from harm, and I obliged.

They went inside while I waited in the dark and quiet parking lot as the Route 301 traffic zoomed by in both directions. Why would they build so many motels on a highway where robbers could quickly get away and get lost in

To Be Loved

speeding traffic? They sure were dumb, I thought. Little did I know that when we would leave the motel lot, if we turned right on Route 301 North, we would pass a Maryland State Police Station. A left turn on Route 301, headed South, would take us past the La Plata Jail. Either way, we were headed to jail. Minutes later, Mitchell and Too Tall rushed back out. Mitchell carried a 13-inch, portable black and white T.V., a little sack of money, and the sawed-off rifle.

As Mitchell entered the car, another car pulled into the hotel's driveway and stopped. The driver noticed Mitchell and Too Tall piling in and got out of his vehicle quickly to look inside the motel office before he came back to his car and began to follow us. I drove away, turned north onto Route 301, and took off. Less than a block away, I stopped at the light to make a left on Route 225 West (towards Indian Head Highway). The car that followed us kept straight towards the Police station.

"Yeah, let's get the fuck out of here!" Mitchell said.

"Damn, how much money did we get?" Too Tall asked.

"I don't know. You think I counted it before I took it?" Mitchell replied.

By this time, a car seemed to be trying to pass us. I sped up, and it sped up, its lights looming larger in the dark. I slowed, and it slowed. I stepped on it. As I sped, it sped up, too. Ahead, a cadre of Police cruisers blocked the thoroughfare with their lights flashing.

On the car that appeared to tail us, Police cruiser lights flared with the sound of its siren.

Father: Ngina Steele

I pulled over to the shoulder of the road near the wooded area as Mitchell tossed the shotgun out the car window, and the Police aimed their weapons at us from the roadblock.

Then a Police bullhorn sounded, "Get out of the car with your hands up so we can see them, and there won't be any accidents!"

Police arrested and handcuffed us, searched for weapons, loaded us into the back of a squad car, and drove back to La Plata Motel for identification. The victim identified Too Tall and Mitchell, but not me.

We were then taken to the Charles County Courthouse and booked for robbery with a deadly weapon. One officer also stated that he followed us at up to 60 mph. He also declared they found in our possession a portable T.V., a Gruen wristwatch, and $150, all belonging to the robbery victim.

Our bond was set at $5,000 each.

My late father's social security, a lump $600 payment intended for my further education, Mama declared, was used for my bond. Mama never mentioned the social security benefit. I guess she had waited for me to settle on something meaningful lest I waste the money. I was glad that money was there; otherwise, I would have remained in jail for about six months before trial.

Once out on bond, I had three months to get all my "licks" in and say goodbye. Police claimed they had found a shotgun shell on me, matching the shotgun used in the robbery. It was a lie, an illegal plant that they had used to connect me to the robbery.

To Be Loved

Being locked up might not be so bad, I wanted to believe. Brothers in prison were probably like the ones in Attica and Soledad Prisons who I read about, united, revolutionary and strong, I wanted to believe.

I went to see Pat and told her what had happened. I thought she would be outraged by the arrest. Instead, she accepted it with calm and empathy. Maybe it was because her brothers, like my brother Mitchell, were career criminals, burglars, and robbers, who did big time repeatedly. Or perhaps she was glad that I would be gone for a while.

While struggling to get a hold of my life, I got hit with a punch that had me sprawled on the canvas. The arrest was a definite wake-up call. I knew that the time on bond should be used so that I could testify in court that I was trying to move my life in a positive direction and that this was a mere mistake; it was. I had told myself that I would not commit crimes anymore.

I had to learn how to fix my early adulthood past of local street culture that compelled me to revert again and again.

***

I went to a United Planning Organization job counseling program called the Washington Concentrated Employment Program at 1331 Savannah Street in one of the poorest, roughest communities in southeast Washington, D.C. My job counselor, Mrs. Montgomery, took a particular interest in me after I expressed my educational interests to her. She referred me to The American Learning Center at 9th and H Streets, N.W., a minimum wage, six-week refresher course in English,

Math, and Typing. Then, I enrolled in D.C. Skills at 5th and W Streets, N.E., a 14-week, minimum-wage auto mechanics program.

They were "social" programs, small fruits of the Civil Rights Movement. Blacks, women, the disabled, and more were increasingly admitted into the mainstream job market. However, the economy couldn't or wouldn't support them. So, these programs were stopgap measures aimed at providing a minimum wage for a short period and to help brush up on basic job skills.

For me, they were paychecks, $144 bi-weekly, and the closest to having a job I could get at the time. It was the first time in my life that I was in school because I wanted to be, and I enjoyed excelling in the class. After a few more paychecks, students graduated with a certificate and warm regards.

The new relationships I enjoyed would be very superficial. I was moving in a different direction, which was significantly uncertain. I might not see anybody except other prisoners and visitors for a while.

***

While in the D.C. Skills program, Federal City College (FCC), another plumb of the Civil Rights Movement, finally responded to my application from nearly a year earlier. I enrolled in FCC, whose main campus was its headquarters building at 2nd and D Streets, N.W. FCC's only criteria for admission were a student's desire and willingness to study. I was ready to excel academically.

If I beat this rap, I thought, I would study psychology; no, I couldn't deal with all the problems people might have. Maybe I would study sociology to help

To Be Loved

fight the drug peril destroying our community.

The D.C. Skills program and FCC kept me earnestly learning right to the day before the trial. I went to D.C. Skills during the early morning work hours, and from there, in the evening, I went to FCC at night.

In September 1971, Mitchell and I were due in the Circuit Court for Charles County, Maryland, for an arraignment. The night before, Mitchell bought some heroin, and we sat up in the living room, reveled, and nodded the night away as Brooke Benton's "Rainy Night in Georgia" played on the radio.

The next day, after a court proceeding, FBI agents asked Mitchell if his name was Michael Lucas. Then, they arrested him as a fugitive from the work release program he had walked away from in January. I cried as they took him away, "Mitchell, you want my money, you want my money?" They took him away. I was reminded of Marvin Gaye's "Mercy, Mercy Me," where he sang, "Things ain't what they used to be." My world turned upside down. I realized that I had all but lost control.

Finally, on October 20, 1971, during the court trial proceedings by a jury of nine whites and three "Negroes," the robbery victim, Mr. Kent Taylor, testified, "I am absolutely sure that Ronald Douglas Steele did not rob me." Again, I hoped justice would prevail.

Mama didn't go to the trial. I couldn't blame her; she had been to court so many times for Mitchell. It's painful for any mother to watch her children get sucked into the system, unable to do anything except witness it, tragically.

Father: Ngina Steele

I had maintained that I was drunk and asleep in the back of the car -- which they could not disprove -- and I knew nothing of the robbery. The victim's statement certainly reinforced my alibi. It was Mitchell's turn to be the big brother and protect me from incarceration by copping a plea since the state had so much evidence against him and Too Tall and none against me.

"A plea would exonerate me," I wrote to Mitchell. He replied, "when you have a record like I have, and you plead guilty without a good reason for doing the crime, you're asking for the maximum." They had the gun, positive I.D., the duct tape in the car that matched the one used on the victim to tie him up, and other evidence, including Mitchell's fingerprints on the weapon. Who was he fooling? Was he that selfish, or was he crazy? He was irresponsible to have a younger sibling out with him on a robbery if he didn't plan to protect me at all costs.

This was his idea. I had tagged along to the wrong place at the wrong time. I felt he had always left me alone to fend for myself.

On October 21, 1971, after instruction by the judge that "if one was guilty, they all are," Mitchell Steele, alias, Michael Lucas, and Too Tall, both age 22, and me, 19, were convicted of robbery with a deadly weapon. If I was guilty of anything, it was an accessory to the robbery; however, they didn't charge me with accessory. This time justice had robbed me.

My court-appointed counselor, Mr. Murdoch, proved incompetent throughout the trial. He didn't ask for a change of venue or a separate trial for me;

To Be Loved

I quickly learned. He didn't challenge the veracity of the officer's claim that he found a shotgun shell on me. Murdock didn't raise the fact of the victim's testimony as he clearly said that I did not rob him. How can they find me guilty of the robbery? I was remanded to the La Plata Jail, for a pre-sentence report, due with sentencing, nearly two months later, on December 16, 1971. Damn!

I recalled with deep regret my brief efforts to become a civil rights activist. Ngina was only three months old; I wouldn't see her grow. I had begun college and was enjoying it.

I couldn't believe this was happening to me. I thought I would not be here if it weren't for getting into an argument with my girl and storming home. If it wasn't for that person coming to La Plata Motel; if it wasn't for those cops planting and lying about that shotgun shell; if Mitchell had only copped a plea; if Mitchell had not pulled up that evening; if Mitchell hadn't walked away from work-release. Then, I realized that an antidote for guilt is to blame. I could have said, "No thanks." Suddenly, I felt like the patient at St. E's must have felt after the cop noticed his trunk of bank loot -- like going crazy!

Inmate

La Plata Jail was a two-story cagy building with about eight cells and a single shower. An elderly couple lived in an apartment adjacent to the jail, and they prepared our meals and provided us with clean linen for our beds. What a life, I imagined. We came out of the cells once a day to go upstairs and shower. Inmates spent days there rapping and looking out the window as people went to and fro, oblivious to La Plata Jail and us inmates waiting to be tried or sentenced.

The Jackson 5 was the reigning top group with "Never Can Say Goodbye," and I wasn't out there. Sly and the Family Stone sang, "It's A Family Affair," and I wasn't out there. There would be lots of songs released before I was free again.

I missed the music and jive-talk of my hometown radio stations: "This is Mel, Mel, Mel of the big (W) O.L." La Plata Jail was too far away to hear WOL AM. So, I listened to WPGC, a white radio station. After a while, I began to appreciate white recordings, too. They, too, began to mark my life. Like: "I Got a Brand New Pair of Roller Skates" by Melanie; "Gypsies, Tramps and Thieves," by Cher, and "Sunshine Go Away," by Jonathan Edwards.

Mama and a couple of family members came to visit me. Standing at my cell door, we talk through the bars. They'd tell me what was going on in the neighborhood.

I couldn't wait to be transferred from that little country jail.

To Be Loved

Occasionally, I'd write to someone at home. In this case, it was my 15-year-old brother, Milton:

November 1, 1971

Hey Brotherman:

How you doing? Don't even ask me, brother, you know I can't be doing too well in here.

I guess Mama told you what went down. So, I won't bother to discuss it. I must forget the past and start looking forward to the future,

Milton, I'll be calling on you to do certain things for me from time to time. As a brother, I'm granting you a responsibility that only you can do. My clothes, as you know are my pride and only possessions. And to prevent the destruction of them, I'll ask you not to wear them. Please understand I'm not being selfish. My books also are my pride and joy so don't lend any out. But if it interests you, you are welcome to read them. Send them and other things only upon my request by letter. It'll be a hell of a responsibility (smile). Do you think you can swing it? Sure you can Bro.

Tell Carlean to stay Blacker than she was when I saw her last. She has the most levelest head on our culture at home now.

Take it easy, brother, later

***

Ronald

November 28, 1971

Inmate

Hello, Mama:

How's all? I hope you are fine. I'm doing O.K, despite the outlook. I try to keep this situation I'm in off my mind. Along with my pessimistic feelings, I also control the power of my mind not to worry about problems until the final days of their existence.

I hope you're feeling the same way. Do that for Mitchell and me. I expected the worst so if given any less, it wouldn't be as hard to accept.

As I stated in my first letter, you are truly a strong mother. Stay that way. Keep smiling. It gives me (I'm sure Mitchell, too) encouragement.

Things aren't going to be as bad as expected up the road.

Really (as I understand) it's what you make of it. So, in that case, it'll benefit me. It can't be any worse than here. Matter of fact (So I'm told) its luxury compared to this joint.

Sure you're gonna miss us both, but it'll only be for a short while.

Love you Mama. Keep smiling.

Ronald

***

My main man, Robert, along with Thomas in his '70 (Ford Lincoln) Mark IV, drove out to La Plata Jail to see me only once in the three months; what a letdown from friends. We had to conduct the visit through that back window, visiting hours were over.

On December 16, my brother Mitchell, Too Tall, and I appeared before

To Be Loved

the judge for sentencing. We were asked whether we have anything to say before sentencing.

"No," said Mitchell.

Too Tall shook his head and said, "No."

I followed their lead. "No, "I replied. Mitchell and Too Tall were sentenced to 20; I was sentenced to 15 years.

Upon hearing the sentence, I was both saddened and elated. Saddened that they would give me such a severe sentence, even though they really didn't prove my guilt. I was glad to be leaving La Plata, however, where this nightmare began. Still, with a sentence almost as long as I had lived, the judge had also coffered upon me "baddd Nigga" status in my neighborhood. For I had to be baddd that he felt he had to sentence me to 15 years to chill.

I staggered out of the courthouse alone as I resigned myself to not going back home. Mitchell and Too Tall were shackled and transported to prison to serve their sentence.

I lay on the bunk and looked around at the small bullet grey, cagey bars and stairs of the jail, the barred window.

I wrote: "The longest day was --- today...when the day ended, I slept with 15 years on my mind." One and one-half years after graduating from high school and street life, who would have thought I would end up in 1972 serving a 15-year-bit? Damn, I sure didn't. My life would be altered forever in a moment of bad judgment.

Inmate

As the days stretched on, I longed for freedom and yearned to be reunited with my loved ones. The world continued to move forward, without me. But deep within, I held onto hope, knowing that someday I would be released and given a chance to rebuild my life.

To Be Loved

Chapter V

No Place to Be Somebody

"The Baltimore Pen," with its gothic architecture veiled in a thick layer of black grime accumulated from over 160 years of pollution, stood as a testament to time. It is the oldest penitentiary in the Western world and the sole maximum-security facility in Maryland. We were escorted by correctional officers, shackled and bound at our waists and ankles, evoking eerie reminders of slavery and our haunting past. Passing through the imposing front doors of the Maryland State Penitentiary, we ventured beyond the visiting room where I had visited Mitchell in the past. Our procession led us to the "holding room," a cramped office adorned with regimented steel bars, gates, and guards stationed every few feet. The space resembled a mammoth institutional hallway repurposed into a reception area for visitors, while just across the hall loomed the presence of a "Police Station."

In spite of the circumstances, I tried to find solace in the notion that things might not be so unbearable. The spirit of social activism from the '60s and '70s had also made its way into the prisons. Uprisings had taken place in Attica, Soledad, San Quentin, and other prisons, where fellow inmates demanded to be treated as human beings. I assumed that incarcerated individuals, especially those who shared a similar background, would be united like the bolts on the Brooklyn Bridge. Society had made it nearly impossible for young Black men to attain the American Dream, even as television tantalized us with its images. The law mandated that we remain on the side-lines, waiting and yearning for "white" privileges. Some accepted their subservient roles, defending the interests of their masters as their own. But we belonged to a unique class of Black men – the field hands who undermined the system, the "Stagolees." We were insurgents, warriors, and we refused to succumb to white supremacy or the notion of our alleged inferiority. Or at least, that's what I tried to convince myself.

For me, being locked up offered respite from the daunting pressures of early adulthood and the consequences it entailed. No longer would I have to plead for employment from white individuals or grapple with romantic dilemmas. I could avoid the agonizing decision of accepting responsibility for a child I doubted was mine. Those thoughts brought a temporary sense of relief because I had yet to learn how to navigate the challenges of early adulthood. I was ill-prepared. However, prison proved to be no escape. Instead, I replaced one set of worries with another, far more perilous and unrelenting than anything I had encountered on the streets.

Descending further into the depths of the facility, we inmates were ushered into a room where we were stripped of our clothes. A guard then proceeded to spray our genitals and anus for lice. Each of us was allocated a pillow, a blanket, and a sheet set before being assigned a cell.

We continued our march through the Pen, eventually arriving at the Maryland Receiving and Diagnostic Classification Center (MRDCC). This tier

To Be Loved

served as a temporary abode for new arrivals until their ultimate placement in a correctional institution was determined.

The Pen resembled a colossal warehouse, with ceilings towering three stories high, grimy lime-colored windows adorned with chipped paint, bars, and two sets of what looked like substantial cages positioned at its center. These cages held five tiers of cells each, one accommodating the main penitentiary population and the other reserved for MRDCC.

The bunks were dimly illuminated by a single bulb, casting eerie shadows against the three steel walls that formed the cells. These walls, adorned with personal photographs and magazine cut-outs, attempted to inject a semblance of warmth into the cold steel surroundings. Colorful towels, hanging like substitute curtains, provided a brief respite from the monotony of grey. Privacy was a long-lost luxury, as anyone passing by could catch a glimpse of my every move, even when nature called.

We walked past the Death Row tier of the East Wing and the main inmate population's floor tier of the West Wing. The second tier was Death Row. Those guys were segregated from the rest of the population, while they waited their date with fate. Many of them looked resigned to their fate. They seemed to study their movements in their cells with great detail and patience, as if there was nothing as important as the moment.

"Hey, Steele!" a familiar voice shouted out to me from Death Row. It was

Timothy, the old Spingarn High School buddy, who had been a hustler.

"Hey, Timothy!" I shouted as we walked, passing 10'x10'x15' cells.

In the cells' ceiling a bulb illuminated the bunks and three steel walls decorated variously with personal photographs and ones from magazines. For a homey effect, colorful towels hung like luxurious curtains, hiding the grey steel walls. Some inmates attended personal matters. There was no more privacy. Even when I had to use the toilet, I could be seen by anyone passing along. "What you're in here for?" Timothy hollered out to me, as we continued to march single file.

"Robbery," I shouted back.

"Whatchu get?" he asked.

"15 years," I said, as if a badge of honor.

You can handle it."

"Got to," I said, "What you're in here for?"

"Murder/robbery."

"Damn! What you get?"

"Death, plus 70," he said.

'Damn!' I thought. I had never heard of a sentence that severe.

"See," he said, "you can handle that 15, can't you?"

"Yeah, man!" I shouted over my shoulder as we continued to march.

"Stay strong, Steele!"

I said, "You hang in there, too!"

To Be Loved

The regulars stared at us new arrivals. While we wore the orange prison jump suits, regulars were allowed to wear street clothes. However, the clothes dated their entry. It looked awful, but to them, I guess it was cool. It was their foundation, who they were. It was one way in which they tried to hold on to the memories of the way things were before they were incarcerated.

I had heard how the old, regular prison heads preyed on the new arrivals, especially the young ones. Brothers have always exploited one another's weaknesses, if only in joaning. Certainly, in prison, unlike on the street, survival would be more intense and for more basic things. So, we all had to show no fear, no weakness. I had to act like I knew my way around at all times. It was like being in Lincoln Heights, again or being at Roper Junior High. I had to carry myself like I had no fear.

I had to learn to suppress my natural tendencies. I couldn't be the jovial, fun person that I was on the streets. I had to stay on guard for the unexpected. I had to be serious, dead serious, all of the time. This was serious.

Prison, I soon discovered, bred a survival instinct that demanded vigilance at all times. The exploitation of vulnerabilities, even if in the form of jest or sport, was an all-too-common occurrence among inmates. To navigate this environment, I had to suppress my natural inclination for cheerfulness and adopt an air of constant seriousness. Fear and intimidation flourished here, and I had to convey an unwavering sense of fearlessness, as if I had always known my way

No Place to Be Somebody

around. It felt reminiscent of my days in the Kelly Miller or at Roper Junior High school, where I had to project an image of strength despite the lurking dangers.

Led by the jangling sound of oversized keys, the guard guided us to our designated tier, using the clanging keys to unlock the steel closet and release the row of levers that opened the cell doors. The sound reverberated down the tier, echoing through the cavernous space. Down on the ground floor, four stories below, inmates engaged in various activities—playing cards, walking, mopping the tier, and others watched television suspended high on the wall.

I walked past the cells, stealing glimpses of their personalized inmate decor until I reached my designated destination—cell B 4 12. Here, within the cramped confines, I would dwell for an indeterminate period of time. The cell housed a double bunk, a toilet, a sink, and walls of cold metal adorned with steel bars, serving as both a barrier and a constant reminder of confinement. I laid my meager belongings down and peered out of one of the tall, dirt-smudged windows, about 30 yards away. Life carried on beyond these prison walls—people walked by on the streets, while children played in front of their government-subsidized homes. It was a surreal juxtaposition, a penitentiary nestled amidst a "growing" community—a testament to the school-to-prison social engineering.

As I began unpacking my meager possessions, the familiar clamor of unlocking doors filled the air once again. It was time for the communal shower, a prospect that filled me with trepidation. I had heard tales of assaults that took place in those tiled chambers. The vulnerability of being naked amid others,

To Be Loved

exposed and defenceless, unsettled me. Yet, there was no avoiding it. Gripping my towel and washcloth tightly, I made my way to the shower room.

The space was expansive, with archaic plumbing pipes exposed in the ceiling. Each inmate, focused on self-preservation, barely acknowledged the presence of others, save for the occasional menacing glare that warned against encroachment. Thankfully, the shower passed without incident, but the tension in the air was palpable—a constant reminder of the stakes at hand.

After I had arrived back at the cell for a couple of hours, the doors swung open once more, with a thunderous bang, signalling suppertime. The clang of footsteps reverberated as we marched single file to the end of the tier, descending the lime-green-painted steel steps to reach the first floor of the penitentiary. The guard led us across the courtyard, enclosed by imposing boulder stone walls and watchtowers that emphasized the prison's gothic fortress-like appearance. Armed guards, ever watchful, perched above, scrutinizing our every move.

Taking our seats on several rows of lawn benches in the cafeteria, the inmate kitchen crew aimlessly dropped portions of food onto our trays. Dinner passed without fanfare, and we were soon escorted to another building—the infirmary. There, we underwent individual examinations, prodded and pricked for any signs of disease. Afterward, we were assigned a number, a new identity that would define our existence within these walls. For me, that number was 112538, a symbol that had to be displayed on my clothes, attached to every piece of mail I sent or received.

No Place to Be Somebody

Back to the main housing area, clad in our orange "kangaroo suits," I couldn't help but notice an older man in a neighboring cell. He unfolded his bunk leisurely and opened a small brown bag, savoring food as if it were a fine dining experience. Time, or rather the length of our prison sentences, began to dawn on me, casting a sobering shadow over my thoughts.

A voice interrupted my introspection, belonging to a Brother named Ray. We exchanged greetings, revealing our origins—Baltimore for him, and D.C. for me. Curiosity led us to inquire about each other's offenses. "Robbery," we both admitted, and then came the question of the dreaded time served. "Fifteen years," I confessed, the weight of the sentence reverberating in my voice. Ray's reply hit me like a punch to the gut—"Twenty-five years." Ray was 17.

Damn. Those judges were handing out time like it was candy, indifferent to the devastating impact it had on families, loved ones, communities. The message to the Black community was clear: "If we commit crime, we'll endure the harshest punishment." I couldn't help but wish I had known just how fucked up prison was, and I would have fought tooth and nail to avoid ending up here.

As I surveyed the surroundings, the cacophony of voices merged with the blaring noise of a TV, reverberating across the ceramic walls of the recreational area. The man in a neighboring cell moved at a slower pace, seemingly unaffected by the passing of time. I couldn't help but notice the outdated clothes some inmates wore, marking how long they have been a prisoner. I longed for this scene to be over, yearning for escape.

To Be Loved

"Follow me," the guard commanded, leading us back to the tier gate, destined for our cell. It was in that moment that I began to resent the relentless passage of time, feeling trapped and on the precipice of depression. Climbing onto my bunk, I sought solace in sleep, hoping that the nightmare would dissolve upon awakening. But deep down, I knew that the torment would persist unless I managed to sleep away the 15 long years of my sentence.

The next day marked my first full day at the MRDCC, where we were granted access to a designated courtyard. Memories of my time as an employee at St. Elizabeth Hospital, a mental asylum, flooded my mind, drawing unsettling comparisons. This time, however, I was an inmate, and suspicion and paranoia became constant companions. I had to remain on high alert, watching my back at all times.

We had arrived at the courtyard. I was curious to see who I might know in MRDC, , when suddenly a door from the cafeteria swung open and an inmate sprang from the building right across the courtyard where we were standing. Another inmate ran after him. The lead guy, having nowhere else to run, surrendered with his hands up, as the guy who was chasing him sprang on him with a knife and began stabbing him, over and again. Blood began to soak the victim's clothes at every point in which he was stabbed before he fell on the ground.

Damn! Again, everybody stood around and watched him stab that muthafucka. The guards in the towers didn't even react. What on earth could he

No Place to Be Somebody

have done to that guy to make him want to kill his ass? A prison guard arrested the assailant. The victim was carried on a stretcher to the infirmary. Living in the midst of constant terror, although I had been there before, was not something I had not counted on. Prison was no place to be somebody.

At night, as silence settled over the prison, I found myself lying awake on the bunk, surrounded by darkness that only faint streaks of streetlight managed to penetrate through the grimy windows. The air was thick with stillness, interrupted only by the distant melody of Marvin Gaye's "Flying High" emanating from someone's radio. The song transported me back a couple of years, evoking memories of a carefree yet reckless life I had once embraced. We had squandered every opportunity, caught up in the allure of crime and drugs, trying to be somebody. We thought our cavalier attitude would last forever. Now, Marvin Gaye's poignant lyrics resonated with a sense of hopelessness that I had come to understand all too well.

"I go the place where danger awaits me. And it's bound to forsake me. So stupid minded. I can't help it oh, I'm so stupid minded..."

Through trial and error, I had traversed the treacherous bridge from adolescence to adulthood, entirely on my own. It was a solitary journey, the harshest rite of passage one could endure. As I turned 18, the consequences of our actions amplified, just as I had anticipated. What I lacked, however, were the lessons on alternative paths, the wisdom of navigating life's pitfalls. I had been cast adrift in childhood, abandoned and grown too hardened to be welcomed back

To Be Loved

into the comforting embrace of parental guidance. Oh, how I yearned for Mama, for my big brother, for someone to show me how to steer clear of life's traps. Daddy, how do you achieve your dreams despite the allure of vices, temptations, and distractions? Uncle, Aunt, Cousin—anybody, please...!

Instead, I was left to grapple with the lessons of survival within prison walls, learning about the intricacies of "shanks" and the harsh reality of life behind bars. Time weighed heavily on my hands, and I pondered how to spend it— withering away like the old inmate who ate alone in his cell was not an option. No, I was determined to utilize every moment in my quest to have my sentence reduced to fit my crime. I acknowledge the wrongdoing of my actions. I should not have allowed myself to be so easily influenced by my big brother. I should have stood up for me and said, 'Drop me off at home, I got something to do.' But, I had no idea that the outing would lead to a robbery, much less that we'd get caught. They had gotten away so many times. We hadn't planned a damn thing that night. How could I have known that someone would drive up on the motel lot as Mitchell and his buddy came out? That's exactly it; you can't plan for the unexpected. That's why you shouldn't do that shit. But, in no way did my poor judgment warrant the police officer planting a shotgun shell on me and me being convicted and sentenced to 15 years for a robbery that the victim testified I did not do. That the victim testified that I didn't rob him should have constituted reasonable doubt in a court of justice. In my pursuit of justice, I engaged in conversations with several fellow prisoners, sharing the details of my case and

No Place to Be Somebody

seeking their counsel on how to rectify the situation. These conversations became a lifeline, offering a glimmer of hope amidst the darkness of incarceration. We exchanged stories of injustice and shared strategies to challenge the flaws and biases embedded within the legal system.

And I wrote on an envelope on December 22, 1971:

To, Mr. Murdoch:

Copy of Request for Review of Sentence

Order for Appeal, copy of pre-sentence investigation report

Copy of Motion for Appeal and Review, and transcript.

To: Judge Whitaker:

Request for Application for Review and Order for Appeal.

Researching and espousing law was foreign to me, but it represented hope.

***

In April, my brother Mitchell, who was serving out the sentence for his last escape from Lorton, Va., before going to Baltimore to do his Maryland sentence, wrote to tell me he had enrolled in a legal correspondence course, and he subsequently gave me legal guidance and, big brother counsel.

I began to read and write for my release from an unfair conviction.

***

January 3, 1972

Charles County Court House

To Be Loved

La Plata, Maryland 20646

Application for Review of Sentence

I hereby apply for a Review of my Sentence in Case No. 3822. I understand, and hereby agree, that after my present sentence has been reviewed, it may be increased, or decreased or left the same, and that any sentence that could have been given originally may be given after review. I further understand and agree that this application may not be withdrawn after receipt of a notice that a hearing is to be held on this application. I believe that my sentence should be changed for the following reasons:

1. Lack of due process of the law;

2. Biased and unequal protection of the law;

3. Uncorroborated testimony which weighed heavily on the decision of jury;

4. Denied the right to a fair and proper procedural line-up;

5. Identification was improper and the procedure, unlawful

6. Denied adequate counsel.

Respectfully,

Ronald Steele

***

Once the application was sent to me, I modified the reasons from legal to moral:

1. That the applicant has no record

2. That the applicant is only 19 years old

3. That the applicant was gamely employed.

4. That the applicant was enrolled in Federal City College until conviction

5. That the applicant was enrolled in three educational programs.

6. The shotgun shell that the testifying Deputy claimed he found on my person was not in fact found there;

7. That the applicant's counsel did not represent him properly or competently.

***

January 5, 1972

Ronald Douglas Steele

MRDCC 954 Forest Street

Baltimore, Maryland 21202

Dear Sir:

Judge Whitaker has received your request for a transcript of the record in your case. He has instructed me to write to you that your previous letter concerning an appeal has been referred to Franklin B. Olmsted, Esquire, La Plata, Maryland, Public Defender. The transcript has not been typed, but your attorney will have the benefit of the transcript when it is prepared.

Judge Whitaker, also, received your Motion for Reduction of Sentence which he regards as a request for him to reconsider your sentence. He requested me to

To Be Loved

write you that you were not given the maximum sentence and that he did consider, in fixing the sentence at 15 years, the facts stated in your letter.

He does not feel that the sentence was excessive under all other circumstances involved in your case.

Very truly yours,

Dorothy Toliver

Secretary dt

***

"He requested me to write you that you were not given the maximum sentence and that he did consider, in fixing the sentence at 15 years, the facts stated in your letter."

I was outraged at the letter. I couldn't believe his words. He gave me a sentence that befitted a seasoned, hardened criminal!

As anger simmered within me, I pondered my response to the letter. Judge Whitaker's words lingered, dismissing yet another Black statistic with a tainted past. But I refused to accept that narrative. If only he would read my letters, perhaps I could appeal to his humanity. I believed I was a good person who had faltered and whose mistake did not warrant a harsh 15-year sentence. The more I contemplated it, the stronger my conviction grew—I had to try. I had nothing to lose, nothing better to do than to devote my time to seeking justice and release from prison. It was a pivotal moment in my journey of growth.

No Place to Be Somebody

English had been a subject I loathed in high school, earning mediocre grades of Cs and Ds. Yet, writing became my lifeline to the world outside. Oh, how I yearned to express myself! I was more than the sum of my conviction and sentence. The justice system failed to recognize my humanity, reducing me to a stereotype. But I was determined to convey my true self on paper. This exercise would utilize all the knowledge I had absorbed from studying Black history and culture, my vocabulary-building exercises, my fascination with the power of words, and my innate ability to find the right ones. The injustice that had befallen me became the catalyst for redefining my identity. I glimpsed the person I aspired to be and started severing ties with the person I once was. Within two months, Judge Whitaker and a former counselor began praising my writing prowess.

I penned letters to anyone who held the potential to aid my cause or alleviate my sentence. Then Governor Marvin Mandell, Congressman Parren J. Mitchell, the Federal Bureau of Prisons, the very victim of the robbery, and even Judge Charles Whitaker himself—no stone would be left unturned.

Meanwhile, the classification process determined that I would serve my sentence at the Maryland Correctional Institute (MCI), a medium-security prison in Hagerstown, nestled amidst the picturesque hills of western Maryland. Damn it! I had hoped to be assigned to the Maryland Correctional Training Center, a minimum-security facility known for its self-help programs. Nevertheless, on that fateful morning of January 20, 1972, I was shackled alongside fellow inmates, herded onto a bus, and transported through the scenic mountainous terrain of

To Be Loved

Western Maryland. Eventually, a building emerged on the horizon, seemingly as tranquil as a college campus. I relished the opportunity to escape the grim confines of the daunting penitentiary for Maryland's most incorrigible criminals.

Stepping into MCI, memories flooded my mind. The atmosphere bore a striking resemblance to my days working at St. E., again. Institutions: tall ceilings, expansive corridors stretching into the distance, officials adorned in uniform with jingling keys by their sides, and scattered offices. MCI, known as Hagerstown's "Old Jail" due to the presence of the newer Maryland Correctional Training Center, boasted a unique architectural design. It resembled a spherical structure, with the administration at the center-front level and inmate tiers radiating outward like spokes on a wheel. Beyond various service buildings housed essential facilities such as the metal shop, laundry, and cafeteria.

Little did I know that within those walls, I would embark on a transformation journey, navigating the labyrinthine realm of MCI while clinging to hope and fighting for my place in the world beyond its confines.

I was assigned to F-2-27, the receiving tier of MCI. This section was a temporary holding area until inmates were allocated their "permanent" cells within the facility. Each tier boasted basic amenities, including a communal shower for approximately eight inmates and a recreation room for the entire tier, accommodating around 30 individuals. Our cells were modest, featuring a tall, case metal window, a radiator, an old government-issued metal cabinet in army green, a single bunk, a seatless toilet, and a sink. While the sliding metal door offered a modicum of privacy compared to the Pen, it still bore a window that reminded us that we didn't deserve privacy. Adjacent to the recreation room stood the shower area, where we could shower at our discretion. We assembled in the recreation room throughout the day until we were assigned a job or enrolled in educational programs.

Within the prison's microcosm, regional factions held sway. Inmates primarily aligned themselves with fellow prisoners hailing from their respective city or in the case of Baltimore, from sections of that city. The next notable group that displayed solidarity consisted of individuals from Washington, D.C., while the white inmates formed their crew.

Immediately, I gravitated toward my home crew, seeking familiarity and a sense of belonging. However, even among your homies, paranoia thrived. Men deprived of intimate connections with women and stripped of their basic human rights, whether deservedly or not, become walking time bombs brimming with anger. I didn't take long to comprehend why stabbings were commonplace among incarcerated Brothers. The sheer magnitude of pent-up frustration, exacerbated by the limited opportunities to release this anguish before a vigilant guard intervened, pushed inmates to the brink. The knife became their outlet, an instrument to unleash their fury before correction officers extinguished the fight.

Prison bred a climate of kill or be killed, where anger and fear ignited swift altercations and definitive outcomes. The assailant, whether acting in self-defense or engaging in an assault, would be promptly "locked down" on the

To Be Loved

segregation tier for a year. In certain instances, if the victim's family pursued legal action, alleging "unequal protection," the victim of the attack might find themselves heading home under the law.

We were expected to harbor animosity towards those who shared our appearance and to trust no one. We had to be prepared to kill or die at any moment, every hour of every day. A rival crew member could be scrutinizing you for weakness, seeing it as an opportunity to exploit. Such vulnerability meant no one, not even your "Homies," would defend you. Showing weakness was not an option. Without a support network, one would inevitably be indebted to someone—a protector. The supposed solidarity of brothers in prison proved fleeting and temporary. The truth was clear—prison was no place to be somebody.

"Hey, Ronald," Brick called out, his voice resonating within the room as he sat at the table.

"What's up?" I responded, curious about his intentions.

"Wanna play some 'Contract' or 'Pimp'?" Brick asked, shuffling the deck of cards.

"Fuck no," I retorted, firm in my stance. "It's that kind of shit that landed us in here. Aren't you all ever gonna learn?"

"Fuck you, man. We're gonna play Contract or Pimp. None of us is going anywhere anytime soon, you dig?" Brick's response held a mixture of defiance and resignation.

No Place to Be Somebody

The conversations rarely revolved around the prospect of parole or escaping the confines of our sentences. Most seemed resigned to serving their time, accepting the bleak reality stretched before them.

***

The tension between my family and I had relaxed. My mother and sisters were very supportive, although, at times, I had to nudge them to do something for me. The time away from each other and my tragic situation seemed to make us forget all the pain and strain we shared. They had to know that even when everything I had done was added up, I didn't need to be caged for 15 years in prison like a wild animal.

When we were kids, my siblings barely talked to one another. My sisters prided themselves in reporting my misbehavior to my mother and getting me whipped or otherwise punished. So, I avoided my sisters. However, it was a red alert if somebody bothered one of them. I'd be angry as all get up and kick as much butt as I had to, to let dudes know they do not mess with my family.

I felt rejoiced to see my family during visits. They visited and wrote to me regularly, with Mama sending her love, money, and stamps and taking care of matters I requested.

***

My sister, Paulette, told me Pat was already making it with another guy. My mind kept telling me to break off with her. Yet, my heart was singing the chorus of soulful R&B balladeer Al Green's latest song, "Let's Stay Together." I

To Be Loved

hadn't been gone for three months. My heart may as well have been tossed on the ground. I felt like I didn't matter to her. Not mattering was a feeling I had tried to counter since childhood. She had written to me repeatedly, pledging her support and devotion to me and only me. I didn't believe her. I'd read her letters, heartbroken, and chose not to respond. I was more inclined to write Sharon Smalls from Sheriff Road for affection. We had always been friendly, nothing romantic. She got my address and began to write, and we stayed in contact. As my heart sought solace and connection through Sharon's letters, a newfound sense of determination began to take root. It was time to confront the source of my unjust incarceration, Judge Whitaker himself. The urge to respond to his dismissive words and present my case with unwavering conviction grew stronger daily. With Pen in hand, I composed my reply, channeling every ounce of frustration and determination into the words I would soon send to Judge Whitaker.

January 24, 1972

The Honorable Judge Charles Whitaker

Charles County Court House

La Plata, Maryland 20646

Dear Sir:

Although I feel, as many others, that the action you bestowed upon me on December 16, 1971, was indeed unwarranted, I have no harsh thoughts about you and hope this letter finds you in the best of health.

No Place to Be Somebody

I wish to first express my appreciation for you deducting the eight weeks I spent in La Plata Jail from my sentence; I apologize for not thanking you earlier. My mind has been in a state of confusion and disbelief of the fact that my life ended on December 16.

I am inclined to believe that the man that sentenced me on that day was not, in actuality, the real Judge Charles Whitaker. No, it was another person, an evil person, a person blinded with prejudice--but he was in your physical form. Your facial expression and action on previous cases told me that in you, there is reason, kindness and impartiality. But, I wonder, what happened to it on December 16? A wave of evil thoughts must have overpowered you. But, where did these evil thoughts come from? I feel rather than from your heart or mind, these evil thoughts were inspired by the immediate environment in which you work. I know that, because I could see through the hatred-filled faces of the stenographer, the D.A., the heavy-set clerk and the deputies. All of them was were there on December 16, although they had no active part in court. Each set quietly in court with expressions of doom on their faces. They all left to have a beer and rejoice. While twenty (20) years of two young men lives, and fifteen (15) years of my life has been slashed away. To you, and that body of Charles County, it was only words. But, to the victims, it was tears, and sorrow in so very many peoples heart, it took me back to the thought of the Slave Market, when above all atrocities, families were brutally divided, advertised "For Sale," priced and involuntarily sold up the river away from their loved ones and to a strange and

To Be Loved

unknown society under different slave masters. But you may feel that I volunteered for this corrupt treatment. No... I didn't. Your sentence was more influenced out of court, then in. You heard and discussed statements concerning me and this incident by, maybe, above other people, my counselor, Mr. Alfred Mudd.

But, Sir, I need not tell you but you would have been acting justifiably if the statements you heard were brought to court and proved. But no.

They were alleged. And you acted on allegations..........I PROTEST........I PROTEST.........! But it is unheard, ignored and oblivioned. So here I am..... Casted out of society into the small and growing world of the forgotten people, denied the opportunity to ameliorate my capabilities and project my thoughts and dedicate myself to our communities where help is greatly needed. I wanted to destroy and conquer the problems of society that I once lived in. But "Thumbs down!" My wants and will have to be forgotten, now, or canceled out.

If the opportunity to go to college here is granted, then NO, I won't cancel out my endeavors. I shall study sociology. And when the oppressing revolving doors of this prison open for me to leave, it will never open again for my return. I shall be prepared to pick up my new-found weapon of knowledge and combat injustices and social problems that inspire people to show hatred and disconcern toward another man because of his physical characteristics which, even if he wanted, he had no power to control.

It is evident that I am the victim of such prejudged thoughts due to Deputy Scofields statement which was never proved.

No Place to Be Somebody

He told a convicting lie or an honest mistake. I can't decide which it was; "I wonder why when a man makes a mistake, instead of moving to correct the mistake and offer relief to the victim of the mistake, he moves to fabricate a justification." His statement of a shotgun shell being in my possession should have been investigated. And in spite of the testimony of Deputy Smallwood and Mr. Cox, his sister, and his fiancee, I was still found guilty. Was the court JUSTIFIED!!!???

Because I believed in you representing the Law of the United States Constitution, I still would have come back in a new trial (if given) subconsciously expecting justice and humanity were as there was ample proof that it didn't exist. Was that foolish thinking? Nevertheless, the motion for a new trial or reduction of sentence was denied. In my Motion for Reduction of Sentence, I only asked for justice. It was denied...

I am pessimistic now, I only hope for the best, but I expect the worst.

Sincerely,

Ronald Steele

***

Two weeks had crawled by, every passing day intensifying my anticipation for a response from Judge Whitaker. The prison walls seemed to close in on me as I yearned for a glimmer of hope and acknowledgment that my plea was being heard. The tension in the air was palpable as fellow inmates shared my restlessness, their hopes and fears mirroring mine.

To Be Loved

Finally, the moment arrived. It was mail call, that brief window of respite when the entire tier congregated in the electrified atmosphere of the rec room. A hush fell over the room as the guard's voice reverberated.

"Ronald Steele," he called out, his words echoing with a weight that could shatter dreams or illuminate the path to justice. The name that left his lips was mine.

Every pair of eyes turned towards me, their gazes a mix of curiosity and empathy. The walls seemed to tremble with the collective anticipation, as if the prison itself held its breath, waiting for the contents of that letter.

I received the envelope, marked with the seal of the Charles County Court House. The weight of possibilities pressed against my fingertips as I carefully tore it open, revealing the words that could alter the course of my fate.

February 7, 1972

Ronald Steele, 112538

Box 2000, Route 3

Hagerstown, Maryland 21740

Dear Sir:

I have read with interest your letter of January 24 and am impressed with the obvious ability you have to express your feelings. Nothing I could say would serve to change those feelings, so I will leave it unsaid.

My only hope for your sake is that time will erase some of the bitterness you now feel and that you will take advantage of whatever opportunities are

No Place to Be Somebody

afforded for the development of your inmate talents and put them to use on lawful and worthwhile endeavors.

Very truly yours,

James Charles Whitaker

Damn, something about the judge's reply excited me. What are "inmate talents?" Or did he mean innate talents? What are they? "*I have read with interest your letter of January 24 and am impressed with the obvious ability you have to express your feelings.*" No one in authority had ever told me I could do anything worthwhile. He, wittingly or not, gave me a reason to write.

***

I was housed at B-1, a tier that included a lot of Washingtonians, including Rabbit, Popeye, Batman, Mickey, Ricky, Jim, Rufus, Smiley, Peanut, Rack, and Brick. I was assigned to the State Use Industries Metal Shop as an office assistant. My typing skills prevailed again, I guess.

The Metal Shop was where, officially, inmates crafted school bus chairs, government cabinets, desks, and other metal furniture. Unofficially, it was the inmate's shank factory. It's the source of almost all the inmate shanks.
In passing the time away in the rec hall, some Baltimore Brothers did a fighting dance, using their Afro comb as a fake knife, like we used to shadowbox on the streets; they were warming up for a knife fight and didn't mind everyone knowing it.

To Be Loved

Across the room, another Brother was a middle-class dude who'd gone astray and ended up here. He appeared to have zapped out. He was on Thorazine; the doctor preferred prescription for whatever psycho shit bothered inmates. The guy was like a zombie all the time; nobody bothered him.

The marble-floored rec-hall had tall, clean windows on either side. Wooden, round picnic benches and tables partially furnished the room. Inmates played cards, walked around, rapped, and or watched a 19" TV hung up high on a wall.

George Williamson, a Moorish science Brother was preaching the virtues of writing to get out of prison to those who'd listen. I was already writing the judge. George's remark was confirmation that I was on to something. Writing to get out of prison impressed me to be a better use of my time, in addition to reading books.

I grew bored of the rec-hall and would check into my cell early every evening to read and write anybody who could possibly help with my case.

At my request, Mama had brought many of my books. *Soledad Brother*, by George Jackson; *100 Years of Lynching; Seize the Time*, by Bobby Seale. From the prison library, I read a biography of George Washington Carver and more. Suddenly, a wealth of information about my heritage was available, and I had nothing but time to read. I began to identify with the writings of George Jackson, and his influence began to manifest in my writings.

***

No Place to Be Somebody

I felt let down by my boys, none of whom had visited me; few had even written me. On the street, it was, "Steele this, Steele that." These are the same Brothers for whom I'd do almost anything. Yet, they didn't even visit me. when I return, I've got to find new friends; who will be with me through thick and thin.

I thought of Mrs. Montgomery, the job counselor I briefly knew when I was out on bond. I liked her. She was an older, caring maternal figure. I could talk to her. I didn't want her to think ill of me; like, I was another problem child whose case crossed her path; I didn't see myself that way. She would also encourage me to write.

***

February 5, 1972

Mrs. Montgomery

WCEP

1217 Good Hope Road, S.E.

Washington, D.C.

Dear Mrs. Montgomery:

Today I received your letter of January 24. It was received with gladness. And so was your advice, though I had planned to excel in life long ago. American Learning Center, D.C. Skills, and New Careers was only preparation or shall I say stepping stones. Yes, my ultimate goal was to continue going to Federal City College and study my damnedest in sociology. Why sociology? The social welfare seems to be my ideology, to be the root of unravelling so many problems we live

To Be Loved

with in our communities. Think on it, drugs, crime, drop-outs, etc. All have some sort of social unbalance. And I feel already that I can help alleviate such problems. So after I leave this place, whether it be 45 months or 15 years I will study, study and study sociology. Even if the government won't accept me, I will still try to be an active leader in the community. The oppressor has slowed me down but he hasn't stopped me. I have determination and self-motivation like a life-long battery that keeps my head raised high and looking toward the future.

You said "We have just about run out of this black sympathy." I don't sympathize with Blacks, I sympathize with whites. They are the people who have been perpetuating the social imbalance. Blacks in tryin' to out-do them have foolishly taken part in this endeavor. We as a people are still feeling the everlasting effects of the early 1800s. They've changed overt, brutal-shackling slavery into still brutal Gentile Slavery. They still own the jobs, we're still the underpaid, first to fire, last to hire people, there's still discriminatory housing, we're still the victims of poverty, while the American Government sends money to other poverty-stricken countries, we still have black sharecroppers, our children still can't get first hand education or the opportunity, our children still have to play in the alley or street with their games while the beasts' kids go to nearby flower trimmed grassy parks and playgrounds. The ugly truth goes on and on. Some of us get by. They become lower-middle-class or upper middle class and WOW they are content, while our overall population here, or shall I say, humanity suffers. No, I don't sympathize with blacks, I sympathize with whites.

No Place to Be Somebody

When I die, I want to die like Martin Luther King, Malcolm X, Medgar Evers, which was for a cause. And if it has to be, I want to die like **Demark** *Vessey or Nat Turner. The knowledge of the latter two is the history of your people that you have been deprived of and like me have been taught white history with the American included and the white excluded as a scheme. My eyes are open, I can see!*

Ronald

P.S. I'm sorry to hear about the now defunct American Learning and TRD. It was a tool for the people.

After that letter, I decided to write Judge Whitaker again. This time I wrote to Judge Whitaker to share what a day in prison is like.

***

February 10, 1972

Dear Mr. Whitaker:

How are you? I hope fine. I received your letter of February 7, with gratefulness.

I had just returned from work here in the metal shop. I was lying on the bunk (can't say it's my bunk) here in my cell with books here and there just thinking. Nothing specific, just thinking. At times (and very often) I think about my future.

I'm sure you have heard the plea of wanting desperately education so many times, that you thought I was (as some do) trying to evade working. But that isn't so with me. If possible, I'd like to go to school all day. You see then, I can

To Be Loved

accomplish a worthwhile endeavor. There, on my job, my mind just idle. I have a constantly exploding desire to ameliorate my capabilities.

But, my incarceration is in vain as it stands presently.

It may interest you to know how ones' life is lived inside these prison walls--well, I'll be more specific--my life.

At 6:00 a.m., I awake overwhelmingly through an unconscious instinct (a steel door that bangs when it opens and closes). Rising from this bunk, I glance at my watch which usually signify that I have about thirty (30) minutes to prepare for the day's activities. I straighten the bunk, and in a small marble-like, white sink, with two hot and cold chrome painted push-button knobs, I wash my body. The sink is adjoined to the wall of my room, cell, cage, "can" or whatever. (To project an image of this depressing cell is needless; you've seen one before, I presume--they're all alike, cells look just like..." jails."

After awkwardly washing my body, I thoroughly brush away the six-hour night dew from my teeth.

Now it's 6:30 a.m. and the officer at the mouth of the tier operates the mechanism that unlocks our doors. Then we walk about 12 yards to a small corridor-like recreation hall where we await the ringing of a designated bell to signify our entry to the cafeteria, or "breakfast" is ready to be "served."

The cafeteria is approximately 20 yards away from the "rec-hall." There, after entering, we are seated at long, wooden, primitive tables and benches, and

No Place to Be Somebody

are allowed 20 minutes to eat the maybe bread, potatoes, eggs, and liquidated powder milk.

After which, the silverware or stainless steel forks, spoons, and knives are collected by a designated inmate and with the watchful eye of a guard. Those are tactics used in preventing the misuse of such utensils. In single file, we walk from the cafeteria to designated jobs.

In the State Use Industry, Maryland Correctional Institution, Metal Shop, I'm a clerk. This building is located about 60 yards from the Housing Units. On my job, I type contracts, requisitions, material release slips, inventory, keep time sheets for both inmates and officers, etc., for FIFTY-FIVE CENTS a day.

"The prisoner has, as a consequence of his crime, not only forfeited his liberty, but all his personal rights except those which the law in its' humanity accords to him. He is for the time being, the slave of the state." Ruffin vs. Commonwealth, 62 Va. 790 (1871).

At 3:45 p.m., the working day ends and we are returned to our designated cells, At about 4:10, the bars in our windows are checked by tier-officers for the prevention of possible escapees. 4:30 p.m., the doors automatically unlock again and into the small rec-hall we return for the bell to indicate "supper" is ready to be served. We are on our small journey back to our cells at 4:50. Between the hours of 5 and six-thirty, p.m. one's own discretion determines how this hour is used.

Me? I read.

To Be Loved

I read because it broadens your mind and manipulates your mentality. I've read quite a few books prior to my incarceration, and continue to do so. I never read fiction, unless it pertains to my studies. It may or may not interest you, but my literature is limited to the social, economic, and political problems of ethnic groups. And lately, law.

So in a way, I might say that I'm, as always, endeavoring to self-educate myself.

I study this limited field of literature because one day, I the so called convict, the criminal, the menace to society, will make a contribution to humanity or our communities. This is determination. It can never be taken away from me--it's mine, I invented it.

It's like an everlasting energized battery which motivates me toward my goal. Someday I will meet that goal. And you can say, "I remember him..., he's the one that..., and I..."

Well, at 6:30 p.m., "Rec-Hall" is called which is ended at eleven o'clock. Again, the doors unlock and this time the small corridor like "recreation" hall, is our destination. There we socialize, play cards and/or look at T.V., which is a useless endeavor because of smooth, ceramic walls richocet loud, disastrous and chaotic noises...

"Inmate days are spent playing cards, checkers, chess, or writing, if he is literate. Many prisoners are not. Most just lie about. The tension becomes great

at times and fights break out frequently." Cook County Grand Jury, Rep., supra note 8, at 15.

I don't mingle with my fellow inmates too much.

You may think I'm paranoid but I sincerely feel (and it is evident) that kindness is taken for weakness.

So I just stay in the 5' by 10' cell reading...just waiting for the next day's activities. "Tomorrow will be just like today; nothing added, nothing taken away. It'll be like that the day after tomorrow and the day after that, and the day after that, and etc., etc.

Very truly yours,

Ronald Steele

The Court summoned me today to review my sentence, the weight of uncertainty heavy upon my shoulders. Four agonizing days had passed, and now, on February 14, 1972, I stood on the precipice of hope or despair. Pessimism threatened to engulf me, but deep within, a flicker of determination burned brightly. Against all odds, I vowed to muster every ounce of strength to somehow turn this nightmarish ordeal around.

To Be Loved

February 23, 1972

Today, a letter arrived, shattering my expectations and pessimism with a single stroke. Its words reverberated through the depths of my being, igniting a surge of disbelief and joy. My sentence, once suffocating in its severity, would be modified and reduced on February 28, 1972. Hope surged within me like a torrential wave, crashing against the shores of my soul. Joy to the world, indeed! It seemed too good to be true, and yet, there it was—a glimmer of salvation piercing through the darkness.

For five agonizing days, I clung to the promise of a brighter future, the weight of anticipation pressing upon me with each passing moment. The calendar pages turned slowly, marked by a growing sense of anticipation. And then, as fate would have it, the day arrived.

A second letter, received with trembling hands, revealed a truth that shattered my newfound hope. Its contents struck like a lightning bolt, searing into my consciousness. The reality before me was stark and unyielding, a harsh reminder that not all dreams come true. The prospect of freedom, so tantalizingly close, slipped through my fingers, leaving me to grapple with the bitter taste of disappointment.

February 28, 1972

DETERMINATION AND ORDER ON APPLICATION FOR REVIEW OF SENTENCE

February 23, 1972

Application having been made by Ronald Douglas Steele for review of the sentence imposed in this case, a panel of trial judges,

...after consideration of the application following a full hearing, has determined that no change should be made in the defendant's sentence in this case.

FOR THE PANEL,

[Signed]

Seventh Judicial Circuit of Maryland Chairman

I was really feeling discouraged. I decided to share my feelings of pessimism with the judge.

February 29, 1972

Mr. Justice Whitaker

Charles County Court House

La Plata, Maryland 20646

Dear Mr. Whitaker:

I am overwhelmed in a depressive mood of pessimism. I haven't really anything to smile or be joyous about. Except when mother comes. But even that depresses me, knowing she has to travel so far. And to share a visit with her lost son, for only one hour.

One hour per month is my only opportunity to see her. Transportation is difficult and sometime lacking. Regretfully for all who'd like to come here for a

To Be Loved

visit, transportation is somewhat difficult. My peers live so very far away...and I am so lonely for them.

However doubtfully, but hopefully, I'll get over this loneliness.

Yesterday I was summoned to Court in Upper Marlboro before the three-panel Judge, as a response to my Motion for Review of Sentence. Your representative, a Mr. Henson, alleges and still contends that I had a shotgun shell on my person as well as Too Tall's wallet. Nothing can be more victimizing and discriminatingly alleged. I still wonder why when that statement was first alleged, instead of moving to correct it, the move was made to fabricate a justification by the Court!!! Now, I'm the victim of...That three-judge panel even failed to bring about constructive possession. And will probably deliberate on mere conjectures and speculation.

In the case of <u>U.S. vs. Bussey 432 F. 2d 1330, 7 CLB 270 (1970)</u>, a young man was apprehended as a suspect in a burglary.

In his pocket was found on paper the commission of the burglary, but the judge said evidence was insufficient and the suspect released!

Do you sincerely believe justice prevailed???

If your answer is, "yes," then it surely didn't prevail for ME!!! If your answer is "No," then Sir, you are contradicting and deprecating the judgement of higher Courts!

And me, I'll just be here...noticing every second that wobbles by...idling...dullening...and, degradingly dieing...

February 23, 1972

P.S. Please acknowledge letters of February 5 and February 10.

Sincerely,

Ronald

A week later, I received a letter from the Charles County Courthouse.

To Be Loved

Chapter VI
On Target: The Judge

March 8, 1972

Dear Sir:

Judge Whitaker has requested me to advise you that he has received and read your letters of February 5th, 10th, and 29th. He does not feel that time out on bond bears any weight in favor of a reduction of sentence.

Judge Whitaker, also, requested me to say that he wrote to the Department of Correction to inquire about the prospect of your pursuing some college courses. He has received a letter from Mr. Hickabon, the Superintendent at Hagerstown, which should be a source of encouragement to you. A copy of Mr. Hickabon's letter was sent to you.

As of this date, Judge Whitaker has not had an opportunity to review the case you cited as being recorded in 432 F. 2d 1330.

Very truly yours,

Dorothy Toliver, Secretary

***

Judge Whitaker sent to me a copy of a letter from MCI's Superintendent. Wow! My writings appeared to bear fruit.

March 6, 1972

Dear Judge Whitaker:

On Target: The Judge

Ronald Steele was received at this institution January 20, 1972 and was seen by the Classification Committee February 1, 1972 for assignment to a program. The present semester for the college program had begun with capacity enrollment January 15, 1972. This program is not an open entry program. Mr. Steele was advised of this and the criteria upon which selection is based. He was also advised that at the appropriate time in his incarceration, if he qualifies, he will be considered for the two-year program.

Thank you very much for the interest you have displayed and hopefully this information is helpful in alleviating the concern you have expressed.

Sincerely,

John Hickabon

Superintendent

Jh:

R. D. Steele

I couldn't allow Judge Whitaker to see Mr. Hickabon's reassurance as the last word. I wrote Judge Whitaker to press my case for college.

March 7, 1972

Dear Mr. Whitaker:

How are you? I sincerely hope fine.

This is a beautiful day of March 7th and in a matter of 18 days I'll be twenty years old. I guess it's' every kids's wish to be of that age-twenty or twenty-one. However, I can't say that I am glad tho.

To Be Loved

Long ago when thinking of my future, I vowed that at the age of twenty-one, I'd not only be a man but a man with ample proof of my efforts and preparation (to be examined) and think to myself "I'll soon be at the peak of my education and qualified to help someone else."

However, it is only a dream now -- a wasted thought. I wish, when the fifteen years of my life was taken, you could have taken my aging away too. Then upon my return I will still be only nineteen and as eager as ever to excel. It may be a childish wish but its' an honest wish. You see, here, my will and determination is in danger. I can only unwillingly weave into this corrupt environment which will inevitably turn me away from my goal, pervert my thoughts and above all, crush my determination.

However, if accepted in the college program here next semester, then I am glad, for I may still be able to look back over a year and examine my progressiveness.

But the thought of me going to school here in the upcoming semester is very doubtful. For Mr. Hickabon has wrote you an indirect excuse for my unwanton lingering. I can never express in words my profound appreciation for your concern of my wellbeing. However, he is avoiding my desperate desire to learn. He has stated in his letter of March 6th, that I was assigned to that "program" (as he has called it) is a needless job that I am assigned to. The job is that of a clerk which I've mentioned prior to this letter. I think I have also

On Target: The Judge

explained to you the nature of my job. It is not only useless to me but its' also deprives me of my pursuit.

It is difficult to explain Mr. Mitchell, but I have a longing desire to help people. Not just a few selfish-thinking individuals, but all. And through clerking, my endeavors will never avail. I want to prepare myself to help the masses. Can't they understand that my learning might someday help others like them, their children or their neighbors? No I don't think they can understand --or won't.

..."At the appropriate time in his incarceration...he will be considered for the two-year program," Mr. Hickabon says. "Appropriate" is a deliberate scheme to avoid revealing the unfair and detrimental procrastination that exist presently. His phrase, "appropriate" truly means that I must wait and idle until I'm at least two years away from my first parole hearing. This is unjust. Am I or anyone who wants education so desparate as I, deserving of this abuse. Isn't it enough to deprive me of liberty, isn't it enough to deprive me of the priveledge to see my daughter grow, walk and talk for the first time in her life, isn't it enough that I will be separated from my love ones at the most needed times...isn't it enough, I cry.

Mr. Hickabon could have explained to you about Maryland Correctional Institution's affiliate, Maryland Correctional Training Center, which is constructed to help those incarcerated to help themselves. There, an inmate can acquire knowledge in almost any field desired. And MCTC (sometimes called)

To Be Loved

would in fact be most credible to me. You, Mr. Mitchell, as well as the staff and others can see my progressiveness and endeavors to excell.

However, time will not allow me to be transfered there--the maximum sentence one can possess there is five years-- or be a distant period of one-and one-half years away from the first parole hearing. So I guess I will have to stop thinking about MCTC and the benefits thereof.

Mr. Hickabon could have wrote you in detail however. He could have told you that this (Maryland Correctional Institution) is Maximum Security and it was constructed to lodge and work hardened criminals and not first offenders.

But I guess that subject wasn't the matter of your letter and he chose not to disclose these depressing facts. However, I want to thank you Mr. Mitchell for your appreciated concern and I hope that Mr. Hickabon's reply will not alleviate, as he has implied, your concern.

Sincerely,

Ronald Steele #119567

***

Maybe mistakenly, due to the lacking arrangement of "program" they conduct for individuals here with sentences such as mine. The judge was very encouraging.

March 20, 1972

Dear Sir:

On Target: The Judge

Judge Whitaker has asked to acknowledge receipt of your letter of March 7, 1972 and to advise you he is still very interested in your case and is hopeful that you will be able to take the college courses in which you have an interest.

Very truly yours,

Dorothy Toliver

***

March 30, 1972

Dear Yvonne,

It is now 8:15 a.m., and most unusually, every inmate in this joint is locked in. No one is told why. The guards just came to our work details and commanded everyone to go to their cells.

I at first thought it hopefully to be a rebellion; a work strike against the sadistic pigs under whom eye we do work of plenty value and are only paid $4.40 a week. If it is a strike, then it is surely to put a hole in the State's ass.

You see, we make those many signs on the highway you ride by; we make the chairs you sit in and the tables you sit at in those government buildings and schools; we repair all of the furniture and official cabinets that the government uses and needs repair; we even made these beds we sleep on! Every movable (although mechanical) supplies needed out there is made by an inmate such as I- for .55, a day!

To Be Loved

Ain't that nothing-we, the do-badders, at one time or another were casted out of society and resultantly society depends on our labors. The thought alone, inspire a mood of adversity toward society. But most know its' only the white power structure that permits this cunning form of slavery.

And they further try to project (brainwash the weakest of us inmates) that it is right for us to work for "nothing" because of our rebellious acts on "extortionists."

Most of us who are committed to these human degradation warehouses should be skillfully trained or mentally trained to meet the financial responsibilities that led us to these ends. As to the unrelated crimes, such as rape, etc., still a different form of rehabilitation should be attributed other than pay less work which is none other than slavery.

Some people think and profoundly believe we are paid so little because we have the accommodations of food and board. If this is true, then I have a Helluva' lot demands to make to my extremely inhumane landlord.

First, I want this "can" I sleep in, painted; I want permission to put pictures of my love ones on these four walls and not hidden in a book; I want this rust-ridden cabinet and table painted; I want a seat and cover on my commode; I want a protective cover on this red-hot radiator so I won't burn myself anymore; I want a rug or permission to put carpet on my dirt-accumulating cement floor; and lastly, but not least, I want them damn pigs to stop bursting into my cell and

On Target: The Judge

intruding my just privacy just to check the bars of my window, for my just, if possible escape.

When a man is receiving room and board and paying for it with his labors, the necessities I just mentioned should come natural without a request. Or petition! And when a pig uninvitingly burst in my pad, I can respond as I see fit.

Furthermore, if you compare our work with the service and lacking comfort we get, then the ratio would read as follows:

Labor	Wage
$10.00	.10!!!

If I had this job I have now, and was out there, my labors would well be worth $7,000 a year. Here, I get not even $100 a year.

So, if a strike is going on, I have every reason to be fully involved.

Well, that's' me and my many brothers unwanted situation, here. How's things for you and Rod? It sounds OK. Your card and picture is very pretty. I hope I'm out there when Lil' Kenny begin to talk, I got some "rap" for him.

Tell Rod I said, "Hi!" And ya'll take it easy. And if you can spare the money, Yvonne, buy or steal (smile) me six (6 fancy, all one color or matching colors) bath towels. Regretfully it's the only means of life we can have in our cell. And the rhythmic rolling pleats of the towel are very comforting and an escape

To Be Loved

from the mental agony of peeling old painted walls. Thanks. And I'm going to close for now and rap to you soon.

    P.S. Just got word, regretfully its' not a strike. Its' foggy outside and I think someone escaped. They locked everyone in to find out who is missing. If all goes well in court, I'll be "missing," sometime this year. (smile). Tell Mama to mail some stamps. The money, .55, we do make spends quickly in the inflationary commissary here. I have to work two days just to afford a small can of deodorant or a small 2 oz. can of hair conditioner!

    Ronald

***

On Target: The Judge

April 18, 1972

Dear Mr. Whitiker,

As ever I hope you are fine. And as for me I guess I'm okay, considering my state of being.

On March 15, 1972, I was transferred from the job as clerk in the State Use Industry, Metal Shop to that of clerk in the Assistant Superintendant's Office here. It should be considered a premium assignment. I am not content, though, for my capabilities extend far beyond the duties of clerk.

However, there, the duties are many and somewhat interesting. It is indeed a very vital organ of the institution. As inmates are received here from the Penitentiary (MRDCC), on a small yellow index-card I type their name, race, religion, commitment number, the nature of offense, sentence imposed, the date the said sentence began, the date inmate was received here and the designated cell at which he'll reside (which is decided by Superior Officers appointed to do such). On that said card there are also some 75-100 job-changes and cell-changes recorded from Request Slips submitted by inmates whom request the said changes. The reasons vary from maladjustments to "Administrative" moves. After the deletion of prior status or location is made and corrected, the cards are to be filed in a small open tray-like container for further use.

Disciplinary cards are also typed in the said manner, however on much larger cards. They are larger for the purpose of recording minor incidents that shouldn't be overlooked, but corrected by the witnessing officer. The incidents

To Be Loved

vary and are minute such as: covering the bars of one's cell to reflect away the rays of scorching sun: covering the small window of the door of said cell for the often needed privacy from others; the said cell may be untidy: inmate may be talking too loud or childishly playing in the corridor-like Rec.-Hall: and undoubtedly the reactionary disrespecting of officers. The correction for the said offenses is an oral notice to the offender that he will be "Locked-in' his cell on the evening of the offense while other inmates exercise the privileges of socializing with others, playing cards or looking (though unable to hear) at the television designated for some 80 inmates. I guess it really isn't punishment, for the activities of the Rec. Hall are few, monotonous and undoubtedly lamentable. To the inmate, "Lock-in" serves no purpose-excepting the offense is recorded and may be held against him when eligible for parole...I guess it does have purpose! I'm designated to record, as clerk, the offense on one's Disciplinary Card.

Coincidently, there are Adjustment Reports. They must be typed in detail as witnessed by the complaining officer. These become indictments. After which, are trial procedures from a body of selected (by superior officers) guards and one civilian (acting as Judge). He (the now defendant) can be represented by fellow inmate or represent himself. He may also call on witnesses on his behalf. The procedures are like that similar to your court with the exception of stenographer, legal clerk, jury, and legitimacy. I say the latter because if I am being tried for cursing an officer (which may never happen), I can't expect his friends to find me

On Target: The Judge

other than guilty! And further they won't weigh the offense on provocation, either, or reaction, but "did you or didn't you!" ...An Impasse!

When one is found guilty by the said group, he is subject to probation, suspended sentences and even indefinite sentence on "Isolation" or "Segregation." The maximum sentence imposed that may be served here in Segregation is fifteen (15) days. Otherwise the inmate is transferred from here to Maryland Penitentiary, Segregation Unit, (South-Wing). Here, Segregation is a regular tier designated for the results of the aforesaid verdict, guilty. Actually it is a suspension of all privileges and twenty-four-hour confinement to one's cell. I shouldn't omit the "Walk." For approximately 15 minutes every day while on Segregation the residents are allowed to walk that defiled tier for exercise. Then, return to their cells until the next day, probably the same time and another "walk."

Isolation is inhabited by those considered a potential "threat" to the Administration and those convicted by the said group for felonious actions committed while incarcerated; such as making a crude weapon (so-called "shanks"). Despite security measures, shanks are hand-made from scrap metal and in the Metal Shop. After stealing the metal, it is sanded to a rough edge and point. Some are as long as (14) fourteen inches. Still they are smuggled into the adjacent Housing Units and passed on to others -- maybe for a pack of cigarettes and inspite of the never missing "skin-frisk" before entering and exiting the main building, here. A conviction rising from possession of the said weapon could mean as much as months on Isolation via complete solitary confinement.

To Be Loved

Incidentally, since my incarceration a "shank" has been thrusted at another inmate. As in this infraction, the incident doesn't always reach the point of a fight. It is generally the first blow... and last. The victim of my recollection was I think, convicted in your court for Breaking and Entering. He was sentenced to the lenient sentence of two (2) years. His name is John Huntington. I met him in La Plata and I didn't know him personally however I still felt the pain and shock of his calamity. He was maliciously attacked by a shank-thrusting inmate. It resulted in his being hospitalized and surprisingly an exoneration from his said conviction. I guess he was lucky in a sense. I neither wish nor desire such misfortune for no one, however it is phenomenally more painstaking to be here...

After pouring my thoughts and emotions onto paper, a sense of unease settled within me. Doubt crept in, questioning the sincerity and effectiveness of my words. Perhaps my letter had been too self-pitying, too desperate, too soon. I had to tread carefully, mindful of the delicate balance that could tip the scales in the wrong direction. Convincing the judge to have a change of heart about my case would require meticulous persuasion, and any misstep could lead him astray. With a heavy heart, I decided not to mail the letter, sensing that it fell short of conveying the depth of my conviction.

Yet, something unspoken, something I needed to convey directly to the judge. Words eluded me, dancing just beyond the grasp of my mind. The weight of what was left unsaid lingered, gnawing at the edges of my consciousness.

On Target: The Judge

Instead of partaking in the usual recreation to distract myself from the tumultuous swirl of thoughts, I enrolled in a typing class. I met Rufus Williams, a man who exuded an air of confident composure. Well-groomed and handsome, he carried himself with a reserved demeanor, yet his bright smile and sense of humor radiated friendliness. Like me, he held onto dreams of a future beyond these prison walls, a world we had planned to conquer.

One day, as we conversed, Rufus shared a discipline that unique to me—he meditated. His eyes sparkled with a distant reverie as he described the transformative power of his mind., He said that sitting on his bunk, and gazing out the window, he could transport himself back home in his mind. His voice carried an unwavering belief, a conviction that no one could imprison his thoughts or spirit. The freedom he found within himself was a source of inspiration.

Rufus had reminded me of the untapped power within every person, the ability to transcend the confines of this physical reality. At that moment, I resolved to tap into the depths of my being to unlock the unwritten truths within my soul. I would navigate the labyrinth of my thoughts, seeking solace and strength amidst the confines of this prison.

***

Pat's letters arrived like fragments of a shattered dream, each a bittersweet reminder of the love we once shared. Despite my best efforts to distance myself from the tumultuous rollercoaster of emotions, her words seeped through the cracks in my resolve. She poured her heart out on paper, weekly,

To Be Loved

vowing her unwavering love and dedication. But with each letter, pain of wanting someone so deeply, yet afraid of their love deepened, and the strain of our relationship became unbearable.

I longed to sever the love that bound us, to find solace in the absence of her words. Yet, the ink on her letters carried the weight of our shared history, a love that once burned brightly but had now dimmed to ashes. Pat, the girl I had loved with all my heart, had become both the source of my greatest joy and my deepest anguish.

Her letters detailed the challenges she faced in integrating our daughter, Ngina, into my family, recounting the unease and rejection she often encountered. She sought to dispel rumors of her involvement with other men, desperately trying to reassure me of her loyalty. But, the betrayal of my first love made me scared of love.

As time passed, the tone of her letters shifted. She confessed to going out, assuring me it would not be sexual. Then came the painful admission of kisses shared with another. The words cut deep, a final blow to the remnants of our shattered bond. And then, with a cruel twist of fate, she confessed that she had fallen in love with someone else, even as she acknowledged the irreplaceable love we had once shared.

***

May 13, 1972

Judge Charles Whitaker:

On Target: The Judge

JOYFULLY, I EXPRESS MY SYMPATHETIC PLEASURE ON ACCOUNT OF YOUR SUCCESS AND GOOD FORTUNE AS AN UNOPPOSED CANDIDATE FOR THE JUDICIARY SEAT: CONGRATULATIONS.

As Ever, Ronald Steele

May 15, 1972, marked a day of unexpected chaos within the prison walls. In the rec room, laughter and conversation filled the air. But the tranquility shattered instantly by the piercing cry that reverberated through the tier.

"Wallace got shot!"

The words hung heavy in the air, electrifying the atmosphere with disbelief and jubilation. It was a moment of surreal irony as news spread that the racist Alabama Governor George Wallace, the embodiment of oppression and hatred, had become the target of an assassination attempt. In a twist of fate, a white man had sought to silence the voice of intolerance. Wallace, in a symbolic attempt to keep his 1963 inaugural promise of "segregation now, segregation tomorrow, segregation forever" and to stop the desegregation of schools, Wallace stood at a school house door, to block the entry of two African American students.

The roar of sudden noise swept through the prison like a tidal wave, transforming the solemn walls into a cacophony of jubilation. Cheers erupted, blending with the piercing whistles and the rattling of doors, an exultant symphony that echoed through the entire compound. In that instant, the barriers that separated us dissolved as we reveled in the poetic justice that had befallen Wallace.

To Be Loved

An assassin's bullet had left Wallace paralyzed, forever curtailing his hateful political career. He championed racially oppressive political ideologies, and rather than getting elected president, it ended his political career, if not his life.

That jubilation was short-lived, for another racist U.S. presidential candidate would surely follow in the form of Richard Nixon.

Having not seen Pat in nearly a year, I realized that, I couldn't shake my love for her. The more I tried to forget her, the more my heart reminded me: I need love.

May 20, 1972

Patricia McIntyre

Dearest Pat:

Just for You My Love I close my eyes and think of you

and it seems as though you're here

But when I open them up again

you always disappear

I think of you both night and day

and that's a natural fact

because the very thought of you,

my dear, Sends warm thrills up my back.

I think of you in the morning

that's how I start my day.

On Target: The Judge

You see, sweet and wonderful memories

help me along my way

I think of you at noon time

as I look at the clouds above

 and thank the man that made them,

Because he made for me -- you to love ...

    Love, Love, Love

    Yours,

Ronald

Within the confines of my prison cell, a rare opportunity presented itself—a chance that felt like a lifeline thrown into the abyss. In May 1972, just five months after my arrival, I enrolled in a prison college program. If I could spend incarceration getting a college education, then the time would be worthwhile. It was an opportunity to resume college that I had started at FCC, while on bond, a flicker of hope amidst the darkness of uneventful prison life.

The timing seemed almost serendipitous as if my heartfelt letters to Judge Whitaker had stirred the wheels of fate. The college program was a coveted privilege reserved for those who were a minimum of 18 months of their first parole hearing. Although I was three years away from that milestone, again, my aspirations were gaining traction.

As I stepped into the makeshift classroom, the prison walls seemed to fade away, replaced by the ambiance of learning. Hagerstown Community

To Be Loved

College had extended its reach behind prison bars, portending rehabilitation, second chances, and redemption. Our instructor, a beacon of knowledge and inspiration, ventured into the confines of our world to meet our desire to learn.

The first course I embarked upon was English 102, a gateway to the world of literature and critical thinking. We delved into Tennessee Williams's timeless masterpiece, "The Glass Menagerie," dissecting its nuances and themes. Words flowed through my pen as I crafted my essay, immersing myself in the ideas and perspectives like never before. The library, though limited, became a treasure trove, fueling the pursuit of my budding intellectual growth.

But as with many things in prison, my journey through higher education was destined to be brief. Abruptly halted, it left me longing for the intellectual stimulation that had briefly illuminated my days. The barriers of my confinement cast their shadow once more, obscuring the path of enlightenment that had briefly opened before me.

Yet, even in the face of this setback, the taste of knowledge lingered on my tongue. It had shown me a glimpse of what was possible, of the person I could become beyond the prison walls. The spark of learning ignited within me during those brief moments and continued to burn unyieldingly.

Although the prison may have curtailed my formal education, it could never extinguish the thirst for knowledge that had awakened within me. The opportunity of a lifetime may have been cut short. Still the fire it ignited would

On Target: The Judge

guide me on my path of self-discovery, pushing me to overcome the limitations imposed upon me and driving my intellectual destiny.

As I continued to navigate the complexities of prison life, an unexpected emergency arose, and in that moment of urgency, only one person could provide the help I needed—Mama.

June 29, 1972

Dear Mama:

I don't want to create any new worries for you, but an emergency has arisen and only you can help me. I hope things are well there.

The administration here has taken off their mask and we are being subjected to the cruelest of harassment. There was a beginning and the story is below. As soon as you've read this letter please don't hesitate one moment to call Prisoner's Aid phone number (Baltimore) 945-0620. Ask for Mr. Charles F. Morgan and read him this story. He's located in Baltimore and tell him I didn't write because we can't mail any letters now and when we can it may be too late.

On Tuesday June 27, they called "big courtyard" as usual at 6:30 p.m. Close to two-thirds of the inmate population usually goes out, and I was one of them. It was a normal situation, then, with no unusual happenings: We went out, some would play basketball, some baseball, and some would just sit on the steps outside and watch. While sitting out there talking to a fellow I overheard a slight rumor that there would be a protest. I also heard that there wasn't going to be a rebellious riot or the destruction of anything. We were only going to peacefully

To Be Loved

express our grievances to Mr. Hickabon, the superintendent. Mr. Hickabon wasn't out there then, and an hour later everyone that was playing sports began to stop.

There was no verbal assault or heckling to any of the guards who guarded the outside post of the fence for possible escape. It was quiet, peaceful and the inmates talked quietly among themselves. The subject of an actual protest was not even on tips of the majority's tongues because it wasn't expected to go to that extent.

When a guard saw us coming collectively together as a group, one leaped into a jeep and drove hurriedly away returning minutes later with shotguns and tear-gas. Nobody blew, we just sat there because as the rumor said, it would be "peaceful" and we took it among ourselves to believe that the many guards riot equipment, now surrounding us <u>would not be</u> necessary and therefore <u>not used</u>.

The guards stood outside the barbwired fence waiting, wanting and itching to pull their triggers. They were oblivioned by us and the inmates still sat talking among themselves without a word of rebellion in their mouths.

A car pulled up at the mouth of the fence, emptying the assistant superintendent, Mr. Nichols. He saw the mass, rode to the rear of the yard (still outside the fence) and returned back to the mouth of the yard calling Mr. Hickabon through his two-way radio in his car. When Hickabon did come, everyone grew quiet presumably hoping Hickabon would call off the riot squad after seeing us sat there without disturbance. He himself, thought it to be as it was--peaceful--because if it was thought to be violent he would not have walked

On Target: The Judge

the 100 yards or more without guerilla escort to the center of our mass to answer our grievances. He came with ease, clarity and without tension because it wasn't a tense situation. Of course he wanted to know what was at the root of this solidarity but because there was an air of phobia of being singled out as a leader no one spoke but one did toss out a scroll-like list of grievances. Hickabon picked it up, read it and replied, "they look comprehensible--give me 10 representatives and we'll talk about it." The representatives of the last protest was transferred to maximum security--Md. Penn. and therefore the masses were leary of jeopardizing more people's chances of ever leaving these places. The group then asked for publicity from local newspapers for security and maybe protecting us from additional harrassment. He refused it, saying, "I don't deal that way." After that denial we asked for Rep. Parren J.Mitchell and Marvin Mandell to investigate our grievances and prevent Hickabon from handling the situations as he has in the past with sheer apathy. He said Mr. Mitchell and the governor, "were not coming and he (himself) would not compromise." He concluded his statement with, "I'll give you ten minutes to select 10 reps." And he walked off. When he had gotten back to his car, he made a call and minutes later some hundred officers came rushing to the scene brandishing 36" riot clubs. We thought they were going to just rush us and start ' whipping heads" (as they have in the past).

Mr. Hickabon knowing he had projected an air of violent aggression resolved that we were the aggressors-and after completely brushing aside our grievances he ordered his gestapo to fire the gas right into the crowd. Beforehand

To Be Loved

someone had stood in the row and said our demonstration would not be violent, and if it would get so, it would be on their part and we were to just retreat to the building.

The officers went berserk. The faster the crowd dispersed toward the building, the more they fired at us. It should have ended right there. We went to the building as he had ordered. But what had begun as a peaceful demonstration to express our grievances was now a nightmare. Officers met us at the door with shotguns, tear-gas guns and billy clubs. We retreated to a rec-hall where we were detained and kept for hours, suffocating in the midst of tear gas and over crowdedness. This wasn't a riot, nothing was destroyed, no hostages, no fire, no disturbances at all and all their get tough tactics were unwarranted and unmerited. After two hours had passed, we were collected together according to tier address and stripped of clothing and searched under the guard of some ten shotguns. After getting our names we were marched with our hands above our heads and through a mill-like line of officers--with sticks--to our tiers and into our cells. No one offered resistance. Hickabon ordered us all placed on segregation-lockup.

We were in our cells for approximately 2 hours, and most were asleep when about 20 officers with sticks came rampaging on the teirs like maniacs talking and laughing out loud and banging on our cell doors telling us to wake up and undress again. This is where the harassment began. With many verbal attacks, they ordered us out of our cells and on the tier with our face at the walls

On Target: The Judge

while they mutilated our cells and humiliated us with riot sticks. They ripped the dust-proof plastic from our clothes and shoes, snatched the pictures from our walls, tore up the hand-made paper toilet covers and threw all of this in the hall. They snatched the sheet off our bunks and threw the mattress on the floor. They took all our personal belongings such as underwear, books, letters, papers (legal and otherwise), records, stamps, soap, deodorant, shampoos, etc., and dumped them in a pile on the floor. After emptying the cabinets of our cell, they then turned it over on the floor and ordered us back into the mess they had created.

Today is Thursday, we've been locked in ever since; our rules have been reduced to 2 hour visits, cutback of all educational and self-help programs, only two meals a day (at 8 and nothing after 7:00), no more yard recreation, segregation and for every inmate who was out there in the demonstration--will go to "court" and be tried. Haven't they committed all the crimes? What can we be tried for? PLEASE COME TO OUR AID AS SOON AS POSSIBLE, OR SEND SOME OF YOUR AID AT YOUR CONVENIENCE!!!!

In the meantime, Mama, please bring me all my books, get phono fixed and sent up or brought up as soon as possible and stick with me.

I don't know what to say about this situation or what to think. But I'll tell you, Mama it's rough, real rough! And it's gonna be rough until I get some legal aid. Call Stanz and see what's going on in court. I've got to have something to look forward too--this bit is trying to get the best of me.

To Be Loved

I'll be on lock-up with most of the jail for I-don't-know how long. I know you'll get that phono fixed as soon as you can but send along with it many books if they'll let it through.

Keep your faith and take care,

Son

Weeks dragged on within the confinements of our cells, the monotony swallowing us whole. There was no escape, no respite from the relentless routine of reading and thinking. In the isolate corridors of Segregation, where time seemed to stretch infinitely, a voice would occasionally pierce through the thick silence. Gator, a Brother from Baltimore, would pass by Segregation, his presence a connection the regular inmate population. A loan him writing paper, a small gesture that may hold significance amidst the bleakness.

After enduring 30 days of lock-up, the day of our parole hearing arrived, offering a glimmer of hope. In an unexpected twist, the panel, reduced my sentence for "rioting" by 30 days, a small victory. Soon, I would be released from the confines of Segregation and back into the bland realm of normalcy.

As I returned to the normal population, the haunting melodies of The Stylistics' hits filled the airwaves, their lyrics weaving tales of love and heartbreak. "Break Up To Make Up" resonated deeply within me, a reflection of the tumultuous vicissitudes of relationships. The fleeting taste of college education had dissipated, leaving a lingering regret. The shut doors of opportunity echoed in my mind, reminding me of the impermanence of hope.

On Target: The Judge

In the laundry room, where I toiled alongside fellow inmates, our hands gripping the edges of sheets as we maneuvered across the room, clad in our prison attire, we became anonymous figures in a sea of grey and blue, blending into the monotonous landscape of inmates.

But amidst the routine, a conversation with Terry, a fellow worker, shattered the fragile calm. His words held a foreboding weight, revealing Gator's ulterior motives for asking to borrow paper.

"Hey, Ronald," Terry, a fellow worker, said anxiously.

"Yeah?"

Terry moved over closer to me for privacy. "I gotta tell you something, man."

"Yeah?"

"You know Gator, man?"

"From Baltimore?"

"Yeah, man. Let me tell you. Last night I overheard him saying he was going to be sweet on you."

"Yeah?" I asked in red alert. I looked around and wondered how many other inmates knew about that shit. I was going to be challenged. What should I do? Did the muthafucka see some weakness in me? I got to move on that muthafucka before he moves on me.

Feigning sickness, I secured permission to visit the dispensary in the main building. Determination fueled my steps as I navigated the unfamiliar

To Be Loved

territories, passing through guarded gates that separated the tiers. Gator's tier loomed ahead, and a confrontation became inevitable. I had to confront him, to face the threat head-on, even if I didn't yet know the full extent of his intentions. I had intended to go to Gator's tier and confront him. I didn't know what I would do, but I had to do something. As I passed his tier, he walked out. The shit was eerie. I had to see this muthafucka right away, and as if he somehow knew it, there he was. Time to act.

"Hey, man, what's this shit I hear that you were saying about me?"

"Whatchu talking about, Steele?"

"You know muthafucka! You telling muthafuckas you supposed to be sweet on me?!"

"No, Steele, I didn't say that, man. No, I wouldn't say no shit like that about you, man. Who told you that?"

"Well, looka here muthafucka, Uma tell you this only once, I better not ever hear you talking this shit again!"

"Naw, man, I ain't say that shit about you, man!"

I went to the dispensary. I was boiling. But, I was pleased the muthafucka copped a plea. If Gator hadn't, I would have declared war, and we would have gone for it. The rules were, when someone's after you, you go after them!

Our encounter was tense, the air thick with anticipation. Accusations flew, and I demanded answers. Gator, startled by my intensity, denied the claims

On Target: The Judge

vehemently. He cowered, pleading innocence, and in that moment, I found relief. A confrontation was averted, and a war was avoided. The rules of the hood dictated that if someone comes after you, you go after them. But for now, a fragile truce was established.

Leaving Gator behind, I went to the dispensary, my mind boiling with mixed emotions. Although a confrontation had been narrowly avoided, a fierce determination burned within me. The rules of survival in this unforgiving environment were etched in my consciousness. I would remain vigilant, ready to defend myself should the need arise. There was no room for weakness or hesitation in this realm of perpetual potential conflict. It was a constant battle, an unrelenting struggle for survival.

In the brutal world of prison, fighting was not enough. It was a realm where blades determined the victor. The thought of whether he possessed a shank didn't matter at that moment, Anger coursed through me, fueling a primal instinct to overpower him, to strip away any weapon he might brandish. If he dared to reclaim his shattered pride, I had to be ready, which meant I needed a shank.

Carrying a shank in prison came with a heavy burden, akin to wielding a gun on the streets. Possessing one meant being prepared to use it, no matter the consequences. If drawn into a violent altercation, it meant automatic confinement in solitary for a year, a mark against any chance of parole. It was a treacherous path to tread, forging compliance and self-defense. In prison, if you weren't

To Be Loved

willing to kill in self-defense, you risked becoming someone's prey, subject to their dominance and control.

With the element of surprise on my side, I struck fear into his heart. My fellow inmates nodded their approval, acknowledging my commitment to protect myself. Their support was earned through demonstrating a readiness to fight and defend myself at all costs.

Batman, a trusted ally, provided me with a shank. Hiding it was a precarious endeavor, especially during the frisking process near the central housing unit. The risk of being caught in possession of a dangerous weapon was unnerving. I carefully concealed it in my boot, knowing that correctional officers were aware of the influx of inmate-made weapons, particularly from the metal shop. It was an unspoken acceptance, a dark truth within the prison walls.

Each encounter with Gator only fueled my wariness. The grit in his demeanor indicated that he hadn't let go of our conflict. In fact, his newfound confidence presented a danger to my well-being.

One fateful Saturday, as the gates separating the rec-halls were opened for cleaning, I was perched on a table, eyes fixed on the television. Only a couple of other prisoners shared the space. Suddenly, Gator entered the rec-hall. Thoughts of my shank raced through my mind, realizing I had left it behind in my cell. My gaze never wavered as he approached from behind.

My instincts found Gator's movements untrustworthy. And I wasn't going to allow anything to happen to me again. I wouldn't be the one lying in a

On Target: The Judge

hospital bed regretting that I suspected him, but took no action to deny him the opportunity to surprise attack me. Remember, I thought to myself, I wouldn't be in this prison if I had stood up for my interests; never, again. I shifted to another area of the room, preparing myself for an all-out assault if he dared to come near me. My fists clenched, ready to rain down a barrage of blows upon him, followed by a relentless barrage of stomps from my boots until a correctional officer forcibly pulled me away. But he left the rec hall.

Word spread the following day, that Gator had stabbed another inmate the previous evening. He was sentenced to a year of solitary confinement, isolated from the rest of the prison population. I was relieved that our drama ended. That victim could have been me had I not moved to an area where I could watch Gator.

The weight of the shank became too burdensome to bear, a constant reminder of the violence that lurked in prison. I relinquished it, relieving myself of the constant fear and the haunting possibility of taking a life.

***

September 20, 1972

Dear Mr. Steele

The Maryland Court of Appeals reviewed the Petition for Writ of Certiorari (the last level of review) and denied the request. This closes the participation which we can have in this case on behalf of the office of the Public Defender.

Sincerely,

Johnathan Stanz

To Be Loved

Chapter VII

All the Way Down to Get Up

Imprisonment had taken its toll on me, draining my spirit and hope. Despite my efforts to appeal for a new trial, the court denied my request, leaving me at a loss for words. Amid my struggle, Marvin Gaye's soul-stirring music from the movie "Trouble Man" resonated with the anger, vulnerability, and frustration I felt as a troubled man. While the world outside embraced the film "Superfly," it was the accompanying soundtrack by Curtis Mayfield that penetrated my soul and offered me guidance through its social commentary on the prevailing issues in oppressed communities.

From my confined cell, I observed the wasteful existence of humanity, surrounded by garbage and longing for the freedom I once took for granted. I envied the freedom of creatures like birds and mice, feeling I was reduced to less than either. Memories of the simple joys of walking freely in nature or feeling the comfort of a tiled or carpeted floor became distant and unfamiliar. A growing dislike for my condition made me question how I ended up in this situation, forcing me to confront my past and the choices that led me here.

I realized the importance of taking responsibility for my life and understanding that unexpected circumstances can derail my best plans. No one had warned me about the harsh realities of prison, and had I known, I would have made a conscious effort to change my ways and take control of my destiny. I had

All the Way Down to Get Up

failed to speak up and protect my interests, relying on others to do so for me. I had to acknowledge that I was the one in the driver's seat of my life, responsible for my own words, commitments, and actions.

A crucial shift in my mindset was necessary, letting go of the "get-over" mentality that sought something for nothing. In a society like America, trying to cheat the system is a trap, resulting in incarceration. I couldn't ignore my dreams of pursuing civil rights, sociology, and Black history any longer. I had prioritized seeking approval and love from others, sacrificing my true essence, which was never a crime. If only I had pursued my genuine interests, choosing civil rights over petty crime, my current predicament could have been avoided. The realization that I couldn't bear a life without freedom grew within me, evoking a desperate desire for change, even preferring death over captivity.

There was a need to be me, and I couldn't. There was a need to relax; I couldn't. I had pushed the real me down so deep into my sub consciousness to survive the hard prison life until I nearly forgot the person I was. When I needed to rely on my senses and instincts, I couldn't connect. I couldn't be me in that place; it wasn't safe. It became challenging to smile about anything. It became difficult to feel connected to anything. In a funk, I wrote "Death & Life's Strife":

"Rather than by life be quit?"

"Suicide, I think, one day, I'll commit."

"But, like everyone, it should catch you Running."

"Want to know when it is coming."

To Be Loved

"Life is sometimes filled with utter frustration..."

"Mmm! Even with your every association!"

"You sometimes wonder whats' after this?"

"Halcyon and calm; peace-even bliss."

"But even there, perchance, to a few of your foes."

"So. For peace, willingly I'll still go!"

"They will possibly consider vindication."

"No. They're tangled in the web of t' mortician."

Wherest thy sorrow, wherest thy blue?"

"Life's dolefulness, sadness and rue."

"...Up one day, the dumps the next?"

"Tired of this fluctuation -- there IS infinite rest"

"But so young, we are, these thoughts are t'morrow's."

"Hmm! Seen too much, we have; felt ever'thing

embellished with sorrow."

"Then pop some pill-obliviously live by thrill!"

"Tho the pill's good thrill, its, too, a shameful kill."

"Well, just get back on the bronco of life and row!"

"To be taken half-way, 'n stopped by my foe?"

"Suicide, I think, one day, I'll commit."

"Yeah. Rather than by life be quit."

My self-confidence had abandoned me; I was depressed.

All the Way Down to Get Up

Dear Judge Whitaker:

Something other than want and desire is compelling me to write this letter. And hoping that this, my plea, won't disturb you or deprive you of much time from your honored work, I would like to express this need in a way, plain and simple, my only way and to your honor's reasoning.

November 16 marks one full year and twenty-five days of my incarceration. Compared to my sentence, it may seem a concise time or maybe not long enough. But to feel a year, every day of this year, and every hour tick away in discomfort due to your environment has levied in me an illness, a constant sense of depression that you'd hope nobody else shares. That I just can't seem to cope with.

I see the dangers therewith and the traumatic effect of suppressing these feelings, which reappear in the privacy of your cell and the restlessness of a still night, is terribly detrimental to me.

The pain I live with every day is torture and I hope that it would go away. Knowing the thoughts of me having another year and more to live like this is enough to contemplate suicide -- an alternative, the only existing alternative, that may release me of the pangs of my mind, clouded with suffering.

This is not an ordinary pain. It's not physical, but mental. But, I don't want to die a worthless death. I don't want to die knowing I've achieved and contributed nothing to life.

And so, I erase away the thoughts of that, and I seek another alternative

To Be Loved

-- a psychologist.

In talking to the institution's psychologists, I've gained nothing much, the results are fruitless and futile. I'm not insane, though, it has been said that a person who contemplates suicide is insane. I have my full senses, but this place is overwhelming them. I've had repeated appointments with him since May 1971. And after each conference, I return to my cell, thinking, hoping, wishing and praying that my depressions will dissolve and I may have a cheerful day, even a moment. But it's out of the question. My senses to "look around" and replace the reality of this prison life with rationale, has been completely exhausted. I just don't fit into this environment, and I can't adjust.

I see this place -- a closet filled with confusion and parked in the farthest and darkest corner on earth, away from everything.

Away from laughter, rejoicing, and even mutual feelings of care. Inside of this place, I see the angry faces of inmates, who are powder-kegs, about to explode on anyone and me who looks at them wrong. I feel the awesome rejection and dejection from people who don't understand this depression I feel and look at it as "weakness," only and one who the stronger will thrive on.

It's a full year that I'm suffering. What's kept me going has been hope in my attorney.

I am a year older, more mature. In April 1972, I enrolled in the 7-Step Program, a self-help program that involves self-therapy. I hear the awful joke of an inmate telling another of his strong-arming homosexuality of another inmate.

All the Way Down to Get Up

And I hear that the only person I could talk to was "shanked."

Your honor, I see the dangers herein. If there is a lesson to learn here for my wrong doings, I have learned it. The rest is a killing.

In July 1972, only two months after my enrollment in the college program here, it was suspended, as a result of a mass disturbance. Since September 1972, I have been assigned and has worked with regret in the institution's laundry, folding sheets.

Please, Judge Whitaker, suspend my sentence. I have been punished severely. With probation, I can prove to you, my mother and myself, my worth.

You will see that the year that I've served and the stigma of my conviction being with me for the rest of my life was enough to correct and rehabilitate me.

When released, I will resume my studies at Federal City College and if you ever hear my name again, it will be for a deed I've contributed to the field of my studies and humanity, not for a crime.

Sincerely,

***

I was desperate, unafraid of anybody hurting me, as much as I feared what I might do to myself. I used everything in that letter I thought I could use to persuade the judge to release me, if not for legal reasons, then out of human compassion, but I never mailed that letter. It felt pitiful and rambling. My depression clouded my instincts, making it challenging to write a letter that satisfied me. It had been a long time since I'd written to Judge Whitaker.

To Be Loved

Nevertheless, I needed to write him again, at least one more time.

I got with an acquaintance, Theodore, to rewrite my letter to Judge Whitaker. Theodore, also trying to write his way out of prison, accepted my request without hesitation or charge.

About six feet tall with smooth pecan brown skin, Theodore wore a big Afro like everyone else. And he wore large eyeglasses that all conspired to make him look like a square who shouldn't have been there. Theodore wasn't square; instead, he was introverted and studious. He got mixed up with the wrong crowd and was sentenced to 20 years along with Batman for a robbery. He used to walk and talk with one of the cooler cats from Baltimore, Charles Dutton. Dutton wasn't into that East Side, West Side shit that characterized most Baltimore inmates. Dutton carried himself like he felt no one was better than him and he was no better. Years later, after Dutton was released from prison, he became a Broadway stage actor and the star of his TV series, "Roc."

I showed Theodore copies of the letters and responses I had written to Judge Whitaker in the past, including the most recent one, so he could sense my tone and direction. Theodore redrafted my letter:

November 1972

Your Honor:

I hope this appeal is received by you in the best of health as well as spirits. Please read this with reasoning for I am writing with all sincerity and need.

All the Way Down to Get Up

Understandably, you may have forgotten me so if you will grant me a few minutes of your honored time, I will attempt to refresh your memory.

On the day of December 16, 1971, you imposed a sentence of fifteen years' imprisonment on me upon a conviction of armed robbery. Subsequent to my sentencing I wrote you several letters, each of which you graciously acknowledged, and expressed an interest in my case. In view of the fact that you never indicated the extent of your interest, I arrived at the conclusion--perhaps erroneously--that you were motivated more by common courtesy than any express interest in my case. Consequently, rather than exploit your benevolence, I discontinued my letters. I'm writing you now in a direct appeal for reduction or modification of my sentence. In spite of the fact that my guilt was not proven beyond a reasonable doubt, I realize that neither was my innocence established to the satisfaction of the court.

So I'm appealing to you on grounds which are more moral than legal. Your honor, if I'm not mistaken, the objectives of incarceration are two-fold; to punish the offender and to "rehabilitate," or reform him--each goal being of tantamount importance. The dictionary defines reform as "to induce to abandon evil ways." I can say with sincerity and honesty that I have no "evil" or "criminal" inclinations. I can't be classed as an incorrigible criminal, not by any standards, and to be considered a threat to society would be a gross misnomer. I know within myself that all I want is a chance to prove that I can be a useful and productive member of society. My attitude can't improve any because I want only

To Be Loved

the right things from life and I have every intention of acquiring these things honestly.

So I don't really qualify for reform because if I changed the attitude I have now, I would be retrogressing. Now as for punishment, punishment is supposed to make a man feel remorse for his crime. How then can you further punish a man whose remorse already exceeds any misdeeds?

I've been separated from the ones I love. I've been denied the opportunity to transcend these deplorable situations. I feel as though I've been the victim of a gross miscarriage of justice. I was suddenly cast into an environment which I was totally unprepared for; an environment of hardened habitual criminals.

The fact that a vast majority of inmates here are recidivists preclude the existence of any--they are more adjusted to prison and can thus agitate the ill-adjustment of the weakness of the first offender.

Programs here are geared toward the majority. Unfortunately, first offenders and other inmates with a sincere desire to become constructive and positive contributors to society are a minority. Only through a primordial instinct for survival have I been able to retain my present character and convictions, which I realize are imperative to one day enter the honest and respectable mainstream of society.

As a result of the proclivity of the State, I was portrayed as a subhuman preying on society; a monster deserving absolutely no compassion or

All the Way Down to Get Up

consideration. But that description couldn't fit me through any stretch of the imagination. It's been said that no man can sink below the lowest in all of us and no man can rise higher than the highest in all of us and I agree. Every man is a potential criminal. I have hopes and aspirations like every young man. I realize and accept the fact that this present situation somewhat limits the heights I can reach in certain endeavors. But there are still many things I can do which would provide a comfortable life for my future wife and my daughter. I can still be a source of pride to my family. All I need is a chance and I'm asking you for that chance. I'm not asking you to take what I'm saying here at face value. If I may be granted a court appearance, I want to talk to you personally. I just want a chance.

Very truly,

Ronald Steele

***

Theodore's assistance transformed my words, imbuing them with sophistication and maturity, transcending mere emotional appeal. His objectivity was precisely what I needed. With the refined letter in hand, I wanted to mail it, but my depression had consumed me, its grip dragging me deeper into an emotional abyss. Mood swings were frequent, with moments of feeling invincible followed by periods of worthlessness. Sleep became elusive, prompting me to reach out to my mother, pleading for sleeping pills. Yet, she ignored my request, never acknowledging it.

As my depression worsened, I contemplated alternative means of escaping this overwhelming punishment. However, I recognized that sinking deeper into this funk could render me so mentally unstable that I would become defenseless in this ruthless environment. After enduring a year of incarceration, even the weakest inmates began to appear feminine, a disheartening realization. After several weeks, the absence of any communication from Judge Whitaker added to my growing despair.

I had to make one final appeal, one last desperate gamble to seek justice and regain release. The dice had to be rolled once more, for I had no other option.

***

December 19, 1972

Sir:

"Trauma: Mental injury caused by an external agent," (says Webster). I know it profoundly. It's why I haven't written, anybody. Haven't been able to think, or live, peacefully. Trauma: The appeal was denied in September, past. The Clerk of the Court of Appeal committed an error, which possibly persuaded the affirmant.

I moved for a Writ of Certiarari, concerning this error. The court, in question, replied that "the Chief Judge hadn't anything to do with that error," or something of that order, period. No more said of it. The lawyer, appointed to me to handle the appellant procedures, wrote me to inform that he had to be relieved, as my counsel, making exoneration virtually impossible for me.

Trauma. When it strikes, it hits hard, nearly crushing its victim (when

All the Way Down to Get Up

it's a decision as this, life or death). I guess I was too optimistic, filled with naiveté. I think I had every reason to be. But nevermore... Trauma. It becomes a killing, a slow and tortuous death, because I can't live in here. I can't live in harmony with others because of weary. And I can't live in peace with myself because of loneliness. There's always an atmosphere of antagonism, tension, hatred, and crude violence, twenty-four hours a day. Everyday... I don't know, I guess I just wasn't prepared for this... But ducking and dodging, weaving and bobbing, I've survived thus far, tho not in complete good health. Fourteen months of it, and over 414 days, when you read these lines, and I'm still alive.

An attempt at college, here, was in vain.

It expired July, past. My administrators couldn't find a better thing to do with my well endeavors than assign me to the institution's laundry, folding sheets. It threatens my mentality, this job, this tense and idle time. Mysteriously, my good interest remains the same. Though its met its peak.

Self-teaching is really difficult, though. Studying, period, is difficult, terribly difficult. The hours I've consumed of college has revealed it, and 14 months of trying to study on my own, in the semi-privacy of this cell, has further convinced me. I just can't study my best in here. It hurts because I can't enjoy the benefits of my full potential, not even in the ostracism of this cell! There's always, and now, a racket on the tier; people arguing, fussing, fighting, "people laughing out loud away their miseries," detrimentally disturbing me. I can't think completely. It has shattered thought. Fully concentration is a futile endeavor,

To Be Loved

tension makes even the easiest studies, difficult. But I keep trying. I've ordered, by mail, a programmed book entitled, 300 Commas," (by Leonard J. West, Ph.D.). I have it here, now. And in the early hours of morn, I've studied it persistently, 30 nights so far, 120 hours, more. (I'll know how to use that comma, soon, properly).

P.S. A different program began on December 7, a crash course in English Composition, 102. Whenever the teacher thinks you're ready, there'll be a standard C.L.E.P. test, the equivalent of three College Credits. This class meets every week: Thursday only. I may even fail it. I'm gonna give it a try, at least.

You know, not- withstanding, is that I never had English, #101. The college, aforementioned, started right at English Composition, 102. I passed, however. And I'll get that English, 101, probably piece by piece, but surely in the early hours of morn. Wish you and yours,

Happy Holidays, and

A splendid New Year.

The Court Responds to My Letters

On an ordinary day in December 1972, an unexpected visitor, a Mr. Kline, arrived and revealed astonishing news. He informed me that Judge Whitaker had requested my presence in court to re-examine my sentence. The sheer disbelief washed over me, making it difficult to comprehend the magnitude of this development. A tremendous weight that burdened me for so long suddenly lifted, but I remained numb, cautiously guarding my emotions.

Having previously experienced the disappointment of court appearances and facing setbacks, I had grown cynical and lost faith in the judicial system. Amid prevailing pessimism, the fact that Judge Whitaker summoned me to court hinted at the possibility of a sentence modification or even a reversal of my conviction. Such a notion seemed improbable, yet a glimmer of hope emerged, gradually eroding the walls skepticism had built.

***

January 2, 1973

Dear Mr. Whitaker, kind sir:

Mr. Kline came in like the wind. And he left. There were words-tho I've suffered from extreme ennui and for so long that it also became manifested that all writers don't write the way they talk, don't talk the way they write -- and I was nervous. Perhaps even away from here...I don't know...It was sudden.

And it was real. My gratitude is yours. Just the thought of leaving this

To Be Loved

place, its contents and doing something real...I can see Christmas, now, and the day has past.

How does a man thank someone for an opportunity for relief of such a pang? There's got to be a way to show it, exhibit it. The phrase "Thank you," I think is quite trite for my profoundest gratitude... I'm in debt to you forever.

Very truly yours,

Ronald Steele

***

Meanwhile, a month of sulking had passed before I received a ray of hope from Mama. Good news, no doubt. My response was subdued. Depression had made being hopeful seem alien.

***

January 20, 1973

Hi Ronald

I feel better today than I have felt since you & Mitchell went away. Mr. Kline called me Fri. And asked me to come to Charles County Thurs 25, of Jan. concerning your release. I'm almost sure you will make the best of it. He called me on the job. I was so excited I had to search for words to answer him (smile). I hope the same will happen for Mitchell in the near future. All is well here & also very happy for you. Guess will go to see him Sun. Will close for now, see you Thurs.

Love, Mom

The Court Responds to My Letters

***

On Thursday, January 25, 1973, in the Charles County Court House, it all became familiar to me again. This time Mama was at court for me; her presence demonstrated that my mother cared about me. There was no jury. There was only Judge Charles Whitaker and other court officials.

"Young man, how are you?" Judge Whitaker asked from the judge's bench.

"Okay." It came out muddled. I was in a funk.

"You want to tell me what happened on the night of June 27, 1971?"

"Yes, sir," I told him the whole truth about that night.

There was silence. Then Judge Whitaker spoke up.

"Are you sorry for what you've done?"

"Yes."

"Do you think you will ever do anything like this again?"

"No, never."

"In view of these circumstances, I hereby order that your sentence be reduced from 15 years to 5 years."

"Thank you, your honor," I said.

Conflicting emotions surged within me as I left the courtroom in the custody of the bondsmen. On the one hand, there was a sense of relief that I had finally revealed to Judge Whitaker, the truth, knowing that my confession couldn't harm my brother or Too Tall, given the overwhelming evidence against them, the

To Be Loved

positive identification, and they had exhausted their appeals. And I realized that from this point forward, it was 'every man for himself.' I had to prioritize my own interests over the interests of others.

Stepping outside the courtroom, I saw my mother and brother, after 15 months of incarceration without bars, standing on the grass in a near-normal. I waved, a symbolic gesture of connection and shared hope. Inhaling the fresh air, warmed by the sun and carried by the wind, I felt a renewed closeness to the prospect of my release from prison.

Comprehending the moment's significance, I realized that in only three months, I would be eligible for parole on a reduced five-year sentence; having served 18 months. It was a reason to celebrate and be celebrated. Without formal training in writing, I had accomplished what lawyers and wealth could not — I had my sentence by a decade through the power of written words. This revelation filled me with a sense of purpose and possibility. I felt empowered. I felt valued. I had a gift. I believed that if untrained writing could unlock prison doors for me, then with specialized training, then with and education, there is no telling what other doors could I open for other deserving people! It was an official acknowledgment that I had discovered empowering myself with my potential as a budding writer and world of opportunities awaited me.

***

January 29, 1973

Dear Mr. Steele:

The Court Responds to My Letters

I have contacted Mr. Kline and the Judge concerning their getting in touch with the Parole authorities concerning your early release- I hope that we will obtain concrete from them soon.

Very truly yours,

Milton Canada

MC:nrs

***

The reduction in my sentence didn't guarantee my immediate release; it simply meant I was immediately eligible for parole. However, I still had to convince the parole board of my readiness to re-enter society after 18 months. On the day of my parole hearing, March 12, I was prepared to present my life in context.

Addressing the board, I confidently expressed, "Now that I have had time to reflect and understand what led me here, my life together, I know exactly what I want to do with my life. I aspire to become a sociologist and help prevent others coming to prison."

One of the board members asked if six months at MCTC (Maryland Correctional Training Center) would better prepare me for reintegration. I responded firmly, "Six more months in MCTC would contribute no more than six more minutes towards my readiness. I am fully aware of my life's purpose and I am eager to begin."

The parole board granted my parole, and the realization of a miracle. I

To Be Loved

will escape this chapter of my life, and reshape the arc of my destiny, just as I had predicted I would in my letters to my brother.

That I had written my way out spread throughout the prison, as if it were announced over the loudspeaker. Instant respect accompanied anyone who was released from prison. Suddenly, everyone was listening to what I had to say, seeking my help in writing letters, as if the power of one letter held the magic.

As my release date approached, I recognized that unforeseen circumstances or jealousy could potentially cause delays. I refused to stay in prison a minute longer than necessary, especially for avoidable reasons. Therefore, once I received my release date, I refrained from going to the recreational hall, determined not to be denied my release.

In one of my letters to Judge Whitaker, I had expressed my dread of turning 21 behind prison walls. It seemed to have touched him. On March 22, 1973, just three days before my 21st birthday, I had my final breakfast with my fellow inmates. Overwhelmed by emotions, I couldn't say much. I wanted to escape from that madness and never return. As we marched out of the cafeteria, an officer pulled me aside. I had already packed my belongings. They would lead me through MCI (Maryland Correctional Institution) one last time, and then I would be free. If I ever had the chance, I vowed to help incarcerated individuals help themselves, although I knew it would likely be the last time, I would see most of my former fellow inmates.

"Later, Steele," the Brothers said as they passed, some extending their

The Court Responds to My Letters

hands for a high-five. I was leaving; the nightmare was coming to an end. It was an unbelievable feeling. When I first arrived in prison, I set a goal of getting out before my scheduled release date, and I accomplished it by firmly deciding that I would and then acting accordingly. That's the power of self-determination.

To Be Loved

Back on the Block

As I rode in the taxi on my way home, I felt emotionally detached, numb to the overwhelming experience of my release. However, as the taxi turned onto familiar streets, memories flooded back. Carmony Hills Drive, where I first met Pat, evoked nostalgia and disbelief. Turning onto Peacock Street, I noticed the bare trees lining the road, a starkly contrasting to the warmth I had felt when my family and I moved there. This community, which I had barely known before my incarceration, I thought I wouldn't see again for another two years and three months.

Upon arriving home, I was greeted by my sister Paulette, and our next-door neighbor, Pamela, adorned in hair rollers and a house robe. Amid the screams, hugs, and kisses, we settled in and shared a joint. returning to the real world meant living up to the promises I had made in prison. I had to resume the responsibilities I had left behind, such as determining my relationship with Ngina and adjusting to fatherhood, as well as providing for her. Being high from marijuana and contemplating my place in society overwhelmed me. A terrifying vision crossed my mind, depicting myself boarding a bus and heading back to Maryland Correctional Institution. After some time, Pamela and I excused ourselves and went to her house. She always understood what I needed, possessing a unique understanding of men that set her apart from other girls.

One notable change I observed upon my return to society was the music. The jive-talking DJs on WOL-AM and WOOK-FM had been replaced by

Back on the Block

emerging favorites like WPGC-FM and WKYS-FM. These stations played a mix of Black and white themed music, hip and upbeat. During my time in La Plata and Hagerstown, I had grown to appreciate music, including "Tiny Dancer" by Cat Stevens, "Taxi" by Neil Diamond, "Maggie May" by Rod Stewart, "Gypsies, Tramps and Thieves" by Cher, "Brandy (You're a Fine Girl)" by Looking Glass, and many more. A musical revolution had occured, with Black artists breaking free from the confines of rhythm and blues love songs and incorporating jazz and jazz-fusion elements, and singing about all else that was our community and our world. It was like desegregation also liberated Black music.

Artists like Barry White commanded attention with songs like "I Got So Much to Give" and "Never, Never Gonna Give Ya Up," featuring a string of moans, groans, and adoring lyrics delivered in his beloved baritone voice that drove the ladies wild. Radio also played more message-driven songs, such as Bobby Womack's "Harry Hippie" and Earth, Wind & Fire's "Keep Your Head to the Sky."

In terms of fashion, I noticed another shift as well. The once popular heels of shoes had been replaced by rising platform soles, which, at first glance, resembled the footwear of clowns. However, platform shoes had become a fashionable trend, and how one wore them determined their level of hipness or clownishness. These shoes perfectly complemented our polyester flare slacks and Tom Jones-style shirts, characterized by long slithering collars and bell-bottomed sleeves crowned by our large Afros.

To Be Loved

I had taken a long, critical look at my life during incarceration, I had undergone personal changes and assumed that everyone else had grown as well. However, as I encountered old acquaintances, it became evident that some remained trapped in their old ways. Rod, Yvonne's husband, pulled up in his Cadillac, embodying the rebellious spirit of his adolescence—smoking cigarettes, driving flashy cars, harmonizing on street corners, and hanging out with the boys. His attire reminded me of the exaggerated fashion style of characters like The Mack or Superfly from the movies. Nevertheless, Rod was cool.

"Hey, Ronald. How you doing?" he greeted me.

"Hey, Rod. I'm doing okay," I replied, extending my hand for a shake.

"Get in," he said. "Let me take you to see the guys."

That was considerate of Rod, but I wasn't quite ready. I didn't want to return to that scene. I was done with that lifestyle. Nonetheless, I got into his Cadillac, and we embarked on a smooth journey, exchanging sporadic conversation. Rod and I never quite clicked. He was Mitchell's friend and my brother-in-law.

"It feels good to be back," I commented.

"I can imagine," he replied.

"So, what have you been up to?" I asked.

"Not much, just working."

I was reminded of how our conversations often began with the same answer: "Not much." Or, 'nothing' seemed to be the default response before

Back on the Block

continuing.

"Well, you know what I've been up to—time," I remarked.

"Yeah, what was that like?"

"I hated it. Prison is no place to be somebody."

We drove through my old neighborhood, where memories lingered, reminding me of the fun we had and the passing of a bygone era that seemed to have occurred in the blink of an eye. Everything we experienced on Sheriff Road transpired within only three years. Instead of stopping at the wall on Sheriff Road, we continued up to the methadone center on Just Street—a new hangout.

Fortunately, none of my close friends, like Robert, Sly, Tiger, David Williams, Tyson, or Gilbert, were there. Instead, I encountered a group of lifeless figures hanging out in front of the methadone center, scratching and itching, stooped and pale, bearing the unmistakable frown of heroin addicts—remnants of the Brothers from the hood I once knew. The sight was disheartening. Even if I had been imprisoned for four years, they would never have come to visit me or even write. Now, they feigned pleasure in seeing me.

I couldn't tolerate it.

"Fuck this."

Sensing my distress, Rod asked, "Are you ready to go?"

"Yeah."

I was shaken, deeply disturbed by the fact that they hadn't progressed. They had the opportunities, which were denied to me, for a year-and-a-half. They

To Be Loved

should have made more significant strides. Instead, they had regressed. It depressed me. We drove back in silence. Rod wouldn't have understood my frustration. He had done me a favor by taking me to my old stomping grounds.

"Thanks for taking me up there, man," I expressed, shaking his hand before exiting the car and returning home.

After a week at home, I finally decided to see Patricia and Ngina. However, as we tried to pick up where we had left off, it became evident that too much time and experience had passed. However, her words made me feel like my love really didn't matter. It hurt to realize she wasn't the same Pat I had known. Although I still loved her, I wouldn't tolerate any more mistreatment from anyone. We had outgrown Carmody Hills and the basement. Pat had changed, but not for the better. I struggled to forget my doubts and assumed the role of Ngina's father again. However, questions plagued my mind. The dates, her light complexion, the hazel eyes, and the countless "I don't know" from Pat made it difficult for me to feel at ease in the role of Ngina's father. She was a beautiful baby, but Pat's whole family seemed to exercise authority over her, another jinx of living across the street from love. I could foresee myself clashing with her family over various matters I might observe from across the street. Who would have the final say in these situations?

Visiting Mitchell had become a family routine. Besides Christmas and Thanksgiving, visiting Mitchell at a prison had become the primary family together. My mother would go around the house, asking who wanted to visit

Back on the Block

Mitchell. Not everyone wanted to go every time, and I used to resent their reluctance. I felt they were being selfish and insensitive. Perhaps my mother had faced similar resistance when she asked them to visit me. It was another example of love and care; values I would demand in future relationships.

We had visited Mitchell in nearly every penal institution in the Washington metropolitan area since we were teens, some of them for a second time around. Lorton Youth Center, Lorton Penitentiary, D.C. Jail, Maryland House of Correction, and the Baltimore Pen. Perhaps that was why the family seemed reluctant to visit him. We would dress up and pile into Frank's car, enduring the journey to see Mitchell. Frank and I rarely exchanged words. I couldn't handle his "step" daddy's authority, and he couldn't control my outspokenness. However, I had changed, and he couldn't see it.

Feeling depressed, I caught sight of the grim Baltimore Penitentiary's structure once again as a visitor. I walked up the street and looked up at the window from which I used to watch children play while in MRDCC. There were no fond memories associated with those walls.

Visiting Mitchell used to feel like honoring a fallen hero, akin to seeing a prisoner of war. Now, it had become something we did without much thought. We would wait 30 minutes to an hour in the waiting room until his name was called. Then, we would enter the visiting room, sitting at long tables that formed a square, with inmates on the inside and visitors on the outside. We watched and listened to other inmates while waiting, engaging in conversation. I used to be in

To Be Loved

awe of the prisoners, wondering if I could be as tough as they appeared to be, enduring the deprivation of everything life had to offer. But now, I looked at them with pity. The facade had been shattered. I had been there and done that. Prison was no place to be somebody.

When we saw Mitchell behind the gate that led to the visiting room, he stood tall and proud as if waiting to be introduced to an audience on a stage. Seeing him filled us with joy. Then, he would step into the room, and I would realize it was worth traveling the long distance and enduring the wait to see him.

We accorded Mitchell the respect befitting a fallen hero. I wondered if he ever felt like a hero, being incarcerated and enduring the hardships. But then, I began to question whether there was something he actually enjoyed about being in prison, too, considering how much of his life—nearly one-third—he had spent behind bars. He wasn't a gangster or a legendary hustler.

I wanted to reprimand Mitchell, to criticize him for dragging me into prison the last time, for subjecting our family to the numerous visits to jails and prisons without growing tired of them or changing his ways. I wanted him to understand the consequences it had on our family. As the eldest son, the first child, his presence at home, helping to provide for the family, and exemplifying the right path could have made a world of difference for him and us. Instead, he had surrendered all of that. While the family struggled, he hung out with the boys in Boys Town, USA. It was as if he had traded one form of addiction for another. Perhaps prison life had become a haven, an escape from the burdens of

Back on the Block

responsibility.

During subsequent visits to Mitchell, I observed his behavior closely. I listened critically to everything he said. I began to challenging his complaints about the ineptitude of the guards, the classification officer, and other inmates, and how unfairly they treated him. I would interject, "Do you think this is the Hilton? Nobody ever promised that this system would be fair. It should make you more determined to get out and never return."

I wondered how he could keep returning to a situation he despised. Was he institutionalized? How could he continue complaining about the unfairness instead of sharing his thoughts on what he planned to do about it? I paid attention to the clattering keys, the bars, the institutional marble floor, the requirement to store our belongings in lockers before visiting, and the hours spent waiting in the lounge, only to hear more complaints about how fucked up prison was.

Mama and everyone else participated in what I perceived as a charade, and I was alone in my criticisms; I was the bad guy again. I couldn't comprehend this picture. I was back to catching hell at home. My mother would tell me, "You can leave!" whenever we disagreed. And during an argument with my sister, Carlean, she lashed out, calling me a "fucking ex-convict."

She was the first person in the family to label me that way. No family member had ever referred to Mitchell as an ex-convict. It enraged me. It didn't matter that I was there with Mitchell or the unethical circumstances that had landed me in prison. My experiences behind bars didn't matter. What mattered to

To Be Loved

her was that I had been there at all. Suddenly, she felt superior to me. Ex-convict—an additional obstacle I had to overcome. Soon, every disagreement with Mama ended with her saying, "Well, you can get your own place. You can leave if you don't like it here!" I heard "You can leave" so often from my mother that it became a mantra whenever I was at home. It was reminiscent of the old days. I could no longer tolerate the personal rejection from my family.

My family persisted in painting me as their scapegoat. My siblings could say or do anything to me, and my mother considered me the problem.

However, I had changed for the better. I wasn't going back to my old neighborhood, and I wasn't going back to the same old dynamics with my family or anyone. It would take time for me to fully understand human behavior. We are shaped by our experiences, and my family had not undergone the same radical transformation as I had. They held onto the memories of my past, incapable of comprehending the extent of my personal growth. They denied it and treated me accordingly.

No Longer at Ease

I sought counseling for my ongoing depression, but grappled with what others might think of me. The stigma surrounding mental health in the Black community made it difficult for many to consider counseling a viable option, regardless of the trauma they endured. We believed that, as Black people, we could deal with our own trauma and heal ourselves, drawing on the strength of our ancestors who survived slavery, Emancipation, sharecropping, segregation, and other forms of systemic oppression. Seeking therapy or counseling was often seen as a privilege reserved for white individuals or the affluent. My friends might have viewed my decision to consult professionals as an indication of my mental instability or an attempt to emulate white behavior.

Nevertheless, I recognized that I had lost touch with my inner self, the part of me that had always guided me instinctively. I had suppressed myself in prison to navigate the paranoia and to survive. But now, I felt utterly disconnected from that inner voice. I longed to reconnect with myself and my instincts, believing that doing so would set things right. Something was stirring within me, waiting to be unleashed, and I knew I needed to talk to someone.

I reached out to social services a local social services center. In hindsight, seeking rehabilitative services was as crucial to changing my life as reaching initiating writing to Judge Whitaker had been. Counseling would not only help me understand myself and confront the root of my depression but also lead to my

To Be Loved

re-enrollment in college.

I was assigned a counselor named Sean McSwain, a white man. I would travel several miles by hitchhiking or biking to express my feelings and frustrations to him. Mr. McSwain attempted to provide the answers I sought, offering empathy and creating a safe space for me to open up about my deepest fears, resentments, likes, and dislikes.

During our sessions, I cried about the unfairness of racism, recounting a recent incident at a concert where tear gas was deployed on the predominantly Black audience. I shared how I felt disrespected at home, with my mother's response to conflicts always being that I could leave. But where could I go?

Before seeking counseling, I had never discussed matters of the heart and mind that troubled me. The culture of silence and the fear of being vulnerable or perceived as weak had conditioned us to keep our pain and embarrassment hidden. We believed that discussing personal matters would become fodder used against us in an argument, etc., and thought it necessary to appear in control and unaffected by life's challenges.

However, the need to relieve the emotional pressure and reconnect with myself became a stronger incentive to talk. Sharing my bottled-up feelings provided temporary relief, even though it didn't solve everything. I still experienced severe depressive episodes after our sessions, making me realize that I had become manic-depressive.

Outside my counseling sessions, I felt emotionally closed off from everyone except Mr. McSwain. I explained to him that I didn't have much to say to people because I didn't want to discuss prison or my past, leaving little room for conversation about my life. But he offered me hope, suggesting that re-establishing myself in society with a job and being able to handle young adult responsibilities would help my self-esteem. Perhaps they could help me get a job, too. The social service that made his counseling available to indigent individuals was a lifeline for many.

Through counseling, I began to uncover suppressed conflicts from my past that I needed to acknowledge, accept, or address. Counseling taught me to express those feelings and rediscover myself. I wanted to move forward and be seen by my family as the person I aspired to become rather than solely defined by their perception of who I once was. I needed them to give me space to grow and evolve in their presence. However, they remained unchanged, unable to see my transformation. reminders of my past and my family's dynamics surrounded me everywhere I turned.

Reflecting on the counselor, I realized that emotional love had been absent with my parents. In 1955, when I was three years old, poverty, fear, and violence permeated our two-room tenement house in the tough Shaw area of Northwest Washington, D.C. The legacies of oppression were constant factors, even within our home.

To Be Loved

Confronting the Past

My father had subjected me, at young age to brutal whippings, resembling the actions of a heartless overseer punishing an enslaved individual whenever I made a mistake.

"Get on your knees!" My father's voice thundered before each of these beatings. I was only three years old, and I couldn't fathom what I had done to anger him so deeply. Tears streamed down my face, soaking my shirt and falling to the floor. Overwhelmed with dread, I sank helplessly to my knees.

"P-please, Daddy," I stammered between sobs, "I didn't mean it. I'm sorry!"

No matter what I had done, all I could do was plead for mercy.

"Please, Daddy," I begged, my voice filled with desperation, "Please, I'm sorry, I'm sorry!"

My father gripped my shoulders, pulling me between his legs and trapping me like a helpless animal awaiting slaughter.

"God damn it, I've told you not to mess up! I'll teach you right now that I'll beat you if you don't do as I say!"

His cursing punctuated each strike of his belt. In my imagination, I saw him lifting the leather belt high above his head as if it could touch the ceiling, his muscles tensing with every motion. The impact of Daddy's strap against my backside would cause my bowels and bladder to betray me repeatedly.

When he finally released me, he warned, "Next time, be more careful, do

Confronting the Past

you hear me, boy!?"

I must have been in shock because I can't recall the pain. Perhaps forgetting is a way for God shields children from unbearable agony. All I could remember, as I sobbed, was the horror and sickness churning inside me, the anger and rejection emanating from my father, and my soiled underwear that accompanied every one of his whippings. It was the first time that I had wished I could become invisible, whenever my Daddy was home.

If my father wasn't whipping us, he was either fighting with Mama or absent. On one occasion, I was caught a violent altercation between my parents. Daddy had Mama pinned against a wall. They both demanded that I hand them the broom, leaving me confused and petrified. Naturally, my sympathy leaned toward my mother's defense. However, my father made the decision for me, snatching the broom from my trembling hands. While I don't recall my father assaulting my mother, though I feel certain he did.

Mitchell and I went to the store to buy bread one wintry day. In the snow, I found a brightly colored miniature toy truck, partially buried beneath the white blanket. I bent down, gently brushing away the snow to reveal the vibrant blue, orange, and white truck. As we continued our walk, I marveled that I now possessed my first toy. I carefully tucked it into my pocket for safekeeping. Upon returning home, I excitedly showed Daddy the toy, hoping for his approval. However, Daddy made Mitchell and I return the toy to where I found it. He believed we shouldn't bring anything home that we hadn't purchased, even though

To Be Loved

he couldn't afford to buy us anything. He viewed it as an opportunity for stealing. Daddy would often claim that he would always be there if we went to jail for defending ourselves, but he would never visit if we ended up there for stealing. Maybe that toy reminded my father that he had never bought us toys or anything.

***

My mother, Ruby Alberta Steele, was born on her father's farm in Harmony, North Carolina, on August 27, 1926. She was the seventh of ten children. In those times, it was common for Black families to have five or more children, perhaps a lingering legacy of the slavery era. White overseers would encourage Black individuals to have many children to use as laborers in the fields or to sell them. The father's involvement in their lives was inconsequential, as it was the enslaver's decision. Black fathers were reduced to mere breeding machines and laborers, forced to emotionally detach themselves from children who might be sold, whipped, or even killed. Even after emancipation and the transition to sharecropping, many Black families perpetuated the tradition of having large families, mirroring the customs of their enslaved ancestors. However, in the 1950s and 1960s, this practice often led to poverty, neglect, and abuse rather than help and prosperity.

When my mother was around ten years old, her mother, my maternal grandmother, passed away. Her father remarried, bringing five additional stepsisters and brothers into the Steele family. The Steele children primarily stayed among relatives, working on their own farm, growing food, and raising

Confronting the Past

livestock. Their education often suffered as my grandfather hired them out to work on other farms for weeks at harvest time. The Steeles were respected church members, who helped to fund the church, with my maternal grandfather serving as a deacon. However, even within his family, there was no room for error. Mistakes were met with whippings and warnings of more, a lasting legacy of slavery.

My parents, being only three generations removed from slavery, grew up in a time when stories of the North as a promised land were still prevalent. The Great Black Migration was a period remembered as a time when Black people abandoned sharecropping, a form of de facto slavery, and the oppressive cotton fields of the South in search of a better life in the Northern cities, albeit still plagued by covert discrimination and racism.

In 1945, at 18, my mother left behind the cotton-picking life in the South for good. Her sister Florene, who lived in New York, helped her secure a. Later, Mama found employment in a clothing factory, doing piecework. Although these jobs were an improvement over picking cotton, she still struggled to make ends meet.

Her family had to repeatedly wash and iron the same clothing they wore weekly. But now, Mama could afford to buy as many dresses as her earnings allowed, transforming herself into a stylish woman.

Mama possessed the heart of a southern belle, yet she was naive to the ways of the North. At 21, she started a family with her companion, John Farrell.

To Be Loved

My eldest brother, Mitchell, was born in January 1949, followed by my eldest sister, Yvonne, in 1950. However, my mother often remarked that Yvonne's father proved lazy and unwilling to work. "He didn't want to work," she would say, recounting her struggles as a single mother of two.

Mama and her sister, Florene, at a house party, met Paul Douglas Locas from Wilson, North Carolina. He appeared friendly and dressed sharply. The two Carolinians quickly struck up a connection.

And on March 25, 1952, Mama and Paul began their own family with my birth in Manhattan. The following year, just before my sister Paulette was born, my parents quietly married at a justice of the peace and changed their surname from Locus to Lucas, a somewhat uncommon choice. In 1954, after the birth of my sister Carlean, Mama decided to leave Daddy. He had become increasingly drunk, profane, and physically abusive. She said she "just got tired of it." So, while Daddy was at work, Mama, fled New York and returned to North Carolina with her five children.

Daddy moved to Washington, D.C., to live with his parents in the Shaw area on Rhode Island Avenue, N.W. He pleaded with Mama to return to him, sending letters filled with apologies and promises. Finally, in 1955, they reunited, this time in Washington, D.C.

Daddy worked as a cook or construction laborer, likely earning little more than the minimum wage, which was around 75 cents to $1 per hour. In 1955, my brother Milton was born, followed by my youngest sister, Audrey, the next

Confronting the Past

year. During those three years, we moved about four times within a 10-block radius. We were evicted from our home at 610 R Street, N.W. when Daddy couldn't find work due to a harsh winter that severely impacted construction jobs.

In 1957, our family settled into a two-room tenement on First Street, N.W., across from Paul Lawrence Dunbar High School, a prestigious institution for light-skinned African Americans.

My six siblings and I shared the same bed in our cramped living conditions. I developed a chronic habit of thumb-sucking and bed-wetting. Whenever I wet the bed, my father would whip me as if I had done it intentionally. One morning, after wetting the bed, I was too afraid to move. Everyone else had already woken up and prepared for school. I knew my father would come for me. Suddenly, he stormed into the room like a raging tornado, shouting and screaming as he mercilessly beat me. I leaped and jumped, crying out in pain with each strike of the leather against my flesh. Then, he grabbed me and threw me against the wall, causing excruciating pain to radiate through my left leg. I lay sprawled on the bed, among the covers, unable to move. I could only cringe and cry as he whipped me.

And just like that, when he was done, he left. Mama, bruised and broken, had to explain to the ambulance and hospital staff how my leg had been fractured. As I gazed up from the stretcher, I heard Mama telling them, "He was playing in the bed and fell."

From that moment on, I began to wish my father was dead. Dead! Dead!

To Be Loved

Dead! It seemed as though our family could only truly live if my father ceased to exist. When I grew older, Mama confessed that she experienced a sense of dread every year around my birthday, as it reminded her of the day I wet the bed, and my father burst into the room, assaulting me and hurling me against the wall.

Starting first grade at Scott Montgomery Elementary School was a welcome relief from the constant tension at home. It allowed me to play and interact with other children, something I rarely experienced at home.

During circle time, I noticed another child playing with a small wind-up metal toy airplane, as students gathered to hear a story. It had rubber wheels and would roll along when wound and released. I became consumed with a desire to have that toy. I longed for it so intensely that I would have done almost anything to possess it. I was starved for any toy. However, I couldn't have a toy. I couldn't have anything, not even a single toy.

One evening in May 1958, three years after my parents had reconciled, I sat on the front stoop, observing the people passing by. Suddenly, a cab pulled up in front of our house. Daddy stumbled out of the vehicle, assisted by the driver. He struggled as he approached our gate and stumbled to the stoop, where I had quickly moved aside. Clarence and Mama emerged from the house, helping Daddy and guiding him to bed.

The following morning, I awoke to my mother and siblings weeping. It was May 25, 34, Daddy had suffered a heart attack and died, leaving Mama, 30, with 7 children. Throughout the morning, Mama Ada, my paternal grandmother

Confronting the Past

whom we hardly knew despite living up the street, along with other family members and visitors, came to pay their respects and mourn. Mama asked me to go to the store and buy some sugar. I climbed onto the stool at the corner store and ordered a pound of sugar.

The counter woman looked at me and said, "You're the boy whose father died, aren't you?"

"Yes," I replied, my eyes fixated on the shiny coins in my hand, secretly yearning to purchase some of the brightly colored candy packages beautifully displayed behind the glass counter.

"I'm sorry for your loss," she said sympathetically. "You must be feeling really hurt."

"Yes," I replied. I collected the bag of sugar, placed the coins on the counter, spun off the stool, and confidently walked out the door, feeling a glimmer of excitement I had never known before.

A few days later, at the funeral, as they lowered my father's casket into the ground, our family and others wept, and I joined them, my tears flowing mostly because everyone else was crying.

"I wish my Daddy would come back alive," a boy around age 5, like me, sobbed, tears streaming down his cheeks.

How could that be, I wondered. How could my Daddy be his Daddy, and I not even know him? I felt anger welling up inside me. He was our Daddy, not that boy's. He whipped us, he prevented us from living, and now we were burying

To Be Loved

him.

"I wish my Daddy would come back alive," he continued to sob. *For a while, I pondered who that boy was, calling my father "Daddy" and why he would want him to return to life when I was relieved, he was gone.*

***

My bedroom became my sanctuary, a safe space where I could freely express my thoughts, ideas, and other innermost feelings that I didn't feel comfortable sharing with others. I had ample time to reflect, and I began to write as therapy. This solitary activity allowed me to mature and question the world and how it impacted my life.

During a period of depression, I attended a job fair. The experience filled me with an unprecedented sense of fear and petrification. Despite my attempts to emulate the lifestyle of professionals, I couldn't help but feel inadequate in their presence. I perceived myself as incompetent, regretting my time spent enjoying my teenage years instead of preparing myself for early adulthood and a successful career. These individuals seemed to have a predetermined path to success, exuding confidence and ease. I admired how some middle-class people could eloquently express their emotions and thoughts, appreciating art beyond simple judgments like "it was baddd!" Which meant it was really good.

Observing successful-looking Black men, I couldn't help but feel deep insecurity, as if I were only half the man they were. It seemed they possessed everything I lacked: two loving parents, access to good schools, friendly

Confronting the Past

neighborhoods, and prestigious colleges. I held these successful men in high regard like never before.

In a conversation with my counselor, I expressed my feelings of inadequacy and insecurity when surrounded by successful Black men. I shared my doubts about my manhood, feeling ill-equipped to enter mainstream society and attain what I desired. The counselor, McSwain, responded inappropriately, suggesting that my concerns didn't imply homosexuality but that we could explore that together if I ever leaned in that direction. Shocked and repulsed by his suggestion, I realized that my quest for self-assurance and clarity had been tainted by his inappropriate intentions. Nonetheless, I continued seeking his counsel, confident that I would defend myself if he overstepped boundaries.

Luckily, the subject never arose again, and McSwain eventually left his position. I was then referred to Ms. Shaw of Glenarden, Maryland, for further counseling.

Throughout my incarceration, Sharon and I maintained correspondence. Although I had always felt she was a bit too young for me, she now seemed like the perfect match. Mitchell and I often wrote about getting out and finding "country" girls who hadn't been hardened by the city. Sharon was born and raised in the country but lived in the city, yet she retained her innocence. She was always neatly dressed, acted like a lady, and seemed grateful for the connection we had formed. I needed her unwavering support, and when I saw Sharon, we would sit on the wall on Sheriff Road, engaging in deep conversations until late hours. I

To Be Loved

walked her to her apartment door, and we shared long and passionate kisses. She became my anchor, providing stability and comfort in my life.

Sharon would lend me her car while she was at work, and I would take it home and wash it. It was intriguing to have a woman who owned a car. While Pat, my previous partner, would walk to the store and rely on rides to return home, I now had the privilege of driving Sharon's car. She wanted us to spend time together when she finished work, and she treated me well. I loved her, but I couldn't ignore the fact that she lacked the fire and challenge that had always attracted me. She was an angel, but she didn't excite me.

Rufus, a brother I had met in Hagerstown, had been released from prison six months before me. In July 1973, I reached out to him. During that time, The O'Jays, an R&B hit sensation, had made a resurgence with their album "Ships Ahoy," featuring a song of the same name about the Middle Passage. The album also included conscious tracks like "Now That We've Found Love (What Are We Gonna Do With It)" and "Money, Money, Money." Covering themes from slavery to love to becoming money-driven, it seemed to encompass the journey of Black Americans.

When we were young, Mama didn't have a social life, aside from occasional visits from Mrs. Sprigg, the insurance lady who collected premiums door-to-door. Mrs. Sprigg had no children, and Mama became a role model due to her ability to maintain her children and home with dignity despite her poverty. Besides the insurance visits, Mama would chat with Mrs. Summer, our next-door

Confronting the Past

neighbor, while hanging laundry to dry. Occasionally, other ladies from a few doors down would visit as well.

Absolute joy came when Mama's siblings, Aunt Lucille and Uncle Bobby, along with their five children, Aunt Lois and Uncle Roy, with their two children and other family members, would visit. Mama couldn't afford to take her seven-member family anywhere, so her sisters from New York and other places would come to us.

Aunt Florene would visit from New York and Aunt Mable and Uncle Barchy from Mama's hometown in North Carolina. Uncle Barchy had a bone-crushing handshake that left us wincing in pain while he laughed with cigar breath in our faces. Occasionally, Mama's sister, Aunt Pat, Uncle Albert, and their children, Dennis, Curtis, Gregory, Patricia, and Tracy, would drive down from New York.

In contrast, visits from my late father's family were rare. Only Aunt Christine and her husband, Uncle Omega, visited us. Sometimes, my father's siblings from New York would visit my paternal grandparents who lived in D.C., bringing along other kids who turned out to be our half-brothers and half-sisters. It took me a while to realize that my late father had been married before and had four sons named James, Eugene, Weldon, and Gerald, as well as two daughters named Pam and Cheryl. The resemblance between them and my father was uncanny, and they looked more like me than my brothers Mitchell, Milton, and Wayne. Harold, around Mitchell's age, and Gerald, born the same year as my

To Be Loved

sister Yvonne were among them. Gerald was the boy who cried at my father's funeral, desperately wishing he would come back to life.

My relationship with my estranged half-siblings never developed beyond encounters during weddings, reunions, or funerals in New York, D.C., and North Carolina. Our physical similarities intrigued us but there was no shared history or familiarity. Distance and pain kept us apart, serving as a reminder that my father had failed my mother and their mother. Our family, flawed but dear to Mama's heart, was her source of pride and pain. Mama's joy was her family and friends. Despite our poverty, she created an environment where we, as children, had everything we wanted. If we couldn't buy something, we would make it. We were never hungry, and although we wore the same clothes multiple times a week, they were always clean and neatly ironed.

Mama was a natural at various things. She had a talent for styling hair, a skill she honed on her four daughters. She would create beautiful hairstyles, emphasizing freshness and style. Mama also possessed a natural knack for discipline and raising a seven-member family alone, without making excuses or seeking pity.

Every Sunday, we had to attend church. Mama would give us pennies to put in the tithing basket. Sunday service was a mixed experience for me. On the one hand, it allowed us to dress up and leave our neighborhood, which I enjoyed. On the other hand, I couldn't connect with the images of Christ presented in Christianity, as they bore no resemblance to anyone I knew. The ecstatic

Confronting the Past

atmosphere in the church, where people seemed to revel in pain, left me baffled. The religion didn't radiate the happiness one would expect from worshiping God, so I endured the church services in boredom.

I didn't mind the 15-20-block walk to and from Burville Elementary School during my childhood. It was an opportunity to venture beyond the confines of our community. However, the worst part was swallowing a teaspoon of cod liver oil before starting the long journey. The terrible taste was like dying each morning, only to be revived moments later by a slice of orange. Each child received one slice, so I would savor the orange in my mouth, prolonging its flavor. Once it turned bland, I would eat it.

I noticed that Mitchell, despite being often reckless, was immune to Mama's punishments. No matter what he did, he never received a whipping, scolding, or reprimand. Mitchell, Mama's firstborn, possessed an extraordinary power within our family. Although he wasn't popular among the neighborhood's most well-liked crew, which consisted of the jocks, he remained loyal to his group of friends. Despite his mischievousness, Mitchell never hesitated to offer me insightful opinions, surpassing what one would expect from a big brother at his age.

***

In August 1973, I landed my first job in the five months since being released from prison. I became an office assistant at Numark Associates, a Black management consulting firm on D.C.'s affluent Connecticut Avenue, N.W.

To Be Loved

Numark specialized in coordinating conferences, special events and helping companies embrace ethnic diversity in the workplace. As a clerk, my responsibilities included handling reproduction, maintaining office machines, managing office supplies, and more.

The storm surrounding the new magazine "Essence" intensified when it featured an interview with Wilt Chamberlain, who claimed to date white women because there were no Black women at his economic or social level. I saw this as a sell-out move. While reading the October issue of "Essence," I became engrossed in an interview titled "Dr. Frances Welsing Tells Why Blacks Can't Love."

Dr. Frances Cress Welsing, a child and general psychiatrist and an assistant professor at Howard University, made a powerful impact on me through her arguments. She contended that when a couple enters a relationship, each person should bring their own proverbial bicycle, which they should keep in the closet. Suppose the relationship no longer enriches both parties and begins to deteriorate into hatred. They should agree that they deserve happiness and say, "You are fine as you are, and I am fine as I am, but we need to find other people to maintain mutual harmony and respect!" According to Dr. Welsing, a couple may need to get on their bicycles 29 times. This perspective seemed logical, raising questions about why couples allow relationships to deteriorate into hatred before breaking up.

Dr. Welsing also argued that Black families often do not act like families

Confronting the Past

in the traditional sense, where caring actions typify their interactions. She attributed this to the lasting effects of slavery and other historical factors, suggesting that Black families tend to function more as "survival" units with shared bloodlines and physical environments rather than embodying the true essence of family.

Additionally, Dr. Welsing contended that white men are not inherently superior to Black men but have acquired a superior societal position through violence, force, and deception. Her insights further deepened my growing consciousness about life and societal dynamics.

***

During my time at Numark, I engaged in a conversed with a female co-worker about the societal message conveyed by new cars. I expressed my observation that a Monte Carlo I saw from the bus had a back panel knocked out as if it were made of plastic and someone had thrown a rock through it. She remarked that I sounded like her son, a photographer. She suggested I get a camera and capture the things that stimulated me. The symbolism of the damaged car resonated with me, representing a decline in quality while prices continued to rise. Although I didn't understand how I had mentally captured the image of the car from the bus, I grasped the concept of capturing stimulating moments with a camera.

By December 1973, Gerald Washington, the proprietor and manager of Numark Associates, requested the staff's resignation due to his frustration with

To Be Loved

the results of his micro-management. We had to reapply if we wanted our positions and explain why we believed we should be rehired.

Meanwhile, Rufus offered to get me a camera along with all the necessary film and development supplies to start a business. Instead of pleading to keep my $2-an-hour job, I seized the opportunity to go into business with Rufus as street photographers. We planned was to pitch our services to downtown commuters, particularly those near the Greyhound and Trailways bus terminals on F Street, N.W. I envisioned becoming rich and famous through this venture, capturing moments and offering customers an album of thirty photos taken at their homes, workplaces, or during leisure activities for only $30.

We established a bank account and embarked on our entrepreneurial journey. Unfortunately, our business endeavors did not take off. Rufus and his network of friends seemed to have driven Drug Fair out of business, and although Rufus and I remained friends, he had spent the funds from our bank account. The short-lived experience reminded me of my affinity for photography and sales. I believed that engaging in sales could help revitalize my depressed self-esteem.

***

During my childhood, Michael and Tommy often joined me in raiding fruit trees when I was eight years old. The wooded areas served as our sanctuary, providing abundant fruit for us to eat without drawing much attention, except from Mrs. Bryant when we misbehaved.

Confronting the Past

Over time, our focus shifted from fruit to items that required money, such as candy and water guns. Michael and Tommy accompanied me on various money-making ventures. We raked leaves for our neighbors in exchange for a fee during fall. Throughout the year, we ran errands for a dime each. When it snowed, we would be the first ones out, knocking on doors and offering to shovel snow for a substantial profit. We earned 75 cents per yard, which quickly accumulated to several dollars. With our newfound wealth, we indulged in Tootsie Rolls, Mary Janes, Squirrel Nuts, Fire Balls, Paydays, Mars, M&Ms, String Candy, Button Candy, Pumpkin Seeds, Bon Ton Potato Chips, and two-for-a-penny coconut cookies for days.

One day, Hank, my next-door neighbor, praised my bottle-hustling skills to his friends. I couldn't bear the pressure of living up to his words of admiration. Fueled by the desire to meet his expectations, I confronted another guy who had brought his bottles to Dotson's store to exchange for cash. I demanded that he give me his bottles or else I would fight him. Intimidated, the guy relinquished the bottles to me and hurriedly left. Although I had resorted to robbery, the need to live up to Hank's praise seemed more important than the guilt associated with my actions. I returned to the neighborhood, proudly showing Hank and his friends the bottles I had collected.

One day in my backyard, Michael rushed toward me, out of breath, resembling a speeding train. Prepared to defend him in case he had been involved in a fight and needed help, I asked what was happening. Between gasps for air,

To Be Loved

he exclaimed that he had found a dollar. I immediately asked him where it was, and he replied, "It's in Jack's." He pointed over his shoulder towards Jack's Carry Out and waited for my response. Eager to investigate, I said, "Let's go!" We sprinted through three backyards and the woods until we reached Jack's.

We burst into the store, only to be halted by Mr. Jack, who slammed a spatula against the counter, scolding us for playing inside the store. Frozen in place, we apologized and resumed walking toward the back of the carryout. Michael led the way, and eventually, I spotted it too – the crumpled and balled dollar bill still lying on the floor. We quickly picked it up and left, feeling like millionaires. As partners in this adventure, we promptly cashed the dollar and split the proceeds equally. I used my share to buy a pack of cigarettes for my mother and still had around 25 cents left, buying me enough candy to last nearly the entire week. Michael could have taken the dollar without involving me, but the fact that he sought me out and shared the discovery made me feel important like I mattered.

In our playtime, we made slingshots using a combination of coat hangers, rubber bands, and a piece of bicycle tire inner tube. These slingshots propelled rocks farther than we could throw them. We skipped the inner tube for a more destructive effect and attached rubber bands to small wire hooks we fashioned from discarded coat hangers. With these makeshift weapons, we would break bottles or windows in abandoned buildings.

The neighboring house became our target for practice. The family had

Confronting the Past

abandoned the property, leaving behind many belongings. It seemed like almost everyone in the neighborhood helped themselves to the loot.

We would sit on the three-foot-high brick wall surrounding the abandoned house's front yard at night. We engaged in conversations and playful banter, known as "joaning," until around 9 p.m. when we were called in for bed. Whether it was for dinner or to go to sleep, we only went home when summoned. There was always so much to do, games, and opportunities to earn money that television barely registered on our radar.

Within my household, it was best to avoid my sisters at all costs. They were the ones who would tell on me, leading to the whippings I received from Mama.

Love and affection between my sisters and me were scarce. My mother was so preoccupied with maintaining our home that she never emphasized the importance of sibling love; instead, I would be scolded if I disliked my sisters. While we shared the same bedroom and meals, we led separate lives, perpetuating a wedge of distrust between us. I often felt besieged around them, as they seemed to exist solely to tell on me and get me into trouble. I'm sure they believed they were doing the right thing, but my mother's responsiveness to their tattling empowered them while leaving me feeling marginalized.

As a result, my home wasn't a place of comfort for me. Instead, I sought solace in the company of friends and preferred to be away from my house and family. Outside, I wanted to excel at everything because it garnered attention and

To Be Loved

positive recognition, making me feel valued – something I longed for but rarely experienced at home.

Positive Thinking as Remedy?

In January 1974, I eagerly applied for a sales job at Sales Unlimited, Inc., a prestigious business consulting firm on the bustling Connecticut Avenue, coincidentally right across the street from Numark Associates. During the interview process, I had the pleasure of meeting Karen Rice, a remarkable woman who, at the age of 27, held the impressive titles of vice president and co-owner of Sales Unlimited. Karen exuded a contagious energy and enthusiasm, encapsulating the essence of vitality. Her magnetic personality shone through with ease, quick smiles, and unwavering confidence in dealing with strangers, including men in the office. Desegregation saw many Black professionals rise in corporate America. In many ways, Karen embodied the direction I aspired to take in my life; she exemplified the path I needed to pursue to make something of myself. Her exceptional communication skills and innate finesse made her a smooth operator, capturing my admiration. As for the company's president, he was a Brother—a distinguished Ivy League type with an athletic build and a crown of wavy, curly hair.

To my delight, I landed the job but faced the obstacle of needing a car. Luckily, Sharon, my girlfriend, offered me the use of her car. Ms. Rice, in her role as my boss, assigned me to assist in selling a cutting-edge telephone interface device that facilitated five-location conference calls for businesses, a forerunner to multi-party conference calling.

To Be Loved

Immersing myself in the product's literature, I absorbed every detail. Additionally, as part of our training, we delved into confidence-building techniques, understanding that we were not merely selling a product but also selling our personalities. The material we studied included an array of positive thinking books and audiotapes. As I engaged with these resources, such as Napoleon Hill's "Think and Grow Rich," Norman Vincent Peale's "The Power of Positive Thinking," "Dare To Be Great," and "Enthusiasm Makes the Difference," I grasped the profound impact of positive thinking as a discipline of self-determination and self-esteem.

Those books introduced me to invaluable ideas and concepts that resonated deeply with me. They emphasized the importance of setting goals, refusing to accept rejection, making one's dreams and aspirations known, and pursuing them with unwavering dedication. Aim high, be enthusiastic, and strive to achieve something every day. Aspire not only for personal satisfaction but also to make a positive impact on others. Recognize that every situation harbors negative and positive aspects, and one's focus determines whether it will be deemed wholly negative or an opportunity to thrive amid challenges. Acknowledge the negative, but steadfastly believe in the power of the positive. Conduct honest assessments of one's strengths and weaknesses, striving to enhance strengths while acknowledging and addressing weaknesses.

This kind of positive thinking played a crucial role in my journey to overcome the limitations of my past. Although I hadn't considered it a discipline

Positive Thinking as Remedy?

until now, positive thinking became the foundation for rebuilding my life. I embarked on a personal healing journey, immersing myself in materials that fostered personal development. While Black literature had initially empowered me, I also discovered that positive thinking had been neglected in my formal education. Determined to defy the legacy of my past and embody its antithesis, I vowed to become a positive, caring, enthusiastic, warm, and progressive individual, transcending the negative effects of my life. Above all, I learned the importance and fragility of self-esteem.

Despite my personal growth, I faced challenges in inspiring my family with my newfound value system. I made concerted efforts to spend time with my nieces and nephews, taking them on field trips to parks and other engaging activities, accompanied by my second daughter, Kwanza. I frequently conversed with my family, attempting to convey the power of positive thinking and offering counsel on resolving their problems and challenges. Sadly, my family seemed resistant to adopting new values, content with the old ways. Some perceived my actions as arrogance or me having a know-it-all attitude. They were unwilling to embrace change in me.

While Sharon had been supportive in my life, her reserved nature didn't align with the qualities I sought in a partner. I desired someone with a wildcat's spirit, with forward-thinking and progressive traits. One evening, after a hard day at the office, I offered Karen a ride home, seizing the opportunity to spend time together outside work. We conversed for a few minutes until she mentioned her back pain.

To Be Loved

In a flirtatious manner, I offered, "Is it anything that a massage might help?"

"It might," she responded with a smile.

To my astonishment, she left the living room and returned with a pillow, wearing nothing but a long towel wrapped around her slim, curvaceous body. She positioned herself on the carpet, lying face down, her head resting gently on the pillow. Playfully, I opened the towel, revealing her alluring, slender figure and captivating curves. At that moment, it felt like my newfound thinking, believing, and achieving philosophy was materializing.

That she entrusted herself to me in such a vulnerable way signified trust. I interpreted her willingness to engage intimately with me as a reflection of the potential she saw within me. Karen could have chosen a more mature and accomplished partner who could offer her more than I could. Yet, she desired me. Every second counted, and I was acutely aware that a misstep or a misguided word could jeopardize this newfound connection. I had to maintain my composure, display restraint, and not succumb to a single-minded focus on physical desires. I admired her beautiful pecan brown curves, the softness of her skin, and the delicate tendrils of hair between her legs, representing a tantalizing garden of pleasure.

Considering the situation, I suggested, "I should take my clothes off too, so as not to get oil on them."

Positive Thinking as Remedy?

"Okay," she replied, her voice cushioned with relaxation. It had been an exhausting workday and workweek, and what better way to usher in the weekend than with a rejuvenating massage? I poured oil into my hands, warming it between my palms before applying it to her back, shoulders, and neck. Beginning with gentle strokes, I gradually increased the pressure, employing a rhythmic caress. The music playing in the background and the harmonious atmosphere made massaging her feel effortless and natural. As I reached the area surrounding her most intimate space, I brushed my finger against it, exploring her boundaries. She made no attempt to stop me; it was evident that she desired me just as much. My hands continued to glide over the area around her garden, her supple buttocks, and inner thighs, as our desire intensified. Finally, we surrendered to the moment's intensity, indulging in passionate kisses and caresses until we both found release on the floor.

Karen and I soon became a couple, although it strained my relationship with Sharon. Sharon had always been there for me; I knew she deeply cared about me. However, I couldn't continue the relationship with Karen while keeping Sharon as a side piece. It would have only prolonged the agony and delayed her own recovery. Reluctantly, I had to break the news to Sharon, understanding that ending a relationship with someone who still had strong feelings for me would not be easy. We sat in her car, and I mustered the courage to tell her the truth.

"Sharon, I genuinely care about you, but we need to break up," I explained.

To Be Loved

Confused, she asked, "What's wrong?"

"I'm just not feeling it anymore," I replied honestly.

The pain on her face showed that love had been abruptly snatched away from her. She accepted my decision without putting up a fight, though it was evident that she was deeply hurt. I assured her that it wasn't because something was wrong with her. As she drove away, I couldn't help but feel a twinge of guilt for ending things in such a manner.

Karen and I continued to nurture our relationship, and one evening she accompanied me to my mother's house. My family needed to meet her, as she represented my envisioned future. Karen and my mother exchanged pleasantries briefly before we departed. Karen's presence in her white Lincoln Mark IV was a testament to the growth and progress I had achieved. She saw me for my future potential; my family saw me for my past. Reflecting on my past experiences, I couldn't help but think that Pat, a former love interest, should have treated me better.

I shared my dreams and aspirations with Karen, expressing my desire to become a successful salesman initially and live a prosperous life. Originally, I had envisioned selling cars and eventually transitioning to selling real estate. Impressed by my ambitions, Karen invited me to live with her—an offer that made me feel like I was going somewhere special.

The women's movement, gaining momentum during the Civil Rights Movement, empowered women to pursue opportunities traditionally reserved for

Positive Thinking as Remedy?

men. Karen, a successful Black woman at age 27, became my muse and inspiration. I, on the other hand, at age 21, became the aspiring younger man in her life. Karen constantly immersed herself in new business ventures and attended various social events, where she was revered by many. Some of these events attracted well-dressed, middle-class individuals, and I often felt out of place, unable to relate to their experiences. Although I longed to be part of their world, I recognized the stark contrast between our lives. I feared they would judge me based on my manner of speaking or lack of middle-class experiences that many African Americans were beginning to enjoy. Despite my inadequacy, I remained present at these events, filled with a sense of awe and a determination to bridge the gap.

    Meanwhile, I continued counseling sessions with Ms. Shaw, a fine and shapely Sister in her thirties. Her wild, red hair contrasted her composed and sensitive demeanor. These sessions helped me confront the consequences of my past and learn how to release tension and stress without harm. Unresolved conflicts and deep-seated hurt lurked within me, and Ms. Shaw encouraged me to let them out—through tears, shouts, running exercises, or any means that allowed me to channel my emotions safely. Although I feared the floodgates of emotion would overwhelm me, each session brought me closer to healing. I peeled away layers of pain, one painful realization after another, and felt a refreshing calm settle within me after each emotional storm passed. Gratitude and freedom replaced the weight that had burdened me for so long.

To Be Loved

***

Television programs like "The Lone Ranger," "The Cisco Kid," "Wyatt Earp," "Gunsmoke," "77 Sunset Strip," and "Route 66" introduced us to a multitude of characters and stories. Although I enjoyed a variety of TV shows, my heart belonged to the cowboy and suspense genres. I yearned for a rifle just like the one "The Rifleman" used, and I immersed myself in those programs. However, despite television's allure, nothing compared to the joy of being outdoors.

Eventually, I received an air rifle as a Christmas gift, although it didn't meet my yearning for a BB gun. My brother, Mitchell, also received an air gun, which seemed like the ultimate BB gun, albeit one that shot air. One day, Mitchell left his air gun unattended in our bedroom, and curiosity got the best of my sister, Paulette, and me. I fired the air gun at a piece of paper on the floor, causing it to soar. With the barrel aimed upward, I positioned the rifle on its butt and encouraged Paulette to rest her chin on it. In my mind, it would only blow a gentle stream of air. However, the rifle kicked when I pulled the trigger, leaving a circular cut on her chin. I hadn't intended to harm her.

Mama sent me outside to gather switches from the mulberry tree—a customary punishment for my misbehavior. She braided them into a formidable whip, which she used to discipline me. At that moment, I realized that my actions, regardless of intent, had consequences. Like with my late father, saying, "I'm sorry, I didn't mean it," held no weight. I understood that mistakes were unacceptable and had to tread carefully to avoid repeating them.

Positive Thinking as Remedy?

Another incident occurred when I was chopping wood with an ax, and my sister, Carlean, innocently leaned over while I was pulling the ax head up. The impact of the ax's butt striking her forehead resulted in a painful gash. It was yet another mistake, and I anticipated the consequences. I chastised myself, knowing my actions had put me in a vulnerable position.

Driven by the need to redeem myself through new challenges, my desire to grow overshadowed my fear of making mistakes. Sensing a hint of indifference, Mama resorted to whipping me for even the slightest transgressions, using electric extension cords or vinyl-covered clotheslines. These whippings, devoid of affection, were the most excruciating experiences I could fathom at age 9—pure torture.

Finally, I received a BB gun, bringing me immense joy. Mitchell and I were playing in the backyard when he suggested we have a BB gun battle. Excitement flooded over me, reminiscent of the battles I had watched on Rifleman. Hiding behind the wall of the adjacent abandoned house, Mitchell and I exchanged shots. I visualized myself pumping the BB gun with relentless force, unleashing a stream of BBs toward Mitchell. Amidst the flurry of shots, one BB found its mark, hitting my forehead. I clutched my face in pain, dropped the BB gun, and surrendered.

Mitchell rushed over, apologizing for the unintended injury. He helped me up and removed the BB from my forehead. Surprisingly, my mother never mentioned the incident, and neither did I. I knew I would be held accountable

To Be Loved

somehow. Oddly enough, my mother didn't reprimand Mitchell either, leaving me with the impression that he was always exempt from her anger. It felt as though, as long as I was with Mitchell, I could escape the consequences of my actions.

To relieve tension and frustration, Ms. Shaw suggested that I engage in regular physical exercise. Taking her advice, I started jogging daily, gradually increasing my distance from one mile to three. However, I soon grew bored of jogging and remembered my love for Ping-Pong. Regretfully, it was never recognized as an official sport, despite my belief that I would have excelled at it. I cherished Ping-Pong's opportunity to strike the ball repeatedly and as hard as I desired, much like my parents did to me. But it wouldn't hurt anyone. It allowed me to release pent-up aggression without causing harm. While Ping-Pong tables were scarce, especially ones accessible to someone my age, I conceived an idea.

Tennis. In fact, what we called Ping-Pong, was officially called table tennis, and the game offered the opportunity to strike the ball relentlessly with all my might.

I visited a Drug Fair and purchased a tennis instruction book, a tennis racquet, and a can of tennis balls. I found a secluded wall at a nearby school and began teaching myself to play tennis. My plan involved mastering ball control before venturing to public tennis courts and engaging with other players. However, even during my solitary practice against the wall, I experienced a sense of relief as I repeatedly hit the ball, channeling my stress and tension into each swing.

Positive Thinking as Remedy?

Six months later, I began noticing a side of Karen that alarmed me. She had kept an 8x11 photo of her brother as a baby on her dresser, even though he was older than me. Karen couldn't have children, and it weighed heavily on her. Although I struggled to understand her perspective, I wanted to support her. She trusted me enough to entrust me with the keys to her apartment and her brand-new 1974 Cadillac Coup Deville, which made me feel welcomed.

However, as I began unpacking my belongings, attempting to make myself at home, Karen imposed restrictions, making me feel unwelcomed. She prohibited me from placing my small Instamatic camera on the living room étagère, treating me like a child—a familiar dynamic I had experienced with Mama. "You can't do that in the living room," she would assert. Slowly, I started to feel like that image of a baby she kept on her dresser. Karen never had children. While Karen showed me love and affection, her maternal tendencies clashed with my desire to assert my individuality. In a moment of frustration, I resorted to an act of violence, slapping her in a futile attempt to reclaim my manhood. I had never learned healthy conflict resolution, and violence had become an unfortunate default. The incident happened in the blink of an eye, leaving Karen in tears, cradling her face in her hands.

Overwhelmed by guilt, I decided it was best to leave. I called home to inform Mama that things hadn't worked out with Karen, and I needed to return. I couldn't wait for Mama's approval, so I contacted David Williams, asking him to

To Be Loved

pick me up and take me home. In a bitter conversation with David, I expressed my frustrations about how Karen treated me and how much I resented it.

Chapter VIII

Confronting the Past: Unveiling Trauma

My family viewed me with skepticism, part of being the family's undeclared scapegoat. They seemed to want to prove that I had not changed. Like always, the best way to avoid arguments and conflicts with family was to avoid contact with them. Where would I go? Since I wasn't comfortable anywhere, I'd go to my bedroom. I would read as I did in Hagerstown and write to express myself.

And when I couldn't take the pressure anymore, I'd call Ms. Shaw and cry out. Mama had long laid down a tract; I was the family's scapegoat. I couldn't get respect at home.

Whenever someone complained about an altercation that involved me, I was wrong. I stopped trying to get justice from my mother as a child. I would never go to her to tell her what someone had done to me; I'd settle it myself. If someone had bothered something that belonged to me or got in my way, I would address them on the spot. That meant having altercations with my sisters. My brothers didn't bother me. My sisters seemed to feel they could step on me because all they had to do was tell Mama. They'd call her at work. She'd come home mad at me and with her mind already made up as to what happened. She never bothered to hear my side of the story. I couldn't have been wrong every time. But that's the way it felt.

To Be Loved

During counseling, Ms. Shaw asked me to discuss my relationship with my mother and father. After reflection, sadly, I realized there had been no loving relationship with either of my parents. My only connection with my father was the whippings, the fear, and then he died. I could not recall any affectionate moments with my mother, either no praise, hugging, or holding hands, no saying loving words to me. There were no tender moments that I could recall. She provided me with the necessities of food, shelter, and clothing. While there is no doubt I admired many things about my mother, I began to feel that there was no basis for me to love her. Before then, I was never conscious of my feelings about my mother or father. But I said it. What a tremendous realization and relief. I harbored much trepidation toward my parents almost my entire life. It was like an abscess I was carrying, never even considering that it was there or how it impacted my behavior. I had never known anything other than the instinctive notion of kinship. I knew we had difficulties, but I didn't realize those feelings ran so deep. Now that I had recognized those innermost feelings, what was next?

The realization that there was no love between my parents and I made me recognize that I may be traumatized or maladjusted. It was like being anti-Christ. You're supposed to love your parents. They were supposed to love their children. Was something wrong with me? Where do you go from this realization? That's why so many people don't delve into their emotions. They fear uncertainties, like being unable to deal with what they find.

Ms. Shaw said, "I really think it would be a good idea for you to invite

Confronting the Past: Unveiling Trauma

your mother to these sessions."

"No way! She wouldn't come," I said.

"Then, you should talk to her about your feelings."

"She would dismiss me in a heartbeat, and probably attack me for feeling the way I do, rather than try to understand me."

***

My girlfriend in 1961 was Stella Thompson. She laughed at all my jokes in class. She was witty and fun, too. My fourth-grade teacher was named Mrs. A.S. Brown. I often wondered whether the A.S. was an abbreviation for ass. She wore too much make-up. She was old, fat, and snobbish and always seemed angry with her class. I couldn't do right by her, either. Once when she had told me to stop talking for the second or third time, she stormed, "Steele! After lunch, I want you to go home and not come back for the afternoon! Tell your mother you've been suspended for talking!"

Thunder struck inside me again. I couldn't go home and tell my mother that. She'd beat me to death. So, petrified, I returned to school but not to class. I hid in the boy's bathroom for the remainder of the afternoon. I didn't have enough sense to hide in a stall when a kid from class came in.

"Don't tell Mrs. Brown I'm here, alright?" I pleaded.

"Okay, I won't," a student said.

I didn't tell my mother, either. I went back to school the next day and was quiet and Mrs. Brown said nothing else about it.

To Be Loved

On the day before the last day of school, I was excited about what I would be doing during the summer, and I'd be in the fifth-grade next year. I was talking to Stella in the line to be excused for the school day when something happened, and she pushed me. I pushed her. She pushed me harder, and I fell over a desk, making a noise. Mrs. Brown's voice growled, "Steele! Get out of here and go home! Don't come back for your report card, and don't be hiding in the bathroom!"

She knew. Would she report both things, my mother? I couldn't stand another beating. Mama had begun whipping me, it seemed, every other day. Some of the whippings I got were deserved, no doubt. However, most of my misbehavior involved seeking positive attention that I craved and missed at home. The more whippings I got, the more I did. Mama knew whippings were not working. I think she believed that more frequent whippings would eventually work like magic. It was unfair to beat me every time I made a mistake. That anger started coming out of me as an edge in my personality.

So, this time, I wasn't going to tell my mother I got suspended from school the day before the last day of the school year. I would just run away. I didn't need a family like that, anyway.

My first stop was across the street from where I lived, behind an apartment building, near the pear trees. I should stock up on some fruit for my journey. Once, behind the apartment, I noticed a little bike lying on the ground. It had a flat tire and seemed rejected and abandoned, like me. I needed a getaway.

Confronting the Past: Unveiling Trauma

So, I got on it and peddled away, careful not to let anybody from my home see me leave the neighborhood.

Eight blocks away, I pulled into the Amoco Gasoline station at Grant Street and Division Avenue and asked for help tightening the handlebar to the gooseneck. They wouldn't help me. The mechanic looked at the bike, then he looked at me and asked, "Where are you going with that bike like that?"

"Home, come on, Mister, you can't fix it for me?"

"I can't stop what I'm doing and fix that bike. You got a flat tire, too."

This was going to be more difficult than I had thought. I decided I would take the tire off and ride on the rim. I was unfamiliar with the neighborhood beyond Division Avenue, so I rode back to my community and Jack's Carry Out.

Inside the store, a known bully girl with two smaller children ordered food. I made my way to the pinball machine when one of the kids kicked me.

"You should tell them not to kick people," I told the big girl.

"What, muthafucka!

Who you talking to?"

"You! That little girl kicked me," I said.

"I'll tell her to kick you, again. Kick him Cheryl!"

The kid kicked me again. I moved to bluff the little girl. Like a gorilla, the bully girl jumped on me, shoving me up against the bubble gum machine stands before Jack came from around the counter and pulled her off me. I left, dejected. Nobody else was playing the pinball machine, anyway.

To Be Loved

Once outside, my signifying neighbors, the Summers, were coming into Jack's.

"Hey, Ronald, we heard you were running away," Brenda said.

I hadn't told anyone. "Yeah, I got into some trouble at school and I'm scared my mother might kill me," I said.

"Well, we bought you some water and this quarter." I almost cried. After having such a rough day, Brenda, and my next-door neighbors, who were often my family's rivals, were coming to help me on this -- no questions asked. No, 'you better go back home!' No, I'm gonna tell I saw you.' It was as if they understood why I didn't want to return home.

"Thank you," I said before getting on the bike and riding away with loose handlebars. Soon, night fell, and I was tired of riding around aimlessly. I put my bike in the front seat of an old car at an abandoned garage right down the block from my house next door to the Williams' home, across the street from two-year-old Drew Elementary School.

Drew doubled as a year-round recreation center that had become our neighborhood's social center. It had the most modern playground I had ever seen, including a sandbox, a racetrack, a baseball field, a hopscotch board, and a full-set basketball court. Inside the recreation center, we played tabletop pool on the kind of table that would flip and convert into a checkerboard. We played ping-pong, or we finger-painted and made gimp necklaces and bracelets. We constructed arts and crafts with Popsicle sticks.

Confronting the Past: Unveiling Trauma

I crawled into the back seat of an abandoned 1955 automobile and went to sleep. A bright light over my face surprisingly awakened me. At the other end of the light were the police. They opened the car door.

"What's your name, boy?" one officer asked.

"Ronald Steele," I said through my slumber.

"You got to come with us," he said.

"Where are you taking me?" I asked.

"Home. Your mother's worried about you."

"Can I take my bike?"

"No, leave it. Come back and get it another time."

I got into the Police car, and they drove me home and escorted me to my front door. Mama opened the door, looking stern and focused on me. I knew she was going to kill me this time.

She said, "Thank you" to the officers, and as if she wanted them to hear it, with one motion, she snatched me in, closed the door, and began whipping my ass with a plastic belt. I wondered why Mama was whipping me with a plastic belt; it didn't even hurt. I jumped and leaped and cried just the same. She reprimanded me. I don't remember what she said. I blocked it out in screams from the lashings. She told me to go to bed and, when I awakened in the morning, to go out and get three switches from the mulberry tree, and they better not be small ones.

"Get on upstairs, you good for nothing piece of shit," she admonished.

To Be Loved

I got to the bed and squeezed in with my brothers. My constant bedwetting weakened and marked the bed, with rusted springs piercing through the worn fabric. Mama didn't beat me for wetting the bed, like my late daddy did. However, I remained on her whipping list for almost anything else.

***

I woke up after my siblings had gone to school. The memory brought back what sleep had allowed me to forget. I began to wish I was dead and didn't have to wake up. I heard Mama coming up the steps to get me. She might as well have been the executioner coming to kill me. I felt dead. "I'm a teach you a lesson about running away!" she warned.

She already had the switches. Three big ones, braided, its knots forming rivets. She whipped me until she couldn't whip me anymore. My body felt like one great big sore.

Those switches, reduced to bits and pieces of stems, lay scattered about my smelly bed. I started feeling better the moment my mother stopped whipping me. So, as soon as she stopped whipping me, I began to heal or would look forward to something fun and forget it. Momma left the room, still angry and cursing me.

It was the last day of school. I would probably stay back in the fourth grade. I sat in the bedroom window viewing our big strawberry and dandelion-scattered back yard, the railroad tracks, just outside the yard and just beyond Mr. Williams' house, Drew School, the source of great pain and suffering for me.

Confronting the Past: Unveiling Trauma

Later in the day, my mother called me downstairs. Yvonne, my older sister, was with Mama in the kitchen. Mama was using a new wet clothes wringer. She threaded the clothes through the two rollers, turned its handle, and squeezed the water into the attached tub.

"There's your report card," Mama said, without looking up, with a cigarette in her mouth.

"You passed."

In an instant, I felt victorious until she said, "I should whip your ass again."

***

Mitchell began doing pencil illustrations of objects around us. He told me we could make money if we drew a picture of the boy on the back of some magazine better than anybody else. That got me drawing. We never entered any contests. I discovered that I liked drawing. There was something very intriguing and challenging about drawing something or someone and comparing its likeness as proof of ability. Over time, I amassed a collection of sketches that I had drawn. I would draw anything, the iron, the refrigerator, my sisters and brothers, and insects.

Around age 10, I was in my backyard, drawing a picture of the entire block of houses, including ours, from the shady perch underneath a tree. My 5th-grade school buddy appeared on his flashy bike. It had left and right turn signal lights, a horn, a headlamp, fender skirts, and a raccoon's tail attached to the back

To Be Loved

fender. I laid my art down, hopped on his bike, and we went riding.

"You could have a bike if you want," Clarence said.

"I could?"

Clarence nodded, looking ahead, straining his eyes as we began to gain speed and feel the wind.

"How?" I asked.

"I'll take you," he answered.

"Where?"

"Where you can get a bike unless you are scared. All it will cost is a little bit of heart."

"Alright," I said.

"You got a bike, then."

We rode on his bike over Eastern Avenue, where Clarence asked, "You wanna do it?"

"Yeah."

We rode through 61st Street, past the District Line hardware store, the District Line Clothing store, and the "Seat Pleasant" D.C. bus line bordering Maryland, the Chinese Restaurant, and Jumbo Food store before we rode into Seat Pleasant, Md., where white people lived. They always seemed to have more of everything: Cars, big yards with toys laid about them. I remember once walking out there and my friend, Michael, saying, "Diamond Cabs don't' ride Negroes."

"What do you mean?" I asked in wonder.

Confronting the Past: Unveiling Trauma

"Watch this," he said, anxious to prove his point.

We walked up to a white cab driver with a stubby beard, and Michael asked. "Can't no colored person ride your cab, can they?"

The cab driver shook his head no.

"Why," I asked.

Michael pulled me along and said, "Cause they don't like colored people." I put a pep in my step as we walked on.

When we went into the stores in Seat Pleasant, whites would never look at us. That was why we felt we could get away with stuff underneath their noses. Michael and I would walk to Seat Pleasant, go inside Dart Drug store, and steal water guns, school supplies, walkie-talkies, and fun things. Clarence and I rode through a Seat Pleasant neighborhood. People were out picnicking in their backyards. In the front yard of one house lay a bicycle.

"There's your bicycle!" Clarence said.

I didn't think they would see me if I rode off with that bike, either. I got off Clarence's bike and entered the yard where the bike lay on the lawn. As I picked it up and got on it, the people out back saw me and came running after me, screaming. What was I to do now, I thought? Clarence took off. I took off, too, right behind him. I'd have to outrun them. I was in Clarence's shadow, speeding up the street in broad daylight. We rode into an intersection. Clarence said, "Let's split up!" You go to the left. And I will go to the right. We went in separate directions.

To Be Loved

I rode down a hill as fast as I could. Once down the hill, I suddenly realized I didn't know my way back home. I took a right turn, rode to a dead end, and was lost. I could have jumped off the bike and run in the woods. Without Clarence, I was lost in getting back home. I couldn't go any further. I waited a while, and when no people came by, I returned down the hill.

As I got halfway down the hill, a car full of white people drove past and slowed down. Then, the car stopped and backed up. They must have noticed me, I pondered, afraid. As they backed up to me, a Prince George's County Police cruiser pulled up.

"That's it," one of the white guys said, getting out of the car. "That's Johnny's bike."

The white Police officer said, "We got us a bike thief, aye? Now, do you want to go to the station with them or me?" I looked at the angry white faces looking at me like they wanted to kill me.

"No, Sir! I want to ride back with you."

At the Police station, the officer said, "I usually kick kids in the ass and let them go back over the District Line and tell people, so no more of you will come over here stealing and stuff. Would you want me to do that?"

"Yeah," I said and stood and bent over, bracing the desk. A kick in the rear was no comparison to what Mama would do to me. I could take anything but having my Mama come out there and pick me up. She'd kill me for sure.

"No, then you'd only go back into the district and tell all them Niggers,

Confronting the Past: Unveiling Trauma

they just kick your ass and let you go in P.G. All you Niggers would be coming over here stealing and stuff," he said to the laughter of the other policemen.

Mama got a sister of a guy she was dating to bring her out to pick me up. That must have been embarrassing for her. Besides, to face those white Police officers in the community where she worked as a domestic was probably a lot for her to bear. To the degree she felt embarrassed, I would have to pay with my ass.

Once home, in my bedroom, I cried for mercy to Mama while she used a rope to hog-tie me naked. With an extension cord, she whipped, fussed, and cussed me until she was tired and hoarse. Welts covered me like short, hardened, and bruised veins. Some of the welts bled. My body felt like a big sore.

Anything I moved hurt.

When anyone was busted for anything, that person became the source of much ridicule, especially from family for days. The next day, my sisters had fashioned a single-lyric song for me, "Look at that Nigga on Johnny's bike," amply irritating me. I would leave the house.

Before that, I got into an altercation with Yvonne, and my artwork disappeared. When found, they had been torn up and discarded as trash. I was outraged. I didn't draw much again after that. For revenge, I slipped a pair of scissors into a couple of her favorite dresses.

*

Meanwhile, Pat began to press me about child support payments. I wanted to pay, but I didn't have a job. I never made any money at Sales Unlimited.

To Be Loved

Without the use of a car, I couldn't continue to learn to make any money as a direct salesman. I wanted to be a parent to Ngina, but the uncertainty from the unanswered questions kept emerging, made more apparent by Ngina's physical features. The pressure was on me to get a job. After I got a job, I could go to college, get my place and get out of Carmony Hills.

After reveling in hurt and anger for years, I learned from my first love affair with Pat that you couldn't love people unguardedly. A woman, "sugar and spice and everything nice," will hurt you. A woman will take advantage of you when you love blindly. Amid my still-brimming anger, I would learn how to protect and control my love and affection.

I occasionally visited Roberta Hall, Carlean's best friend, and my adolescent best friend, Robert's sister. One day she called and asked if I would take her to her high school senior prom.

"Thanks," I said, "But I don't have the cash.

"What all do you need?"

"Probably a jacket."

"I'll take care of it," she said.

We went to Spingarn's '74 Prom and began dating. One night, Roberta and I stayed up late, joking around. We went to the basement, where Robert and I used to shoot pool and hang out. We were kissing and caressing one another, and I wanted her badly. It was dark in the basement with all of the lights out. I peeled her clothes off while kissing her. I took my clothes off, too. We could

Confronting the Past: Unveiling Trauma

hardly see one another. But I could feel her warm, smooth body touch and warm mine.

We got it on. I was wearing Roberta out when she came, and her scream ripped from her throat before I could cover her mouth. Afterward, I asked, "Weren't you afraid your voice would travel through the vents up to your mother's room."

"I don't care," she answered.

***

Once you enter the penal system, its conditioning and stigmas tend to trap you forever to stay in it. In and out of prison over and again until you either find a way to overcome it or accept it as a way of life. Recidivism rates were up to 80 percent. Prisons are in the business of self-perpetuating themselves at our expense.

In August 1974, at age 22, I went to apply for a job at the Government Printing Office. I hitch-hiked up to the Seat Pleasant bus line and caught a bus that sluggishly rode its passengers downtown.

Many stores on that route had put up insulting, handwritten signs in their windows that read, "Soul Brother," to ward off the looters six years ago in '68. It didn't work. Blacks knew which of those stores the whites owned; whites owned all the businesses, except the corner Mom and Pop stores.

***

I went inside the red, somber-looking Government Printing Office

To Be Loved

building and applied for a job as an apprentice printer stripper. I didn't know all that a stripper did. But I knew it was related to printing; it paid well, and I needed a job.

The interviewer seemed impressed with me until he got to the application's questions about whether the applicant had ever served time for a felony. "Explain."

"I recognize that I made a mistake," I reasoned. "It was not unlike you coming out of the house and falling down scoffing your knees. Do you lay there in pity, or do you get up, brush yourself off and continue on your journey? I'm trying to get over my mistake and get on with my life," I pleaded.

"I'm sorry, Mr. Steele," the interviewer said. "I understand what you are saying, but I don't know, maybe it's my upbringing, but I don't feel that the U.S. Government is a social rehabilitation agency."

I was outraged. This muthafucka was probably a bigger thief and plunderer of the government than I could ever dream. And, now, he felt at liberty to speak for the government and to protect it from me. Didn't I serve my time?

"Sir, I broke the law and I've paid my debt to society. The government spends $3 billion a year on prisons. When prisoners are released, it is society's obligation to give them a chance to restore their communal rights. If denied, they are left with no alternative but to revert to preying on society, and that $3 billion gets not only wasted, but increased."

"Mr. Steele, I know," he said, "you're right. I'm sorry, but it's just the

Confronting the Past: Unveiling Trauma

way I was brought up."

I left the office. Getting a job would be as tough as getting out of prison.

***

I went on another job interview for a file clerk position at the Small Business Administration on L Street. It was August 9, 1974. I had been back on the streets for 17 months, almost as long as I had been incarcerated.

The GOP allegedly burglarized the exclusive Watergate Hotel in Washington, D.C., particularly the office of the Democratic National Committee headquarters. A host of White House officials were implicated, up to the president, Richard M. Nixon, who was scheduled to resign from the presidency on that day under the threat of impeachment.

The SBA office interviewer greeted me. The official leaped to his feet, lifted his hand to greet me, and said, "Come back to my office."

Several men, watched on TV Nixon's unprecedented resignation and departure from the White House.

How ironic, I thought.

In the face of all the protests, unrest, and assassinations of the 1960s, Nixon and his vice president, Spiro T. Agnew, were elected, partly for their pledge to bring about "law and order." In a twist of fate and exposure of hypocrisy, they both resigned from the highest offices of the land amid charges of breaking laws. Vice President Agnew, former governor of Maryland, was charged with taking kickbacks from contractors throughout his political career till he became vice

To Be Loved

president. President Nixon was about to resign in the face of the House Judiciary Committee's debate on impeaching him for obstruction of justice, abuse of power, and contempt of Congress. They both resigned to escape impeachment and a possible conviction. Congress let them escape, I believed, for fear that their impeachment and conviction might have been the "last straw" that would damage beyond repair the nation's '60s-scarred moral psyche. Not only were some of the nation's leaders were criminals, indeed the founders were criminals, but also little people like me, who did far less were sentenced to 15 years or more. Social disintegration had already set in.

The interviewer offered me a seat next to his desk. During the interview, he asked me about the robbery. I recounted the story, wondering if I would have to do this each time I applied for a job. I confessed again that I had made a mistake and paid for it. It seemed that I would always have to live it down.

He reached into the drawer of his government-issue desk, probably made in some prison, and pulled out a Bible.

"Now, for your sins," he said, "If you will repent, right now, I will give you the job."

I looked into his face for a punch line. All I saw were his blue, self-righteous eyes set in his pale face and fixed on me. He had gotten worked up from Nixon's resignation and probably acted out what he felt should have happened for Nixon.

'I will give you the job,' reverberated in my mind. I got down on one

Confronting the Past: Unveiling Trauma

knee while placing my hand on his Bible.

"Now," the interviewer said, "say you repent before the Lord!"

"I repent before the Lord for all of my sins," I said, as the tears flowed down my face for dramatic effect.

He reached for my hand, helped me back onto my feet, and told me to report to work on Monday at 8:30 a.m.

He believed I had repented, not on my free will, but upon a coerced invitation. I guess he felt that the proof would come later. He was tripping, I thought, as I went back outside, in the summer heat, amid the heavy pedestrian lunch traffic on Connecticut Avenue and K Street, N.W., during lunch time.

Whew! I'd better apply for at least one more job today. Take one more shot at finding some other job. This time, I vowed not to tell prospective employers about my past. They were not ready for it. If an employer found out, after a couple of weeks, months, or years, I would have at least earned a paycheck and had a chance to demonstrate that I had moved my life beyond the mistake. I regained my composure, walked right around the corner to the International Association of Fire Chiefs, 1735 K Street, N.W., and applied for another job as a file clerk.

The interviewer was a redhead, twenty-something white guy named Larry. He was absorbed in making his computer generate mailing lists to send out the association's membership dues. The computer mailer was acting up. Larry was trying to figure it out and was being stretched thin. He reviewed my

To Be Loved

application amid telephone interruptions and had to leave the interview at one point. I followed, and he said, "You sit tight."

He said it like he was comfortable telling me what to do -- like I got the job.

The interviewer returned to the office and asked, "When can you start?"

Damn, it was music to my ears. I got a fucking job. I didn't have to relive my past! I wouldn't have to pretend I had repented.

"I can start Monday, thank you!"

"Okay, Monday at 9 o'clock," he said, reaching to shake my hand. Then, looking down at the application again, then up to me, he said, "And Ronald, don't be late."

"Thanks, I won't."

***

Mama didn't care when I came or went. I appreciated that. She didn't seem to care much about what I did if she didn't hear about it. It gave me freedom, and an outlet to vent through building, playing, making things, trying things, owning things, fighting, and getting respect.

I got into many defensive fights. For example, when people tried to take something from me. Or, I'd end up having to fight to protect one of my sisters and would almost always get the best of the other kid. My reputation for kicking butt had spread, and sometimes I'd be out, and some kid would say, "is your name Ronald Steele?"

Confronting the Past: Unveiling Trauma

"Yeah."

"I heard about you. I heard you could fight."

Occasionally, I'd have to defend my reputation as a fighter on the spot. Some kid would push or challenge me, and I would kick his ass. There was no room for fear, as I learned from the past. Fear encouraged even a chump to try you. I tried to help another classmate by telling him he showed too much fear. I told him that would get him in trouble with the bullies. Don't let them know you're afraid. Fear makes other people bother you, I told him.

***

While crossing Drew's playground, I saw Snook and his buddies. They were older than me, about Mitchell's age. I said, "Hey, punk-ass-Snook!"

"What you call me, you little smart-ass Nigga?!"

And, to my surprise, the group came running after me. I turned and ran in the opposite direction. They split up. Half the guys came at me from one direction; the other half came at me. I ran near some steps, near the school's wall, saying, "Okay, okay, okay, you got me," laughing at the thrill of being in play danger. Snook was serious. He grabbed me by the shirt and slammed me headfirst against the school's brick wall! I was hurt and stunned. He walked away, cursing me out. Why in the fuck did he slam me against the wall like that? I got up stunned and walked away, clutching the now big knot on my forehead.

"Now, muthafucka," he said, "next time keep your smart-assed lip to yourself!"

To Be Loved

They walked on out of sight. I think his buddies were just as shocked at Snook. I had no idea why he had slammed me like that because we had always joked around, and nothing much came out of it.

I had learned to laugh at my shortcomings and laugh at others. From practice at joaning, I could zero in on the most embarrassing aspect of a person's personality and portray it in the funniest terms. It helped me laugh at my faults and get over them.

I went home and told Mitchell about it.

"You shouldn't have fucked with him," Mitchell responded conclusively.

What could I say? He was right. That act told me that Mitchell also was making it clear that I had to fend for myself; he would not fight for me. I had to fight my battles.

***

Mama gave me two of the worst house chores anyone could have: cleaning the filthy, maggot-crawling, smelly, slimy garbage can and cleaning the bathroom weekly. Also, I had to wash dishes on Sundays and Tuesdays -- when I thought it was girlish for boys to do "girls'" work. Mama probably thought that if she could make me feel humble about myself, I wouldn't be so aggressive; I'd chill instead of always being in the center of controversy. Mitchell didn't have to do anything; he never had any chores that I can remember. So, why did I have to do that shit? It just wasn't fair to me!

Confronting the Past: Unveiling Trauma

All I had ever seen of Mama's passion was when she was whipping my ass or telling me I wasn't this or that and ain't going to ever amount to shit. Mama was like an overseer to me. Our only relationship became her punishing me. She expected me to know and do the right thing, and when I didn't, she'd whip me. She was how pain looked—whippings, reprimands, threats, etc. I tried to stay away from her as much as possible.

***

Every so often, Mama would call everybody in from play. The social worker was at the house and had to count heads. We'd sit around while Mama and the lady would talk. Then, upon a word, we'd rush back outside to play.

Once, after the public assistance people left, I asked Mama, "When the welfare people come again would you have them take me away?" I thought by suggesting it, I would do her a big favor.

Nothing I could say to Mama would solicit understanding or the positive, empathetic attention I sought. I wanted her to sit me down and talk with me and tell me that she loved me and appreciated me and didn't want me to go away.

"Okay," she said as she resumed ironing clothes.

To Be Loved

Rebounding

Hearing my name called at the IAFC evoked the same fear and anxiety I remember feeling whenever my mother called me as a child at home.

As weeks went by, occasionally, I would worry whenever my name was called for fear that someone was calling me to tell me I was fired for not revealing that I was an ex-offender.

What will I do? How would I explain? What would all these friendly people think of me?

The IAFC was a small operation with about ten employees. I was responsible for running the copier, packaging, and mailing out brochures and other pamphlets to members. A Black Xerox technician about my age came in to fix the machine periodically. He was very articulate like he was a product of the middle class. He was down to earth, like he was from southeast D.C., yet full of self-confidence. When he would come to fix our machine, we'd rap and discover that we had an instant rapport. He had overcome the hood, and I was overcoming it. He may have seen his past in me; I saw my future in him. He once invited me to hang out with him on a weekend.

His name was Robert Harris. Robert had grown up in Southeast. he lived in Alexandria, Va., way out. He picked me up in his '72 MG Midget, an unusual car for a Brother from the hood in 1974. We drove Northern Virginia's long, winding, tree-lined roads as we talked about growing up in the hood and having what we wanted despite everything. We arrived at his townhouse. He ran

Rebounding

an extensive electric train set. We loved similar music, mostly jazz, except he would buy only master recordings. And we both loved the company of a woman. In his MG, he would drive me around Virginia to mostly white malls and stores and show me around as if there was no racism and we had as much right to those stores as any other customer. In Northern Virginia, they had the best merchandise for the lowest prices. It seemed so unethical that Blacks would pay much more for the same or lesser quality merchandise than whites, even though whites had more disposable income.

We'd driven back to his house, listen to one of his albums like, "Return to Forever," by Chic Corea and talk into the early morning about politics, racism, positive thinking, and the power of self-determination. In Robert, I had met a friend with whom I could talk about my innermost thoughts and feelings and get a meaningful response. Robert and I would sometimes listen to his master-edition LPs and rap all evening, exchanging deeper and deeper vibes.

Sometimes, when we would pause or draw the evening to a close, I would feel like we had explored so many thoughts and ideas about politics and personal values that I felt we had soared beyond conventional thinking. It seemed dangerous to think that free. I felt that the rest of society had been trapped into maintaining the status quo, never venturing beyond the typical reaches of reality. I was shaping my values and future, realizing and articulating my wants and desires, and then pursuing them.

***

To Be Loved

The beauty of nature inspired me. I went to Livingston's Pawn Shop on H Street, N.W., and bought a used Minolta SRT 101 single-lens reflex camera, my first 35mm camera, to frame and capture the beauty I saw around me. I also bought a book on 35 mm photography and began to study it. I wanted to provide photographic services commercially through the viewfinder of a camera -- family activities, trees, animals, creeks, buildings, and models -- everything that seemed beautiful. I would photograph my family gatherings over a 40-years; capturing babies who grew to become parents, and grandparents, and family members who passed.

***

Pat began pressing me again for child support. She seemed not to understand or care that I was confused about whether I was Ngina's father. However, I gave her money on a couple of occasions. When she came to me again about a month later, I said, "Look, I ain't giving you no more money until you answer my questions."

"We could get a blood test," she offered.

"A blood test won't prove I'm the father. It only proves that Ngina and I share the same blood type or not. That doesn't mean she's my baby. I really want to know why did you lie about how many months you were pregnant? Why did you lie about when you were due?"

She was silent. Out of frustration, I said, "Okay, okay, look, you arrange the blood test, and even though I don't believe in it, whichever way the needle

Rebounding

falls, I'll go with it, okay?"

"Okay."

She called me the next day to tell me that she had arranged for us to get a blood test the following Friday.

That Thursday, she called me again. "Ronald, my mother said that I shouldn't have to prove anything to you. So, I'm not going to have the blood test." She hung up the phone.

My heart tightened and sank. She must be trying to drive me crazy or something. I said I'd go with it. If she was sure that baby was mine, and this was all I was asking for me to begin providing regular support and being a father, then I think she would have done it. Instead, her cancellation fueled my worst fear: that she was not sure Ngina was mine. I was ready to walk away and leave the situation alone, forget about it.

***

Robert Hall and I would hang out occasionally. He had recently been released from the U.S. Army. We would get together and discuss old times with an eye on the future. I suggested we get a place together. But Robert didn't seem serious about the responsibility of an apartment, and I also could see us: two guys, neither cooks. Who would shop, clean, etc.?

Meanwhile, his sister Roberta, whom I was dating, got an apartment. I needed to get the fuck away from home. I needed to break with my past. Roberta became all the more attractive.

To Be Loved

Roberta had protruding, pretty lips that, when she smiled, would reveal a spread of white teeth against her walnut-brown complexion. Accentuated with an Afro crown, she had a gold-plated, shapely body. She reflected something inside me: she represented what was good about the hood. Like me, she was reaching beyond it to the future. Also, to fulfill her mother's dream of becoming a teacher, she enrolled in Federal City College.

Roberta reflected the new school of women. They were radically more assertive in life, pursuing the same careers as men, becoming more competitive with men both in the world and in the home, and holding Black men responsible for men's past sins. Roberta didn't believe in laying back and letting a man do everything. She helped. She didn't mind working, like my mother.

"I need to find me a place," I told her one evening while visiting her at her apartment.

"You want to come live with me?" she asked, with a big 'ol cautious smile, like she knew she wanted it but would understand if I wasn't ready.

Before then, I hadn't even thought about living with her. It took me approximately one second to consider the offer. "Damn right!" I said. We broke out in laughter.

Yes! I was getting out of my family's home! I needed distance. I needed to grow.

***

I looked up to the guys who had paper routes. Tommy Washington got a

Rebounding

paper route first. Frecks delivered the "Daily News." The tabloid featured a light tower as its front-page logo and a cash prize crossword puzzle on the inside. Later, I heard that Dixon, in his thirties and one of the oldest newspaper carriers, was retiring from distributing the "Washington Afro-American" newspaper. Dixon had one of the Afro's most extensive paper routes in the area. I applied for the job and got it.

***

I'd ask my brother's friends to teach me how to drive a car. Near the end of my paper route was an abandoned vehicle in the back of apartments on Jay Street. Every Tuesday and Thursday after I delivered the Afro, I'd get into that car and go through what my brother's friends had told me were the first steps to driving:

- *Adjust the seat and the rear-view mirror.*
- *Turn the ignition.*
- *Release the brake.*
- *Put the transmission in drive.*

I was determined; the day was coming when I would graduate from go-carts and bicycles to automobiles.

***

I loved that paper route. I saw the neighborhood, delivering papers and making money. The "Afro" soon announced a 'favorite paper boy' contest.

To Be Loved

Each newspaper included a coupon worth 100 points, clipped, and sent in. Whoever accumulated the most points would win, as first prize, $100 and a cruise trip somewhere. I leaped into the contest, carrying a pair of scissors in my paper bag and asking all my customers to help me win the contest by giving me their coupon. Before long, I was leading the competition. The Afro arranged to photograph me as the frontrunner for a story the paper had planned. I was winning something significant for the first time, which felt strangely good. But, soon afterward, the Afro called to tell me that the interview and the photo session were canceled, that the family of another boy had gone out and bought up a bunch of papers, and he was the new frontrunner. My family went out and bought extra papers, too. It was the first time they came together for me on anything, or maybe it was the first time I had done anything that warranted their support. I dropped from first place, and my instant fame faded.

My family's efforts helped sustain me a third-place finish and a prize of $25; I bought school clothes and supplies. Soon afterward, I quit the paper route.

***

During the fall, I awakened early each morning to walk Mitchell and Yvonne to Kelly Miller Junior High School at 49th and Brooks Street, N.E. After bidding Mitchell and Yvonne goodbye, I'd return to my school, Charles R. Drew Elementary School. I looked forward to attending the big school, Kelly Miller Junior High School, next year. I couldn't wait.

Drew's principal, Mrs. Crab, used to stress the value of education by

Rebounding

telling us she almost fainted when she had recently observed at a funeral that they were using tractors to dig graves rather than laborers. She said jobs that don't require a high school diploma were becoming scarce.

Mrs. Crab and the school's entire faculty could discipline a student whenever they saw fit, and that would be that. She would also have someone go and get her switches, and she would swing them through the air and ask us, "What does that sound like?"

"Pain," we would answer.

"Right, not wind, but pain!

You know, Mrs. Crab doesn't want to have to use her switches, right?"

"Yessssssss."

***

The grown-ups seemed sad when it was learned that President Kennedy was assassinated in Texas during a motorcade. On television, the newscaster, Walter Cronkite, appeared to hold back tears as he told the news repeatedly. I went downtown to the Capitol with a family from my neighborhood and watched the funeral procession.

***

Spunky and I went to the Drew playground one summer night in 1964 to play basketball. We quit when night prevented us from seeing all but ourselves. Spunky lit a Winston filtered cigarette, lay on the ground looking up to the sky, and smoked that thing like it was as natural as breathing. He drew the smoke

To Be Loved

deeply in. Smoking is what the big guys did; the cool guys always smoked. It became a symbol of toughness.

"I can do that," I said to Spunky.

"Here, try it."

I puffed the cigarette, with nowhere near the cool in which Spunky had. The cigarette smoke was bitter, almost nasty. With practice, I knew I could smoke like Spunk demonstrated and all the cool guys on television and in the neighborhood.

At age 12, I felt grown up, like I would do whatever I wanted and not get caught. I started smoking at least one cigarette a night or as frequently as Spunky would give me one. One of the good things about hanging out at the house on the corner was that none of my family did check on me. As soon as the word traveled that I smoked, Paulette or Carlean would suddenly appear, spot me and tell. Once, Mama called me in because someone told her I had been smoking. When I got inside, Yvonne asked, "Can I have your boiled egg from dinner."

"No," I said, sticking the whole thing in my mouth to camouflage the cigarette odor, and I nearly choked myself. It didn't work. Mama smelled the tobacco, anyway, and she whipped my ass good.

***

A few newspaper carriers were sitting around on the porch of the abandoned house next door, smoking cigarettes.

T.C. asked me, "You got a bike," He puffed his cigarette, and smoke

Rebounding

snaked through the air. He let the smoke roll off his lips and inhaled it.

"Yeah, I got a bike," I said, "Hey, T.C., you inhale good. How long you been inhaling cigarettes?"

"About a year," he said as he blew the smoke out indifferently.

Yeah, I bet you I can do that, I thought to myself.

"Let me get a puff, man," I told T.C.

It was customary to ask for a puff of a buddy's cigarette. It was like a ritual among friends, like taking a sip of a friend's soda pop; you didn't wipe it off -- it implied a bond.

T.C. passed the cigarette to me, and I took a smooth puff and inhaled it. It made me dizzy, but I did it!

And, the next thing I knew, I was hooked on Winstons. When Spunky wouldn't give me a cigarette, I would smoke stale butts that passengers tossed to the ground before boarding the D.C. Transit Bus.

***

Hank, my next-door neighbor, began to change his view of me.

"Something's going to happen to you! You ain't gonna make it 'til you're 18. Watch what I'm telling you!"

I took his comments like Mama's when she was chastising me. I didn't see things that way. I would wonder ever so often, what did he see about me that I didn't see that made him think that?

Mama got a call in the middle of the night. It woke everybody.

To Be Loved

The following morning, one of my sisters told me Mitchell and Hank were arrested by the Police and charged with a yoke robbery of our community paperboy. Mitchell and Hank were 17.

Mama had to go to the Police precinct and get Mitchell out. Maybe I wasn't home, but I never heard that my mother had a fit with him over the yoke robbery. Mitchell had something -- I didn't know what it was -- but I would have died or killed to have it -- Mama didn't whip him, much less yell at him for robbing the paperboy. That made me feel like Mama didn't punish me because what I did was wrong as much as it was me doing wrong.

Hank had dedicated his future to playing professional football. First thing in the morning, he'd be up with the dawn, at the foot of his backyard, just before the railroad tracks, tossing an imaginary football at a target for some National Football League team.

***

I moved in with Roberta, against her mother's wishes. Very religious, her mother thought we should marry first. I thought "shacking" was the best way to determine whether you wanted to marry.

Their first daughter and I became a young couple in the community. We were from the hood, trying to get out of it and take advantage of the opportunities of the Civil Rights Movement. We did everything together, grocery shopping, planning our future, sitting on the steps, and talking. We had opportunities to go to college and become professionals, like our older admirers never had.

From Ex-Con to College Student?

Ms. Shaw, knowing of my desire to enroll in college, recommended that I check with the D.C. Social Rehabilitation Center about a Lorton Prison College Program.

This would be another mountain to climb. Am I ready for college? The mere word conjured up mammoth challenges and doubts. Could I handle college? What if I couldn't and failed? No one in my family had ever even enrolled in college, much less talked about it. Roberta had. Why did I think I could? She was no smarter than me. Roberta was handling it, and so could I.

I went to see Ms. Briggs. She said, "Under the LPCP, SRC would pay for your tuition and books, plus give you a monthly stipend if you enrolled full-time."

'Well,' I asked, "All I would have to do is attend?"

"And maintain a 2.0 grade point average."

"What's that?"

"Maintain a 'C' average."

"Oh, no problem!"

It was too good to be true. Ms. Briggs directed me to Dr. Donald O'Connor Fagon, the director of the Lorton Prison College Program at Federal City College, headquartered at 2nd and D Streets, N.W.

Damn, I felt like I was about to consume something too good to be true.

To Be Loved

How could I say no when they were paying me to enroll? It was a no-brainer; a Godsend.

Dr. Fagon, casually dressed with a Caribbean accent, gave me a brief, informal interview. There wasn't all that rapt, stuffed-collar crap associated with colleges whose "qualifications" become hurdles used to exclude rather than include. While drawing up the paperwork, Dr. Fagon asked what I was convicted for, how much time I had served, where and when I was released, and when my parole expired. He didn't even ask me to relive that eventful night. He blew me out of the water. No hurdle. No, prove how sorry you are. No, demonstrate how badly you want to do this. Just come on in, Brother; the water is warm.

Dr. Fagon said that the way the LPCP worked was, after I became a junior, if I maintained a minimum 2.0-grade point average or better, I would become eligible for the Start phase of the program, in which I could compete with other LPCP candidates for an internship at the then U.S. Department of Health, Education and Welfare, a.k.a. HEW. Then, I thought, 'despite everything, God must love me. My whole life was about getting what I wanted. I was still doing it despite everything. What I wanted now was much more meaningful, and I was getting that, too.

In 1974, a year after being released from prison and depressed, I was destined to become somebody. He was rescuing my life. He had pointed me in the right direction, and I would take advantage of His offering.

If I had not pursued counseling, I might not have found out about LPCP.

From Ex-Con to College Student?

It's amazing how life works. One step helps you see or leads to another one you can't even imagine until you take that step. Therefore, you must pursue what you want in life, even though you may have reservations; pursue it anyway.

Much more grateful and appreciative for the opportunity, I would apply the positive thinking and determination theories I had studied in sales to college. I was choosing to commit myself to the potential of big gains that involved relatively small risks. College was all gain; there could be no loss. I was about to resume my efforts to apply myself academically as I had done just before incarceration.

Inspired by Alex Haley's *Autobiography of Malcolm X*, I wanted to major in writing novels. Somehow, I was sent to the school of Communicative and Performing arts rather than the English department. When I told the professor/counselor what I wanted to major in, he said, "Writers starve for 30 years before they even begin to make money.

"You should major in journalism," he told me. "It's a writing skill and you can use it to make money as soon as you graduate. You can always come back to fiction or write it on the side."

It made sense. I told him I wouldn't be starving 30 years after college. With a degree, I can get a career over a job and expect to get paid according to my growth.

Roberta and I celebrated: we were both college students. Ronald Steele, college student.

To Be Loved

Damn, I liked that ring. It sounded a helluva lot better than "ex-convict." College student sounded like I had become somebody after all. I was taking charge of my life and, consequently, control of my future.

***

Mr. Henry came around to see Mama. He was over 6 feet tall. Wavy hair. Friendly. With a big, quick smile, he made everybody feel important. He liked us and was courteous enough to speak to almost everybody in the neighborhood when he walked by. When walking with him, cars would honk, or people would walk past and speak to him, and he'd respond, "Hey, Senator, Hey Governor," with a big laugh or grin. "How you doing?"

It was in jest, but everybody seemed important to him by the surnames he assigned them, and he seemed important to everybody else. Mr. Henry was a shoemaker, the son of a prominent family in the community who was very active in Beulah Baptist Church. In addition to making old shoes look new, Mr. Henry could play piano. He was also a World War II veteran and an alcoholic.

I would go up to the District Line, to a store, and I would see Mr. Henry in the shoe repair shop window doing his thing, or at his next best stop, sitting on the side of the DGS (District Grocery Store) in the shade, not far from the liquor store, hanging out with the boys, drinking with abandon.

Occasionally he came over to our house drunk, and Mama wouldn't tolerate him. She'd fuss at him until he left. So, when he came to our house, he knew he had to be correct and sober. He would come frequently. He'd be there

From Ex-Con to College Student?

when we came in for bed and be gone by the morning.

Mama soon became pregnant. She didn't tell anybody; she just became huge in the stomach. I knew how a woman got pregnant. I also learned a couple should be married before they have children. Mama's pedestal was cracked, and I felt shame.

***

During joaning sessions, a dude had to be good at night, or he'd be embarrassed and fight or go home crying. One had to be knowledgeable about that person's embarrassing business, or his family's, and be funny! It was a free-for-all. Anyone could attack anyone in the group at any time. We'd have runs of continuous laughter for minutes at a time.

Once targeted with a joan, during others' laughter, a dude had to come out firing with a sharper attack to shift the focus.

"Your lips so big, if you was in water, you'd float!"

"Your lips so big they look like a butt, sideways!"

"Your mother's ass so wide when she walks there are earthquakes!"

Everybody and everything you cared about was subject to ridicule: your father, your brother, your sister. I learned I had to respond immediately on the offensive and hit people where it hurt and tickled. We were boxing with words. Dennis, who was about my age, around 12, lived in the corner house. I wouldn't dare tell him what I knew about his sisters, Karen and Nita. But, it seemed, he had an older sister, Brenda, who was pregnant by a different man every year. All I

To Be Loved

would have to say is, "Brenda had a baby, Brenda had a baby!" which would drive him mad. This night, however, he turned that anger at me, "So! Your mother is having a baby! Ruby's having a baby, Ruby's having a baby!"

I laughed along with him and the guys. But I was stunned at the thought. I was joaning about his lost sister, and he put my mother in the same category. He mentioned my mother having a baby because, like his sister, she was not married. I was angry with Mama. She was always making me feel that I was good for nothing and always doing wrong things, and yet, she did the bad thing, too, and it embarrassed me. In my bewildering emotion, I laughed to hide the pain. I had to think of a sharp offense against Dennis.

"Everybody in your house is pregnant," I declared, "including your whore dog!!" There were a couple of snickers. "You live in a pregnancy house," I said, not letting up, "If you don't look out, you gonna be pregnant next!" Everybody laughed, getting up, falling, rolling down the hill in the grass and dirt, and laughing. Dennis jumped up and threw up his fists as we began to fight.

I could never understand why he would want to fight me, knowing when he would hit me, I would hit him three or four times. Maybe he was taking advantage of the fact that if I had beaten him badly, I would not be welcome to hang out at his house anymore.

I drew my fists in a fight stance and began my dance. Everybody stopped joaning to watch. I would jab saliva from his mouth through the summer night.

Style was important in a fight: You had to look cool when you threw a

From Ex-Con to College Student?

punch, even as you blocked and swung fast. It showed confidence.

I jabbed him again without getting hit. I just wanted to show that I was the better fighter, and soon we would quit and return to being friends. So, fighting was a show of strength to me rather than hurting someone. After a few missed swings from him and a few jabs in his face, he turned and angrily left. The rest of us returned to joaning, hiding our shame and making fun of each other's pain.

On my way home that night, I felt good about joaning. 'Gave more hits than I took, and I kicked Dennis' ass again. Damn, I was still reeling from the embarrassing mention of my mother's pregnancy. Nobody in the family talked about it, yet everybody in the neighborhood suddenly seemed to know it. It was a shock because Mama was one of the community's standard bearers of virtue, hard work, and family. That girl on the corner was always pregnant because she always had men around, so she always got pregnant. Not my mother. I wanted to say, "Mama, you have made a terrible mistake, like all the times I have. Go get me the switches!" Just kidding.

Mama soon had to go to the hospital, and our family stayed with the Walkers, the light-skinned couple who lived a couple of doors up the block. They had two children who were shy and didn't come out and play in the neighborhood

Mitchell and I spent the night on D.C. General Hospital grounds in July 1964, anxiously peering through each window, looking for Mama. Finally, after we had taken turns dozing off to sleep that morning, we found Mama. She arrived in her room after having our little brother, Wayne. We talked through the window

To Be Loved

to a recuperating Mama. After we knew she was okay, we went home, walking more than 17 blocks, with the good news: we had a baby brother.

***

For good or bad, my antics helped make the Steele name popular. I had to be as good or better than the next person at joaning, fighting, playing games, building, etc., because that's how you matter in any group.

We walked to distant swimming pools during the summer, like Lincoln Heights. Whenever we left our community, we had to walk among crocodiles showing no fear. The locals would likely challenge outsiders. If there were no incidents, after swimming, we'd go to Safeway, steal lunchmeat, cigarettes, bread, mayo, and soda pop, and go to our hut or a stoop in the woods and have lunch.

On the way out of the Safeway once, the manager stopped me. He asked me to come into his office. He frisked me and found a new pack of Winston cigarettes. I had just stolen them from his store.

"Where did you get these?" the white store manager asked, holding the pack of cigarettes.

"I bought them," I said defiantly.

"Get out of here!" he responded, "You're too young to buy cigarettes!"

"Somebody bought them for me," I said.

"These cigarettes have a seal on them. They came from this Safeway. I'm going to call your parents. No, I'm going to call the police. And they are going to call your parents."

From Ex-Con to College Student?

When the Police arrived, they wanted a confession. I wasn't going to admit to anything.

"Where did you get the cigarettes from, boy!"

"Somebody gave them to me."

"Don't lie to me boy, I'll whip your little ass!"

Shit, I wasn't supposed to be smoking. I was busted again as the policeman escorted me to his car and drove to the precinct. It dawned on me that "Ronald Steele" increasingly meant trouble.

Mama began to accept that I would defy her and keep doing wrong, and she kept whipping me, only harder.

***

I had learned not to expect much of anything that I wanted for Christmas. I was happy with whatever I got. However, Mitchell took care of us for Christmas. He bought me a portable FM-AM radio, which opened a new world: music. I had all the music in the world right at my fingertips. And wherever I went, I could take the music with me. Hits like "You've Lost That Loving Feeling," by the Righteous Brothers, "It's All Over Casanova," by Ruby Andrews, and "Beechwood 4-5789," sung by the Marvelettes, "you can call me up and have a date, any old time, dun-dun, dun-dun, dun-dun."

Music entertained and soothed me, reflecting who we were with melodic style, grace, and intimacy.

I took my radio everywhere to allow me to escape, to take me on rhythmic

To Be Loved

vibration journeys alone or with buddies. It added style and rhythm to whatever we did. At the kickball and the basketball court, joaning, my radio would be sitting just off from us, streaming out the songs of the day, including "Dancing in the Streets," by Martha Reeves and the Vandellas.

New dances seemed to appear every other month, and everybody naturally competed at doing them—the "Mashed Potatoes," the "Jerk," the "Twist," and more. I didn't aspire to be a good dancer, but I loved music and watching others dance and have a good time.

Fear and Intimidation Constants

I went to Kelly Miller Jr. High School in the seventh grade in the fall of 1964. I stopped sucking my thumb when I began the seventh grade. Fortunately, I could still hide that I still wetted the bed. Mama, unlike Daddy, didn't whip me for it. Somehow, she must have understood that it could have out of my control since my other siblings were late bed-wetters, too.

I gingerly made the daily trek to Kelly Miller through the various housing projects. Some of the most notorious stories of bullies emanated from those projects. As I came down Brookes Street towards Kelly Miller, I noticed a hill, which rose high above the backfield of the school's playground and adjacent swimming pool, where the Lincoln Heights boys hung out. They were on fenced-in school property. Lincoln Heights was one of the most feared projects in the area. One of the boys broke from the crowd, ran down the long two-block hill right up to me, and asked, "You from here?"

"I'm from 58th Street."

"You know anybody in Lincoln Heights?"

"No."

"I like that string tie you are wearing. Can I have it?"

"Hell no!" I said, trying to sound tough.

"If you don't give it to me, I'm a get my boys to come down here and help me take it from you!"

To Be Loved

I gently unfastened the tie that had given me so much pride and bid it farewell. I wasn't about to start school being the target of a gang.

Kelly Miller required boys to wear neckties or string ties and girls to wear dresses or skirts. If the teacher asked, I would tell them what happened.

It seemed that the Jackson family of about four or five brothers ran the Lincoln Heights project gangs and, therefore, the kids at Kelly Miller. You didn't bother anyone connected to the Jacksons, like Winky, Doc., and others. The rumor was they hung a man on a swing at the playground, leaving him for all to see. Some days after school, a badly beaten student lay on an embankment of someone's yard, an apparent victim of a Lincoln Heights gang-jumping.

When violence broke out, faculty stayed out of it. Fear and shock at the frequency and extent of violence paralyzed them and empowered the perpetrators. Faculty members were afraid to stop a fight, fearing the wrath aimed at them or their car.

Walking up to Kelly Miller every day, now that I had to, was dreaded. Mitchell had never told me about this. You had to learn to carry yourself as if you were unafraid but respectful, making it easier to be unseen and unheard again.

***

I could never do right or say right to my mother. Once, on a rare occasion, I asked my mother for a nickel.

"I don't have any money," she said, tearing me apart. She won't give me money other than the pennies for the Sunday church service. I could go out and

Fear and Intimidation Constants

hustle bottles and get more than a nickel. Nickels were everywhere. She wouldn't give me even a nickel! I guess she didn't like me. I didn't deserve it from her, I thought. I felt so bad that I was careful never to ask her for anything again. Other than the necessities.

Meanwhile, Mr. Doggett, a neighbor who almost always wore a brown and beige Sealtest milk company uniform and almost always smoked a smelly cigar and would be alone and mumbling like he was drunk, would give me a quarter every time I saw him, just for the asking, even though he didn't know me. I would ask him straight out, "Mr. Doggett, do you have a quarter?" And he would mumble something as he always did while fumbling through his pocket, his teeth clutching the cigar, as he pulled out a quarter.

I couldn't do enough to win my mother's positive attention or approval. Her words of anguish and anger had stung me one time too many. I began to do the dreaded: talk back; sass.

"You always whipping me, for nothing, every time I make a mistake," I would retort. "Others make mistakes. You do, too. You ain't always whipping them!"

"You never whip Mitchell for anything!"

"I wish I was never born!"

"I wish I was dead!"

"I didn't ask to be born!"

"When the decision was made to have me, I wasn't consulted."

To Be Loved

"I wish you would have me put away!"

***

Late one night, while hanging on the corner, listening to the street corner harmony, I noticed a man across the street, sprawled on a lawn, apparently drunk. I went over to him to inspect. He was a big, burly man in a soiled beige construction uniform. He was drunk all right, almost out cold. I carefully patted him down to see if he had any money. I felt his wallet. I pulled the leather bundle from his pocket and searched it for cash. He had money in it. I looked around, and nobody noticed me. So, I dashed home. I opened the wallet again and saw all this money in it. I had to tell somebody. I told Mitchell.

Mitchell walked me back outside our house. We sat on the wall next door, and he began to tell me what big trouble I'd be in if Mama found out about it. He said with all that identification and money, the Police were sure to look for the wallet and who took it. Mitchell said his fingerprints were downtown, and his fingerprints were on the wallet. He said for a man to lose $90, he would return to comb the neighborhood, looking for it. I believed Mitchell as I felt impending danger surround us.

"You ain't got to worry about nothing, though," he said, "cause I'm gonna take it back!"

"Okay," I answered, relieved he didn't ask me to return it.

A couple of days later, I was sitting on the wall when I tumbled over and fell into the yard. As I braced myself to get up, I felt a lump on the ground. It was

Fear and Intimidation Constants

the old, drunk man's wallet, with everything except the $90. Mitchell had duped me. I mean, I had taken advantage of the old man, and my brother had taken advantage of me. He laughed when I confronted him. He said Mama had fallen on hard times, and he gave the money to her. I couldn't be mad at Mitchell. What was I gonna do? Ask her? I didn't bother. In retrospect, though, I should have.

The eighth grade was like the seventh, except for one difference: Helen Cassidy. In class, I happened to notice a girl staring at me. She just stared like she couldn't get enough of watching me. I've never been the subject of so much positive attention before. There was Roberta, who I had a great affinity for but grew bored with when she wouldn't give me any pussy.

But this girl in my class, Brenda, was checking me out. After class, we introduced ourselves and talked. I walked her to her next class.

One Saturday, Paulette came to tell me that I had a visitor. It was her, Helen Jones. No girl had ever visited me. She just wanted to hang out with me. We sat around talking. I would take her to the recreation center or Jack's Carry Out and listen to the latest Motown hits—a dime for a song play, three for a quarter. Then, I'd walk her home.

Weeks later, we became a constant duo. Along the way, walking her home, we'd enter the abandoned project houses at 56th and Foote Streets, condemned in preparation for the eventual construction of Woodson High School. Someone had conveniently placed a mattress on the living room floor of one of the abandoned project houses. Five years after the first time, I was set to have sex

To Be Loved

again. We wouldn't even take our clothes off. She'd pull her panties off, and I'd pull my pants down, in case we got an unexpected visitor and needed to dress quickly. I would lie on top of her to penetrate her, asking, "Is it in?" occasionally.

"Up," she said, with her eyes closed. "Over to the left...No, your left!"

Once I was in, oh, man, it felt indescribably good. We were young 13-year-olds. There were many taboos used to discourage sex, like: 'it's nasty; you could get stuck like a dog; if a girl did it and let somebody know or did it with more than two guys in a community, she was regarded as easy, if not a whore. But none of this quelled our desire for that good feeling. It wasn't a romantic thing. I liked Helen a lot. She was the first female to show me, love. But I didn't love her or know how to love since I had never experienced it. One thing for sure: Helen would give me anything I wanted from her. She asked for nothing more than to be with me as we explored the neighborhood. Helen was the first girl to make me feel valued as if I mattered to someone.

***

One day, I overheard Hank, my next-door neighbor, say, "If you ain't Q-ing, you ain't getting no pussy."

I found later that "Q-ing" meant "cuming." And, as much pussy as Helen gave me, I wasn't cuming. His remark had me concerned that I wasn't getting any pussy.

"Mitchell," I said one evening as we sat on the curb near Drew school. "I think something's wrong with me."

Fear and Intimidation Constants

"Why you say that?"

"Because! I'm getting all this pussy and I ain't busting a nut, yet!"

He laughed.

"I'm serious, man. Oh, you think that shit's funny, huh?"

"No, all jokes aside.

Don't worry about it. Some people cum at the age 12, some at 15. It's like a girl coming on her period. Some come on at 9, and some don't cum 'till 12. You never know, but if you keep fucking, you'll eventually cum."

That made sense to me.

We stopped at the abandoned projects on another walk to Helen's house. Helen and I went inside a building and got busy. Then, pop, I felt something even more sensual than being inside her. It seemed to tickle with a cool, warm sensation I'd never felt before. I was nervous that something had gone wrong. The feeling rose to a crescendo, blossomed, and faded. It mushroomed in and out. I felt both glorious and paralyzed temporarily. And, then, I was exhausted; I had cum.

After that, I'd bust a nut in her every time. Helen gave pussy anytime I wanted it. I wanted it like a kid who wanted candy, all of the time. It made me feel mature. We became inseparable. We'd do it in all of the woods in the area. Almost every day, I walked her home; we would stop in the woods and do it.

***

Aunt Florene died from breast cancer in New York, and her funeral would be in North Carolina. Mama took almost everybody in the family except

To Be Loved

Mitchell and me. I invited Helen over. We wanted to do it. My bed was too smelly, So Helen and I got busy on Mama's bed. I couldn't get caught since Mama was in North Carolina. When they got back, Helen told Paulette, and she told Mama; Mama whipped my ass.

In class, she continued to stare at me so much. It embarrassed and distracted me, bringing unwanted attention and snickering from the other classmates. I told her I would charge her 25 cents whenever I caught her staring at me. No problem, she said. At the end of the class, she would owe me a couple of dollars or more. And would pay up!

***

After walking Helen home, we'd stand on the corner of Division Avenue and Grant Street, N.E., under a lamppost, the site of the Amoco gasoline station that refused to fix my bike when I had run away. I held Helen close to me and kissed her lips long and passionately. She would blush and stare up at me when I'd let her go like I had a spell on her. Helen made me feel like I was somebody very special and important. It reminded me of Martha Reeves and the Vandellas singing from her hit song, "It's in His Kiss," "If you want to know if he really cares, it's in his kiss, that's where it is..."

I had outgrown huts, bicycles, and go-carts, and Helen filled the space. We'd hang out at Jack's Carry Out, playing the jukebox and eating fries, or she'd watch me play the pinball machine. She was always by my side. Smokey of the Miracles sang from the jukebox, "If you feel like giving me a lifetime of devotion,

Fear and Intimidation Constants

I second that emotion..."

Once, when we broke up, she wanted the relationship to continue. I pretended not to be interested. Then, Jason Bar stepped in to claim Helen, and she wouldn't talk to me again except to tell me she and I couldn't be together anymore. She couldn't just leave me like that! We were constant companions for so long and with so many experiences, so much growing up. I did love her; I realized as I was losing her. I was missing her. With Jason Bar, I guess it was like a promotion to her. She became Jason's chick. Music from the radio almost always seemed to speak to me. I could hear J.J. Jackson singing,

"You can hurt me, but it's alright,

One day you will see you'll never find a guy like me,

Who will love you right, both day and night."

***

Mr. Henry had stopped coming around. He couldn't get a hold on his drinking habit. He lost his job, and all we would see of him was when we walked past the DGS near the District Line. He'd be on the side of DGS drinking until he nearly passed out.

***

In February 1965, I walked down the street and bummed a cigarette off the paperboy. The newspaper's cover page featured a photo of a Black man who lay dead on a floor, shot many times.

"Who's that," I asked.

To Be Loved

"I don't know," he said, "Malcolm X?"

"Damn, what the X stand for?" I asked.

"Damn, if I know!" he said.

I began hanging out with Barry around then. He lived on 55th Street in an apartment with his mother and older brother, who was about Mitchell's age.

Barry was a cool fat boy. He smoked cigarettes like me. He acted like he was in control of everything. And he was funny, like me. Besides, his mother would allow us to shoot crap in the living room, her way of keeping a watchful eye on her son and keeping him from doing such things in public places like the laundry room. Also, when his mother was not home, he and I would hit her small but potent liquor chest. One shot, and we would be good for the evening. We'd go and hang out with the Smith family of attractive girls, play some records, and dance, with the hopes of getting the ultimate, some pussy.

Harry McNair, the younger brother of Mitchell's buddy, Rod, the do-wop singer, hung in our crew sometimes. Tall and shy, yet humorous, he liked to Click a lot, and we all connected at the Smith's house.

Click also began to hang around there. He and Robert Briscoe began learning karate around this time. They practiced in an apartment laundry room. Briscoe would become a gay minister and a World Heavyweight martial arts champion.

One evening Harry had gone to the 7-11 Carryout on Eastern Avenue, on the Maryland side in Chapel Oaks, and was sneak-attacked with a brick, hit in

Fear and Intimidation Constants

the back of the head. After lying in a coma for months, Harry died, another God-forsaken community tribe thing; it trailed us wherever we went.

***

Mama, who had worked in white folk's homes in Seat Pleasant on weekends for extra money, stopped around 1966 when I was 14.

To make extra money for Christmas, Mama got a part-time job at the then Hickory Hut Carry Out on Benning Road, N.E., where one of her customers was a regular, Frank Gaynor. Frank was a grumpy, used car mechanic who chain-smoked non-filtered Pall Malls and worked on junk car lots. He'd come by to see Mama. He'd sit and talk to only her, even when we were around. That was all right with me. I didn't want another Daddy.

When we were old enough so that Mama could leave her family alone, she enrolled in adult night school for cosmetology. Everyone complimented her on how well she had always styled her daughters' hair.

***

Mitchell was so generous. He would share much of his money with his friends. One summer, Mitchell got a job as a cook at a restaurant on K Street. The money was good for a 17-year-old. He was helping money-strapped Mama. He decorated our home -- new linoleum, new living room furniture, and even toys for Christmas.

However, Mitchell, by age 17, would not return to finish high school his last year. I was let down. Dropping out wasn't even an option for any of us. That

To Be Loved

put a blotch on his image: "dropout." I looked for Mama to fuss and make him go back. But she didn't. She needed the extra money he would provide.

On another occasion, Mitchell, Biscuit, and I caught a bus to Lafayette Square, across from the White House. From there, we walked to a restaurant to burglarize it. We conveniently found a crowbar and broke into the restaurant through its cellar door. What we found was a kitchen full of food. We stopped and ate. To go in the walk-in refrigerator and eat sliced meat out of the wrapping was privileged stuff. Then, we followed Mitchell through the main dining room and went to the bar's cash register but found no money. We took miniature bottles of liquor and cigars and went upstairs and broke into a cigarette vending machine, took packs of cigarettes and coins, and left.

We boarded the bus at the Lafayette Park bus stop, sat in the back with windows opened, lit our cigars, and rode our getaway ride home. For the next few days, I smoked Tereytons cigarettes from the restaurant.

In the middle of the night, the phone rang. Mitchell and his buddy Biscuit had been arrested and charged with burglarizing Fairmont Heights Junior High School. Mitchell was subsequently tried for the burglary and convicted. Mitchell went to trial alone, and he didn't come back home. The court sentenced my brother to 18 months in Lorton Youth Center.

The first night at home without Mitchell upset me. The only time I could stay up late was with him. We watched TV until programs went off the air, with the marching Marines and flags waving. He would, on occasion, cook us a snack.

Fear and Intimidation Constants

I was heartbroken and wondering what I would do the first night, so I went into the kitchen. I thought about trying to cook a snack like Mitchell used to do, but I quit in tears.

***

A minor league football team drafted Hank, my next-door neighbor. Everyone walked taller in the confidence of knowing that someone from 58th Street could become famous for something good. I was slightly jealous that it was a Summer, not a Steele. Our families always had close rivalries. A couple of months later, Hank, the only guy in a family of girls, was drafted to fight in Vietnam. He came home from the minor league team determined to fight for America. He said, "I'm going to come back with more metals than you can shake a stick at."

***

I was getting the direction I must have been seeking all my life. Some say it took prison, even though I had enrolled in college before and during incarceration. Prison does not deserve credit for my or anyone's reform. It fails the inmates more than it corrects them. Up to 80 percent of ex-convicts return for committing other crimes or violating parole. Unfortunately, I selected prison, as did most of my pals from Sheriff Road, except Robert: Tyson, Smooth, Tiger, Sly, Thomas, and more, grew up and went to jail. That's systematic, not genetic. I believe it took me getting away anywhere. Being away allowed me to look at my past and evaluate it. Racial discrimination, no doubt, narrowed my options. Others go live in the country, get sent to another city, go to college, visit another country or join the military. Each of my old buddies felt alienated from their family. There was either a weak or absent Daddy pattern among us. We were strong-willed young men with no adult male guidance to become responsible young men in the '70s, with opportunities -- both good and bad -- our parents had never dreamed.

***

The Lorton Prison College Program offered me an opportunity to make being an ex-convict work for me rather than against me. All I had to do was keep doing what I was doing, which was a breeze. I was beginning to find myself again. I knew where I wanted to go and felt I was on track to something big time.

I was going somewhere.

I discovered that the real power is within; our choices determine that power. I was learning to anchor my life with a vision, a long-term goal, and a plan, and a determination to achieve them. Taking control of my life felt strangely good, better than any drug.

***

My bouts of depression were beginning to let up for more extended periods due to counseling and my taking steps to make something of my life. There would be weeks that I would go without depression. Then, bam! It would happen all over again. I would be down and out, didn't want to see and talk to anybody, and was just very introspective.

Ms. Shaw wanted me to attend a group session at a church downtown.

Fear and Intimidation Constants

She thought I was ready for it. It amounted to a milestone in my treatment. I would have to be comfortable with expressing my most intimate fears and problems in a group. I would see my issues from others' perspectives and in context with their problems.

I attended a couple of group sessions. Throughout the individual counseling sessions, I learned that something had gone amuck with my emotional state, and one has to address pain and not suppress the trauma. My problems were not as severe as the problems of other group members. The group sessions were like an outpatient clinic for an insane asylum. Hearing all the maladjustments of others depressed me more than it uplifted me. I would draw my strength and inspiration from others, like Ms. Shaw, who seemed to have it all together. Belonging to a group of people with all sorts of problems made me question my identity. They were I, and I was they; I just stopped going. I would have to do the balance of my healing myself.

***

One night, Mitchell said, "I want you to go somewhere with me tonight, Ronald."

"Okay," I said.

"You think you're up to it?"

"Sure, where are we going?"

"Drew School got some shit in there I want you to help me get."

I never even considered danger when out with my brother anywhere. We

To Be Loved

climbed up to the top of the roof of the recreation center, entered through a window, and were in the school. I had a chance to reap revenge on all the teachers who ever reported me to Mama. I insisted that we go to Mrs. A.S. Brown's classroom. Once there, I opened her grey cabinet and pulled out the plain white cardboard box of delicious oatmeal cookies that other kids got to eat while drinking a carton of milk. I could never afford either. As I stuffed the cookies in my pockets and ate them freely, I marveled at the prospect of Mrs. A.S. Brown going into the gray metal cabinet the next day and wondering, "Who took my cookies?"

We walked through the dark building as memories flashed through my mind. I remembered once admiring another kid for the clothes he wore and telling Mitchell in the hallway, crowded with other students, "I wish I was him."

"Why you say that?" Mitchell asked.

"He wears some nice clothes."

"So! You don't ever wish you were somebody else," was Mitchell's stoic reply. "You wish you had what they had!"

What a difference, I pondered. I could never be that person, no matter what. But, someday, I could have nice clothes. Hanging out with Mitchell was always the most coveted, even then, walking through the dark halls of Drew Elementary School. Once in the projector room, Mitchell used a projector stand to haul the loot, including the projector, many cases of school films, and other stuff. We pushed that cart out of the schoolyard, under cover of darkness, up Eads

Fear and Intimidation Constants

Street hill, lifted it across the railroad tracks, and then carried it across the back yards that were our playgrounds and into our house.

In the middle of the night, Mitchell turned our dining room into a mini-theater. We kicked back and watched school film after film. Mama was awakened and came down from the bed to see what was happening. She poked her sleepy face in, asking, "What are ya'll doing this late?"

"Showing some films. I got some films of Joe Louis," Mitchell replied.

Mama left. She would never scrutinize anything Mitchell did. Mitchell's cool or something else made him ride above her reproach. I just wanted to have it or be around Mitchell. Mama had always warned us against crime. This time she said nothing. If my Daddy had been alive, we wouldn't have been able to bring that shit home.

***

I worked at IAFC for a year. I had peace of mind that they would never find out that I was an ex-convict. When I told the staff I had enrolled in college, they congratulated me. They talked about their college days and wished me good luck like I was going on a journey.

I had planned to begin 1976 with a new job in sales. I still liked sales. I thought I should still pursue my ambition as a salesman to have another career to fall back on. I needed an income while I learned. So, direct sales were out. I thought retail would be a warm-up for the real thing.

A tall, skinny, suited Brother named James Washington, who wore an

To Be Loved

equally towering Afro, interviewed me for a job at Regal's Shoe Shops at 1345 F Street, N.W.

Regal's trained their salesmen to bring only one shoe out at a time to a customer: probably a tribute to my and other boosters' past.

"You can make it in this company," he tilted his head toward me and said, "if you are willing to work hard. See that guy up there at the counter, that's my assistant manager. He's worked here only six months as a salesman. See, you can make it here."

"Well, I'm anxious to start."

Two weeks later, in January 1976, I bade farewell to the IAFC staff, especially happy that they had never found out about my past and hopeful that Regal's would never know, either. I wasn't going to tell them.

I had hoped retail would be my proving ground for a sales career. Next, I would learn to sell cars, perhaps, and then houses. Additionally, I had hoped that being in service to the public and thinking persuasively on my feet would help heal my self-esteem.

At Regal's, their salesmen would stand in the store's doorway not only to be the first salesman a customer noticed as they approached the door but also to see the latest girl show at the intersection of 14th & F Streets, N.W. That intersection was like a model runway, featuring the finest ladies of every shape, size, and hue. Occasionally, one of the guys would run out there to meet a babe, get a phone number, or bomb out and come back inside the store empty-handed

Fear and Intimidation Constants

and embarrassed.

***

Federal City College was a hotbed of ideas for students. Students from all over, many of whom may have never had the chance to go to another college because of admission requirements, were chasing dreams and ambitions with passion at FCC. A group of guys would gather in a vacant classroom amid roaring and intellectual debates, questioning, affirming, and debating about almost everything in society. I never dreamed that college and studying could be so gratifying.

***

When Frank was home, he would listen earnestly to his radio scanner or the Washington community activist and radio personality Petey Greene. It was probably the equivalent of Frank reading a newspaper; he was illiterate. He hid it well. He had learned auto mechanics without reading.

He couldn't believe I could have written myself out of prison because he couldn't read. He argued, "Sometimes, when judges sentence people, they put a little note in the file to let the person out after a while."

Determined to affirm what I already knew; I got Judge Charles Whitaker's telephone number and called him.

"Hi, Mr. Whitaker, how are you?" I said nervously.

"Who's calling?" Judge Whitaker responded.

"This is Ronald Steele. I'm extraordinarily in debt to you for having

To Be Loved

reduced my sentence.

"Oh, I remember you. What are you doing these days?"

"I'm in college, majoring in journalism."

"Oh, good. That's a good field. I studied journalism before going into law.

"What are you doing these days?" I asked.

"Well, I'm retired," he said.

"Good for you," I said before asking," Mr. Whitaker, why did you reduce my sentence?"

"For the things you laid out in your letters."

"Thanks, I needed to know that. Goodbye."

"Good luck."

"Thanks."

Later I told Frank. "Boy, get out of here!" Frank replied. "You must be crazy to think I am going to believe that. You ain't called no judge, nothing. And I don't care what you say, you didn't write your way out of no prison!"

In Search of Love: Roberta

After living together for nearly a year, constantly arguing and making up, Roberta called me at work one day to say, "I'm pregnant."

"Oh yeah?" I asked, surprised and disappointed.

"Yes," she continued, waiting for a reaction.

"I thought you were using birth control," I replied after a long silence.

"I was."

"What happened?"

"I forgot."

"You forgot!" I exclaimed as my eyes wandered around my office/stock room.

"Yeah."

I was seething. Again, I had that haunting feeling of being forced into raising a child without being consciously involved in the decision to have a child, not to mention by another woman I was about to break up with.

The female custom of using pregnancy to keep a relationship hadn't occurred to me. After getting to know me, I could not comprehend that someone could think that getting pregnant would keep me. We were on the verge of a breakup. I will not live with a woman I have to argue or fight with constantly to get along. There was something wrong with our relationship because we repeatedly argued so much about the same damn things. How could she forget to

To Be Loved

use birth control when we had such a rough time in our relationship?

"Talk to you later," I deadpanned and hung up the phone dejectedly.

Trusting females. It still had not occurred to me that a man's number one line of defense against the designs of females, willing to have children, for imature reasons, was a prophylactic. We were taught that females were more mature than males. What does that mean? They considered raising families while males were still "sowing our oats." I had never learned that if you don't want a baby, it's not enough to tell a girl that. You used a rubber and ensured she didn't get pregnant by you. My old experience kept guiding me 'you used rubbers to prevent disease when that dog in you led you to be with a slut.' You tell a babe you don't want to have children; they will understand since they're more mature.

Roberta and I hung in there, arguments and all. I settled into the prospects of parenting again. I began to look forward to our newborn.

Kwanza

Kwanza

Roberta and I drove around town in our blue '69 Oldsmobile F-85, which her parents gave us, visiting bookstores in a vain search for a book on African names. We found only one. I was angry. Don't they know we exist at all in Washington, D.C.? We're only the majority population. We stopped by a fledging African American bookstore, the Liberation Information Distributing Co., a forerunner to what would become the Pyramid Books Store, up to three stores that specialized in African-centered books. LIDC was out of such books. At least, they carried them. It was nice to see an African American bookstore. Before we left, Roberta purchased a card. If we had a girl, Roberta would name her; if a boy, I would name him.

Once again, I had settled into becoming a Daddy and trying to build a family. I would love this baby from day one. I would adore it and raise it right. Like school, I would put my best into raising this baby. I would do all the right things and more.

On December 12, 1975, our healthy baby girl was born. We named her Kwanza Reina Steele with so much hope and promise. Kwanza is from Kwanzaa, the African American holiday. Kwanzaa is Swahili meaning the "first fruits of harvest," Reina was Roberta's late grandmother's name.

Kwanza would become my joy. I wanted to be involved in her life to the fullest. I would do right by her. Every evening after work, I'd pick her up, cradle

To Be Loved

her in my arms and walk her through the apartment, telling her about my day at Regal's.

Fallback Career in Retail/Sales

Regal's had a wall chart in the back of the store, ranking salesmen on their sales volume. Soon, my rankings would hover around the top, if not at the top. Sales was an industry that allowed me to determine the heights I could achieve by how hard or intelligent I worked. I was pleased. I had successfully applied the experience of my brief foray into direct sales, which was paying off in retail.

The D.M. approached me one day and asked if would I like to become assistant manager. Wow. They were serious. It was my first promotion ever. Boy, did that feel good. It was a sign that taking control of my destiny was already bearing delicious, succulent fruit. I wanted this, more money and more responsibility. Assistant managers were the manager's virtual slaves. I was in my sophomore year of college and was on track to graduate in about four years. I didn't want anything to jeopardize that. So, I asked the D.M. if I could have a few days to consider it.

Later, I told him that I could not take the offer. I feared that doing an excellent job of assisting the manager would consume all of my time, and I would have to quit college. He seemed to understand.

"Congratulations," he said, "That was a smart decision."

It seems that as you become self-determined, others see it in you and want to add your energy to their team to help them pursue their goals, which may be fine, but it's energy that you should be applying to your goals. But determination meant you didn't allow yourself to be distracted from your original goal. Quitters don't win; winners don't quit. Having a purpose in life meant having direction, a means of judging whether an offer is an opportunity or a detour from your primary goal.

A Father's Need to Know

I received a summons from the court to establish paternity in Ngina's case. Pat had gotten on welfare, and the D.A. had come after me. I regretted that it came to this, but I was somewhat relieved that I would have my day in court. Undoubtedly, the court, after hearing what I went through with Pat, would agree that Ngina was very likely not mine. The truth was on my side; hell, I didn't need a lawyer to tell the truth. The assistant district attorney represented Pat. No problem, I'd represent myself.

Pat took the stand.

"Almost every day," was the answer she gave to the question of how often we had sex. The judge asked if I would like to ask any questions. Sure. With occasional directions from the judge, I asked Pat whether she recalled that we broke up during the last week of July 1971 and why.

How long did we break up? How many months pregnant did she first say she was?

"One month." She lied. How could she have known she was one month pregnant? She initially told me she was two months in September 1971 and that the baby would be due in May. Instead, Ngina was born in June, meaning she was conceived in August when we were not together.

"Didn't you change the number of months of your pregnancy a couple of times while you were pregnant? Didn't you say that you were expecting the

To Be Loved

baby in May, then turn around and tell me that the baby might be premature? Was Ngina born premature? Didn't I tell you that I would go whichever way a blood test directed us, only for you to renege at the last minute?"

The jury found that I was probably the father of Ngina without ordering a blood test. And I didn't have the sense to request one, either. I thought the truth, as I knew it, would prevail. I was shocked. I could barely hear the judge telling me I would have to pay child support for Ngina, who was six until she turned 18."

I was only making around $500 a month after taxes. Then the judge called me to the stand and whispered, "I hope you are studying law in college; you're pretty good." He nodded to the court clerk who called the next case.

I was stunned as when the judge sentenced me to 15 years. Where is justice? Nobody asked for a blood test. I didn't think I needed one. I was quick to learn some things; slow to understand others. Finally, I realized the saying: a 'person who enters a court to do business without a lawyer is represented by a fool' is true. I started child support payments, but that's all. I still wasn't convinced that I was Ngina's father.

On Holiday: Back to Prison?

On Holiday: Back to Prison?

In 1976, the year that Alex Haley published "Roots: The Saga of an American Family" and the year of the Soweto massacre in South Africa, Rufus, his brother, Richard, and a friend named Robert Cain, picked me up for a Memorial Day swimming pool outing. We were the "Four Rs," as our names all began with an "R." As fate would have it, we never made it to the pool. Instead, we ended up at District 13 Police Precinct, charged with assault with intent to kill a Police officer.

We had stopped at what was then a Kentucky Fried Chicken carry out on Martin Luther King Avenue, S.E., not far from the house of the great slavery abolitionist Frederick Douglas once lived and down the hill from St. Elizabeths Hospital, the national insane asylum where I worked the summer of both 1968 and 1969. It's one of the poorest and most troubled precincts of Southeast. Inside the KFC, while we ordered our food, a white guy came in and obtrusively shoved his order at the waitress before me and shouted, "You didn't put my French Fries in the bag!"

The lady appeared stunned and embarrassed. I said, "Wasn't that rude of you to come barging in here like that, pushing us aside and demanding you get help before us?"

Robert stepped up and asked, "You heard him; weren't you rude?"

The white guy stepped back, raising his hand, and before he could get a

To Be Loved

word out, Robert knocked him flat on his back. Then things went south. In an instant, Robert, Rufus, and Richard jumped on his chest as they ran out the door. I was stunned at how quickly things had gotten out of hand. I ran, too.

When we got to Robert's car in the KFC parking lot, someone shouted, "Halt! Police!"

A policeman saw us running out of the store to the car, and aimed his gun at us. Other police arrived and surrounded us within minutes. One Police officer with his gun trained on us asked whether we knew the guy we had stretched out on the KFC floor was a cop.

"No," we said. *A cop? I thought that guy appeared to be a drunk or an outpatient patient from St. Elizabeths Hospital.* However, the Police responded as if it were an attack on the station from out-of-towners. Williams had North Carolina tags. Moments ago, we were out on a holiday celebration, and in an instant; we were on our way to jail. Although my friends overreacted, the initial action was in self-defense until they decided to run.

The Police handcuffed us and took us back to the nearby 13th District Police Station, on Mississippi Avenue, S.E., the drunk and disorderly policeman's station. The police photographed, booked, and fingerprinted us. Then they took our possessions, snatching the necklaces from our necks. They charged us with assault with intent to kill a Police officer. We chose not to talk to the Police without a lawyer. A detective told us, "We're going to have an interview with each of you until you tell us." Who hit that officer? Within minutes, Rufus

On Holiday: Back to Prison?

screamed in pain as he was knocked, kicked, and hit about in the cell for several minutes.

An officer returned to where we were and asked, "Who's next?"

I stood up. It was terror, hearing the screaming and waiting. I wanted to get it done. Detectives and police officers marched me to the cellblock into the cell with Rufus, who sat curled on a bench in a corner, his head wrapped in his arms, his fingers extended and swelled.

When I entered the cell, the Police began hitting and kicking me. When I fell, the officers stomped me and beat me while repeatedly shouting, "Who hit the Police officer?" repeatedly.

"I didn't hit him!" I yelled as one shinny-shoe caught me in the face underneath my left eye. I grabbed it, feeling it swell in my hand. I had not been an angel in my life. But I never thought I would ever witness a whole Police station acting like a vigilante gang. Who would believe us?

"Well, who hit him, then?"

"We have a right to call a lawyer," I shouted.

They continued beating me. Then they stopped and whisked out of the cell. I looked over at Rufus, who was on a bench. He had welts and bruises over his face and head.

"I think they broke my hands," he said.

Then, we would hear the Police beating, stomping, and kicking Robert and Richard in another cell.

To Be Loved

Rufus sustained the worst damage. The Police assault broke the fingers on both of his hands. The rest of us suffered welts, bruises, and sprains.

Upon release on bond, at Rufus's suggestion, , we talked with civil lawyers to begin filing a police brutality suit. At the offices of Max and David Cohen, attorneys Rufus had known. The attorneys photographed our injuries and took a deposition from each of us to begin a suit against D.C. Metropolitan Police for brutality.

Roberta sympathized with us. I appreciated her faith and belief that we were not the culprits of this fiasco. Back at Regal's, my limping impaired my work for a few weeks.

**

For one of the first hearings on the charge of assault with intent to kill a Police officer, Rufus, Richard, Robert, and I arrived at Superior Court in D.C. a few minutes late and were summarily locked up for the day for contempt.

We went to court again, and the charge of assault with a deadly weapon was dismissed since no weapon was cited in the charge. We were happy, but the celebration was short-lived. Our lawyers informed us that we would probably be indicted, again, for assault, a lesser charge, but one that still carried 15 years.

Facing 15 Years in Prison, Again

D.C. officials subsequently indicted Rufus, Robert, Richard, and me for simple assault. A breathalyzer test on the fallen officer at the hospital revealed that he was intoxicated at ten times the legal limit. The charges against us were dismissed again. We celebrated and started planning what to do with the wealth we would win from our civil suit.

We had signed a 50-50 agreement with Cohen's legal team. I didn't agree with the 50-50 arrangement; it was patently unfair -- the police did not assault the attorneys. The case was clear-cut, the cop was drunk and disorderly, the photos of our injuries, and our synchronized depositions. The Cohens balked at first. I persisted. The attorneys later agreed to re-write the contract at 60-40. Still, it wasn't the traditional 33 and 1/3. However, they stood to get 10 percent less, and we stood to gain 7 percent more.

***

Federal City College was a land-grant urban college. It was located not on some sprawling green campus with grand buildings. FCC's campus in 1977 comprised of rented space in buildings located randomly throughout downtown D.C. We would have a class at one building at one location: and another class at another building, some 30 minutes or more away, in another part of downtown. So, my classes were often planned by their building's proximity to one another rather than by sequence. If there was a mandated prerequisite, I had to wait and

To Be Loved

take the course when offered in the same proximity as my other classes. Therefore, I took several courses out of sequence.

That inconvenience, as well as other circumstances, led many students to quit college. White media negatively publicized and magnified FCC's every mistake and discrepancy.

It wasn't enough that thousands of Black people were pursuing higher education to become productive citizens. Now, they were comparing the recently established college with long-established ones and parading the difference as inferior education at FCC. I thought their racist mindset tried to label us 'misfits' in our firm and honest pursuit to self-development against all odds.

Suing the MPD

After living together for nearly a year, constantly arguing and making up, Roberta called me at work one day to say, "I'm pregnant."

"Oh yeah?" I asked, surprised and disappointed.

"Yes," she continued, waiting for a reaction.

"I thought you were using birth control," I replied after a long silence.

"I was."

"What happened?"

"I forgot."

"You forgot!" I exclaimed as my eyes wandered around my office/stock room.

"Yeah."

I was seething. My mind gleamed over the haunting feeling of being forced into raising a child without being consciously involved in the decision to have a child, not to mention by another woman I was about to break up with.

The age-old custom of females becoming pregnant deliberately or carelessly to keep escaped me. After getting to know me, I could not comprehend that someone could think that getting pregnant would keep me. We were on the verge of a breakup, but neither knew when. I had decided not to live with a woman I constantly argued with and had to fight to get along with her. There was something wrong with our picture because we repeatedly argued so much about

To Be Loved

the same damn things. How could she forget to use birth control when we had such a rough time in our relationship?

"Talk to you later," I deadpanned and hung up the phone dejectedly.

It still had not occurred to me that a man's number one line of defense against the designs of females, willing to have children at the drop of a hat, was a prophylactic. We were taught that females were more mature than males. What does that mean? They considered raising families while we were still "sowing our oats." I had never learned that if you don't want a baby, it's not enough to tell a girl that. You used a rubber, which ensured she didn't get pregnant by you. My old experience kept guiding me 'you used rubbers to prevent disease when that dog in you led you to be with a slut.' You tell a babe you don't want to have children; they will understand since they're more mature.

Roberta and I hung in there, arguments and all. I settled into the prospects of parenting again. I began to look forward to our newborn.

I ran into a childhood girlfriend, Karen White, who was also enrolled at FCC. We had a brief fling as kids. She had always liked me. She was always kind of buxom, but attractive. Now, she was voluptuous, shapely, with a matching big pretty smile. But she wore lots of makeup and a flowing wig. Those combinations usually stood out like a red flag to me. It's not what you have but what you do with what you have. Some ladies who wore wigs and heavy makeup did not really hide short hair or bad skin. They were masking something more onerous: deep, emotional conflicts within themselves that were often reflected in insatiable insecurities.

But, I was willing to be wrong. Karen was quick to smile and had an effervescent, attractive personality. I liked that. She seemed to be someone who cherished the joys of life more than the pain. We'd talk about old times and our dreams and aspirations. She would offer me a ride home, since she lived out my way. She drove a beautiful, Burgundy 1968 Lincoln with matching leather interior. It was really slick. She'd give me a ride home from school and we'd sit in the car, outside of the apartment and rap. She was so expressive. I liked feeling, expressive babes. They seemed easy to get along with and freaky, too. I would imagine such a girl's expressiveness in bed. But, I wasn't feeling that way about Karen.

In an argument with Roberta once, she said that she saw me get out of the car with Karen once and she accused me of having an affair with her, which wasn't true.

"Can't I have any friends, without being accused of doing something I didn't do?" I countered. "What are you afraid of?" Are you doing what you supposed to be doing for me? Then, you shouldn't be worrying about my friends as long as I'm coming home to you. Between college, work and family, where am I going to find the time to two-time? I don't have time even if I wanted to."

I wanted to be trusted. I really had no plans to have anything more than a friendship with Karen. If I was going to have an affair, I would have been a

To Be Loved

great deal more discreet. I wouldn't have had her drive me home and sit out front talking with her.

Roberta and I were not getting along. The arguments were growing, again. Our baby, Kwanza, had given us a brief reprieve. But, we were going at it again. I began to wonder could I live with this arguing all the damn time, for the rest of my life. The answer was emphatically, "No!"

I began to consider getting my own place. I thought about Kwanza. Maybe I should stay for her. What would the neighbors think, who looked on us with so much pride. I can't stay for the neighbors and it wouldn't be fair to precious Kwanza to raise her in the environment of anger, by two parents who no longer loved each other. That would be selfish and the greater wrong. If all she saw was anger, which would soon give way to hatred, where would she learn to love herself and to love others?

Roberta and I talked about it. We agreed that I would move out. There was the vain hope that after a brief separaltion, we'd realize how much we missed and loved each other and get back together stronger than ever. But, I knew it was over. I was sad for Kwanza. The dream of Roberta, Kwanza and me living happily ever after, achieving our aspirations together, I thought, would be nevermore.

I bought some home furnishings and now four years at home, at age 25, I went looking for my first apartment, alone. I found one, efficiency, rented by William J. Davis, not far from Roberta, at 1342 Eastern Avenue, N.E., right down the street from Sheriff Road.

Suing the MPD

Occasionally, I would run into one of the fellows from Sheriff Road. Everyone had scattered; gone in different directions. Those who were still around were locked in the past. I didn't want to talk about the fun we used to have. I was trying to make it in a different world. I wanted to exchange what we were doing now to manage our present and move on into the future.

"Hey Sly, what's happening?" He was still the epitome of fashion.

"My man, Steele, how have you been?"

"I've been good. I'm in college and working as a salesman at Regal's Shoe Shop."

"Damn, man, that's alright. Damn, you always were smart."

"So were you. What have you been doing, man?" He should have become a buyer or merchandiser for a big department store or something. Instead, Sly's skin was ashy and his front teeth were missing. There was foam in the corner of his mouth. He was obviously still fucking with heroin. He just didn't get it.

"I ain't been doing too much. You know, *Robert* is locked up."

"Yeah, I know," I acknowledged sadly.

"And, Mercury, he lives down the street on a big empty lot. He's homeless."

"Mercury?"

Sly nodded his head.

"Damn! That's fucked up."

To Be Loved

I was saddened. It would pain me every time I would run into the old guys. My heart pulled at the old. I insisted on the new. But, those guys who I once thought were invincible were falling apart. A short while ago, we were like hood celebrities. Now, most were bombing out. The transition for many from adolescence to early adulthood, without preparation and guidance, meant peril, perhaps for the rest of their lives. I planned to be ready for the next transitions of life. But, many of my homies could not survive adolescence. I saw Nutbush once, as I was driving through Southeast. His skin was a pale, his eyes red. He stumbled along, like he was drunk. My heart wouldn't let me stop. I drove on.

***

I remembered that it was William J. Davis, a slumlord, who owned much of the apartment buildings and houses in my childhood community on 58th Street, when I was a kid. Now, as an adult, he owned my home, too.

The first-floor apartment had a small kitchen and an adjacent dining area, with space for a dinette set. That's where I would put my bed. I put mirrors on the wall as a headboard. I imagined that my babe and I could eat at the kitchen dinette and for dessert, go to bed. On the other side of the kitchen wall was the living room, the full length of both other rooms.

Roberta helped me settle in. She cleaned and swept and helped me put things away. It was like her down payment on continuing to be the first lady in my life after the split. We agreed that Kwanza would spend every other weekend with me. I had planned to continue to be an integral part of her growth and development, the best that I could in spite of her mother and my separation. But, I was really sad for Kwanza. I wanted to give her little, innocent, precious self-everything and raise her right. Now, I was planning to maintain as much of a presence in her life as possible, even though she and I would no longer live together.

      I really looked forward to spending weekends with Kwanza for many reasons. I loved her dearly. My caring for her demonstrated that I was not shrinking from responsibility by breaking up with her mother. And, I wanted to offer Kwanza all the love and wherewithal I could. I wanted to demonstrate that showing interest in her, playing games with her, talking to her, checking her homework, taking her on trips and walks and more, would exemplify my beliefs that love and guidance helps to raise a healthy nurtured, motivated human being. Yes, I wanted to give her all the love and attention and direction I didn't have. In fact, we'd spend a portion of each weekend at the playground, the library, at kiddy plays or movies or doing something else I thought would amuse, entertain and expose her to useful information and events. I would teach her alphabets, numbers, how to read and how to write. She would grow up not only knowing her father, even though her parents had split, but she would be close to her father and love me. I would teach her to love herself before white America conditioned her to hate herself. Besides, with a mother like hers, she really needed me. She needed to be exposed to a father who had all the positives going on as I. I would be her rock. I would steady her aim and try to always guide her. Bathing and

To Be Loved

feeding her, changing her diapers, taking her to visit my mother and family came naturally. My love for my baby and my desire to get her off to a proper start grounded me. All I had to do was the opposite of what was done during my early upbringing.

When I would get involved with a young lady, Kwanza was the person I talked about most. She was my pride and joy. She could do no wrong. She promised me a life away from all the other struggles to achieve. It was a life of love. In fact, I had aimed to learn a deeper love through her; one I had never known but craved to try: an unconditional love; a "love-to-love you because-you-are-you type of love. I loved to hear her voice, especially when she said or called out, "Daddy!"

***

Promotion Offer: In the Suburbs

At Regal's, the District Manager died from a heart attack and was replaced by Mr. Malone, another Italian. Italians seemed to run Regal's parent company, the Wohl Company.

"Yeah, we sell the shoes, the white boys get paid," I told another salesman in the back of the store, amid shelves of shoes, one day as we waited for customers to arrive.

"What you mean?" he asked.

"We hump our asses off in this store, but only the white boys are gonna move up into upper management. You got to be white to move up. Not necessarily talented, but white."

"I ain't letting nothing and nobody hold me back," he responded.

"You must be leaving Regal's. You see any black people beyond the manager's position of one or two of their biggest stores, Harlem and here?"

"Nope."

"Okay then."

***

The new District Manager fixed his eyes on me as I gathered a customer's purchase of new shoes and began my spiel to sell other accessories. The DM was particularly interested in how well I pitched to white people, who comprised about 25 percent of our customers.

To Be Loved

The next day, the DM took me out to lunch. Mr. Malone didn't take salesmen out for lunch unless he would fire or promote you.

He sat across the table, smoking a cigarette and looking around, rather tense.

"I heard the conversation you were having with Harvey yesterday."

"Oh? What conversation?" I asked. That's all we guys do is talk when customers are not around.

"Well, what you said was not true. I'm gonna prove it to you."

"What conversation?" I said, smiling, hoping he'd pull me in on the conversation.

"How would you like to become the Window Trimmer for this region?"

"The Window Trimmer? Really?"

"It's an executive position, like the managers. You'll have 11 stores, and you can set your own schedule."

"Sounds good," I said, and. I could set the work schedule conveniently around my college schedule.

I had worked at Regal's from 9:30 until six every day except Sundays and then went to college at night, often until 10 p.m. Getting home 10:30-11 p.m. meant I had little time to study, except on the weekends. With the promotion, I could work to benefit my college.

Wow, I was so proud to be promoted. When you try and take that first

Promotion Offer: In the Suburbs

step, you don't even know, but God will make way for you. I turned down that assistant manager's offer; ordinarily, one would have thought I had made a mistake, rejecting my first promotion; yet another more suitable opportunity was now possible. Had I not believed in myself, rejected the first offer, the second, better one may have never materialized.

"I would like that very much. Thank you."

"See, you were wrong, I told you." Mr. Malone said with a sheepish grin.

"Wrong about what?"

Mr. Malone laughed and said, "Forget it. You got a car?"

"No," I said.

"That's a problem," he said.

"I can get one," I said, thinking of Karen's car.

"Then, it's not a problem," he said, and we laughed.

As we approached the glass doors at Regal's, I thought these would be the last days that I would know these guys. Days later, I remembered that Mr. Malone referred to my conversation about discrimination at Regal. He was trying to make a point by giving me an opportunity. I appreciated it. His stroke of goodwill did not change the system at Regals or the racist policies that guide American culture.

Karen agreed to let me use her car, provided I would pick her up daily to return it. No problem.

Almost right away, I was asked to start going out with Steve, the window

To Be Loved

trimmer, to learn the ropes. Steve was 6-foot-6 tall people-person who store personnel liked. The window trimmer was like a jock of the chain of stores. He was on par with all of the managers. The window trimmer duties included keeping the window area free of bugs, dusting the shoes, propping them up, and displaying them at an angle in symmetrical patterns. Seasonally, I would replace the backdrop for the windows theme. Generally, I would service one or two stores daily, with my work day ending by 2 or 3 p.m.; perfect.

No doing shoe inventory, no "Can I help you?" anymore, or staying at one location all day. Boy, what a sweet job! I had to live up to expectations. I had to know the window business, as well if not better than Steve; many white boys at Regal's wanted that position.

After two weeks of providing me with on-the-job training, Steve moved up in the company's hierarchy to become a buyer. Within a week, I visited all the stores, met their managers, and tidied their window displays. A couple of the managers were cool, likable, shit-talking guys -- my kind of dudes.

It would be hot as hell in those store windows. Pedestrians outside would wave, comment, with their hands or try to tell me to move something over or give me the "A-Okay" sign.

That friendly image of whites belied their role as oppressors, terrorists, and exploiters. They seemed so polite, social, and pleasant. Except for only a few occasions, I had never met a white person who openly expressed their hatred for Blacks. In contrast, the white majority-led government and every societal

Promotion Offer: In the Suburbs

institution were oppressive or hostile to Black Americans. It was what whites did when there weren't any Blacks around that worried me. So, their smiles and courtesies couldn't be trusted to mean anything except that they could be cordial when it suited them.

Propping those new shoes on the little translucent plastic blocks was an art. The full display of shoes, boots, and sneakers reflected symmetry. Never show the instep. The heel should be raised and the toe floored. They called it marketing, and I liked it. It was communications.

As we came closer to fall, I would work like a slave in those windows, stripping store window displays and exhibits and replacing them with ones that reflected the new season. Those installments could take all day, working in each store's cramped, hot, unventilated window.

Except for one of the stores in Baltimore and the two in Prince George's County, Md., all the other 9 Regal Shoe Stores were white-managed. Sometimes, I would feel very uncomfortable in those stores. Especially in stores with no customers, when the white manager and I had to converse.

I learned that our cultures rendered different interpretations while we spoke the same language. I believe when most whites experience Black people, they seek to confirm what they have been taught about us all their lives; absent or negative, except for sports. The media and our fabricated absence in school textbooks reinforced the stereotypes and notions of Black inferiority and white supremacy.

To Be Loved

They feared that we were going to take something from them. I feared they would stand in the way of my progress. Our value system was so radically different that I felt they'd misinterpret and belittle anything personal that I would share with them, except for sports stories. I had rarely been in environments where I was the only Black person. For the first time, I felt like a minority, alienated in America.

Those managers, while polite, never invited me to hang out with them; we understood that our relationship was cordial.

The 14th and F Streets Regal, like the store in Harlem, New York, were Regal's crown jewels for style and the volume of sales. Both stores had a predominantly Black customer base, exemplifying the temples Black dollars build for others, juxtaposed against their role in our community compared to our role in their economy. We're a commodity, like shoes.

Love & Tragedy

On my way home from the Manassas, Va. Regal's, I raced down the highway, and suddenly I saw what looked like Roberta's smiling face up in the clouds. I realized then that I loved that woman and had to get us back together. I picked up Karen from work. She dropped me off. I called Roberta and invited her and Kwanza to my apartment for dinner.

When I saw her and Kwanza, it was magical. That was where I belonged. I was going to make that evening special. We had dinner and listened to records like "Got to Give It Up," by Marvin Gaye, "Stayin' Alive," by the Bee Gees, "Boogie Nights," by Heatwave" and "(Every Time I Turn Around) Back in Love Again," by LTD. I beat some musical sticks together to the rhythm of the music and the joy in my heart. The three of us danced almost in a frenzy of joy, celebrating our union, when Roberta stopped and began to cry.

I stopped playing with the sticks. "What's wrong, I asked

"There's something I've got to tell you," She cried.

I turned down the music and inadvertently bumped the needle across the record, a fitting departure from the love high I was on.

"I've been to bed with someone else," she cried as she sat down, with two-year-old Kwanza still rocking and oblivious to adult tribulations.

My stomach began to tighten. I felt like I was shot in the heart with memories of the last girl I loved, Pat, and her dallying around. If Roberta was

To Be Loved

dumb enough to do that, she should have been smart enough not to have told me. Now, I knew she had betrayed me. Yes, we broke up three weeks ago. Shouldn't there have been a grace period? There was still a chance we would get back together, and she's gone and gotten intimate with someone else already; while accusing me. I couldn't forgive that shit! Besides, I expected her to have more restraint, especially given how she would tell me 'no' when we were in love. I was feeling too good about her and our family getting back together.

"What happened?" I asked as I sat down beside her.

She sobbed. Her once charming, Afrocentric-pretty face was one of pity, no less than Step 'n' Fetchit or some other damn fool. She had been hitching a ride to work with a girlfriend who would meet at her house and began sobbing. Sometimes the girl's boyfriend, the driver, would arrive early and wait for his girlfriend. Instead of Roberta having him stay outside in his car, she invited him in; one thing led to another, and eventually, she stooped so low as to fuck her girlfriend's boyfriend. Where was Kwanza when this shit occurred, I wondered.

See, she can tell me "No," to sex. Fuck that! I don't have to take that. I could never trust her again. It was over. I was shattered. She might as well have left my apartment; she did; so much for a nice dinner at home with the one you love.

I grieved for weeks, wondering if I should forgive her, asking everybody for the advice. I was so troubled; I even asked white managers what they would do. Almost everybody said I should forgive her. I couldn't. After a few weeks

Love & Tragedy

of drying out, I started healing by getting into Karen.

After doing window treatments somewhere totally sterile, it was great to hit the Baltimore Washington Parkway South in her 1968 Lincoln Continental at 80 m.p.h. until I arrived in the city downtown to pick up Karen. We'd hang out and ball for the rest of the evening.

To Be Loved

Holiday at Take It Easy Ranch

Friday, July 1, 1977, Karen and I packed up the Lincoln with a weekend of clothes and picnic food and drove to St. Mary's County, Maryland, to the big 50 acres, "Take It Easy Ranch," for a weekend of R & B concerts. There were tens of thousands of people, cars, vans, motorcycles, Winnebagoes, lawn chairs, picnics everywhere, campfires at night, and mass bathing showers. It was wonderful to run into friends and see the multitude of styles, attitudes, rhythms, and vibes when Black people come together. I could see and feel the power of our unity, the way we dressed, from the latest fashions and blends of colors, all appearing bright and colorful, complementing our full spectrum of skin hues.

We were sitting on lawn furniture, talking and cooling it in the woods, when word would travel that the *Brothers Johnson* would perform at one of the two concert stages.

The *Brothers Johnson* was called "Thunder Thumbs" and "Lightning Licks." They showed ease and skill when they played the base lead and lead guitars. Their musical duos were about love and happiness -- soft, rich, happy vocals of the seventy's music fame. Later Roy Ayers and Lou Rawls would perform, and, man, it was one party after another, the whole weekend.

***

Later, Roberta wanted to talk. We met. I told her what had to be said. I couldn't forgive her for cheating, especially with her girlfriend's boyfriend. Ugh! She cried and lunged at my face with her nails. I threw my arms up in shock, and her fingernails dug in and clawed my arms. She assaulted me for breaking up with her for cheating on me; go figure. I turned and walked away. Breaking up was always hard to do. But it had to be done.

For years, Roberta would seek revenge for any hurt feelings she suffered from our breakup through her callous treatment of both Kwanza and me.

***

After steadying my aim and making accomplishments for four years in counseling, both in college and work, things began to come together. By 25, I felt like I was coming into my own, or better, taking control of my destiny. Life wasn't perfect. But, I had a job. I was recognized at work and school, which enhanced my self-esteem. I could see I had a bright future. The manic depression episodes were lessening further apart. I was misled, but I wasn't a criminal. I was much more than that, and I was proving it. College was fun, pure, and simple.

White supremacy for me was always threatening; I was always fearful that my commitment to fighting racism might get me in trouble, perhaps even fired.

The average FCC student was like me, around age 25-27, who had a family and one or more jobs, aiming to triumph through their dreams and hard work. It was in an inspiring environment. I felt challenged by each class to learn all I could and would earn "A"s, especially in the communications and literary courses, from interpersonal to public speaking, advertising, logic, and philosophy.

To Be Loved

Each semester presented an opportunity to learn to empower and enrich my expertise -- man, I was in a zone!

Working for the Government, Again

I would soon pursue the Start phase of the Cooperative Education program, the internship. Back in the government, I recalled just six years earlier GAO's plantation culture, and I dreaded rejoining it.

While working at the U.S. Department of Health, Education, and Welfare, I would get hands-on experience in the premium Office of the Assistant Secretary for Public Affairs. Outside of work, I also planned to pursue my still-emerging writing skills. I tinkered with writing prose and read them to my friends for inspiration.

To Be Loved

GENIUS

Genius is the one

Who senses the most

And acts on it.

POTENTIAL

I read this morning's paper.

It heralded a guy

Who had done something great.

He has talent, I thought.

I closed the paper and went out to work.

Everybody likes to do one thing better than another.

Therein, lies the potential of our talent.

Everybody Has talent.

But it is not emerged until it is recognized

And developed by you, individual.

Make time for and do the things you like most and

Surely you will notice your talent, too.

Everybody has talent.

If you don't work your potentials,

You will not notice your talent.

If you work your potentials,

Working for the Government, Again

You'll exercise the Godly creator in you.

SELF-INVENTORY

We have to be constantly mindful

Of what resources we have,

So we will know what we need

To get what we want.

DESTINY

Where do you want to go in life?

You have a destiny.

You're going somewhere in life;

One life to choose and accomplish your destiny

Oh yeah, you select your destiny.

All perception is selective.

Probe your step

As you walk down Fulfillingness Street.

Be selective...every step will take you

Closer to your destiny, or further away from it.

No choice is a choice.

You decide where in life you will go and when

Your life will take you wherever you will go.

How often do you ask yourself: Where in life do

You want to go? Where are you going? Where will you be

To Be Loved

Five years from now?

You decide.

CAUSE I LOVE YOU, FUTURE

I love you,

'Cause I am you, but

I have to leave you, Ghetto.

I don't know where I will go

'Cause the future don't know, but

That's where I'm headed.

***

By sticking to my goals and building on them, I had created many options and, more importantly, a future with bright prospects. Rather than waiting or wishing for an opportunity, I believe you create an opportunity by preparing for it.

***

During the fall semester in 1977, I met with the LPCP coordinator at FCC, Mr. White. Although approachable, a slim brother with glasses, and a big afro, always seemed remote, indifferent. I was a junior and inquired about my eligibility for the internship. He was about to resign and would be replaced by Ms. Arias, a very patient, sweet, enthusiastic program coordinator.

"Yeah, we're recommending you. There should be some openings coming up in October. Would you be interested?"

Working for the Government, Again

"Hell, yeah, let's do it. Great! That's what I have been looking forward to."

***

Ms. Arias made an appointment for me to be interviewed at HEW on Independence Avenue, Southwest, at the foot of Capitol Hill. HEW's building conjured the spirit of GAO's plantation; too many similarities. The building had wide corridors and big automatic elevators. Whites were in control. Blacks kept powerless at whites' whim. Six years after I had left the government, few Blacks were now graded beyond the GS-7 level, including a token sampling in management.

Management still appeared to be 99 percent white and male. However, that ratio was changing slowly. A very jovial, dapper-dressed, suited Brother who, like Mr. White, was ready to leave the Cooperative Education program, too, interviewed me. He seemed polished and smooth. He would arrange my interview for the internship.

He sent me to Melinda Blain, the administrative officer for the Office of the Assistant Secretary for Public Affairs. In explaining my background and goals to her, I said that the offense happened when I was 19 and out of control and that I was then 25 and in control.

I got the internship. I wanted it, even though I was a little leery.

To Be Loved

The Green Sheet

Vincent was a short, pecan-brown, cherubic Brother who smoked frequently and managed the Green Sheet's production. Often called a (news) clip sheet, the Green Sheet was a compilation of news and editorials clipped from a broad sample of the nation's top white print media, which impacted the mission of Health, Education, and Welfare. A news digest is a vehicle that senior staff in almost all federal departments use to monitor and influence their agency's presence in the white print media. Its distribution is limited to senior staff, members of the White House, and Congress.

Work began at 6 a.m., reading 11 top newspapers, including regional clippings, Wire Section, and Daybook (Calendar), then assembled, reproduced, and on Secretary Joseph Califano Jr. and his senior staff's desk by 8 a.m.

Much of the department's work was putting out media fires, giving speeches, and granting interviews to advance the Administration's positions and manage the media's perception of the organization. The Secretary and staff would have to spend precious time daily reading all of the papers before they started their day, or their day could be constantly interrupted by revelations in the media. So, they would have people like us begin each workday early to monitor the representative print media, excerpt the articles of particular interest to the department, arrange them in order of worthiness, and paste them down into a five-sectioned, 8 x 11 magazine, lending to portability. That way, by the time senior departmental staff would have their 8:30 a.m. meetings, they would have already

The Green Sheet

had an opportunity to go straight to the critical stuff --right up front-- along with all the other news they needed to know.

At work, my duties involved monitoring a cross-section of the nation's print media, including the *Wall Street Journal*, New *York Times*, *Washington Post*, and Washington *Times*, etc., and magazines like *Newsweek*, *Time*, *U.S. News and World Report*,

BusinessWeek, *Nation*, and *National Journal*, etc. Having the opportunity to read the work of talented writers was a treasure trove for an aspiring writer. I also learned that reading one writer's version of a story hardly tells the whole story. One would have to read at least three versions of the same story to get closer to the entire story.

I also monitored news clips sent from the department's ten regional offices. Just as importantly, I noticed more of the racial subtleties of the print media that profoundly impacted the image of people they write about and how others perceive them, how they perceive themselves, and how they respond to one another. The white media are Eurocentric. Many Black people subscribe to Eurocentric media with high expectations of objective news coverage, including our news, and we get misrepresented almost all the time.

After suspecting the negative pattern, I surveyed the newspapers I read at work. I found that white coverage of the Black community was usually negative or insignificant, placed subordinate to other news, in the back pages or sections of the papers, mainly in the metro section. The media's portrayal of Black people helped comfort racists in the workplace, housing, cultural institutions, and education throughout society. The white media industry, including its subgenres, maintain a constant lynching of the Black public character in America. On the editorial pages, Eurocentric views about everything are dallied around like ping pong balls, leaving little room for the Afrocentric view. The white media typically rejects many of the African American counter-views. They will not print or broadcast them. The white press has Black writers to reflect Eurocentric views on issues. The Eurocentric view isn't necessarily correct, but they have might; they dominate and control public communications.

People follow the information they consume, assuming certain things about the subject and acting accordingly. Before establishing a meaningful relationship with anyone outside our national community, Black people generally have to disprove all that harmful disinformation the white media has fed them.

The problem is not only the white media's racial supremacist slant but that it goes almost unanswered by the Black or other rational-thinking white communities. If Blacks had a more robust media that could counter white supremacy propaganda, we could leave it up to the public to decide. But, their viewpoint is given credibility by its predominance and that it is broadcast or published to the broadest audience. At the same time, the African American counter-view is disseminated to a much smaller audience.

Near his retirement, Vincent was paid at the rate of a GS-7. He had trained and supervised Rudy, a student intern from Howard University, and I to

The Green Sheet

put together the daily front section of the Green Sheet. We also selected and arranged clips from HEW's ten regional offices and assigned them to three "Stay-In-Schoolers" to pastedown.

One of them, Roberta Harris, I found very attractive, but at 17, she was much too young for me. Roberta was packed on a slim frame. Most young girls come to their first jobs giddy like they're in high school. Roberta hardly smiled. She had an attitude.

'Such a little thing,' I used to think, but she carried herself like she dared anyone to challenge her. Despite her 'baddd' attitude, it was apparent that she was showing more shyness and lack of familiarity with the environment; funny how we see people. Underneath, she was among the giddiest, most charming girls I had ever met. I wanted her. But, damn, she was so much younger than I. I settled for being a big brother-type friend to her, taking her around to meet people and offering to teach her how to drive my new 1978 Chevrolet Chevette. She began to like me just as well, despite our age difference. Occasionally, I'd tell her that if I had the chance, "I'd take you to the moon and back." She'd slip me a quip, like, "I've already been to the moon. I don't think you got the equipment to take me to Mars." Or, she'd say, "You're too old, and I'm too young, and that's that." Then, we'd both burst out laughing.

In 1977, six months after she began working at the U.S. Department of Health, Education, and Welfare, Roberta graduated from high school and found a job at the U.S. Department of Justice. Damn, I would miss her. But we would call

To Be Loved

one another occasionally over the years.

***

The White House had demanded integration at federal agencies. President Jimmy Carter appointed Eileen Shanahan as Secretary Califano's assistant for public affairs. We, interns, were being used to bulk up the minority staff quota among the predominantly white male professionals. Moses Newson, the former senior editor for the *Afro-American* chain of newspapers, was the lone Black professional hired. I told him that I once sold the Afro-American newspaper. It didn't occur to me then, but all of us students were relative chicks surrounded by seasoned veterans, foxes, and wolves. We had no power. You can't integrate with power unless you have power. We were assimilating.

In addition to producing the *Green Sheet*, I would assist Ms. Ellen Hoffman, editor of *HEW Now*, the department's newsletter. I assisted in the full newsletter production, from interviewing and writing HEW employees' profiles to writing headlines and photo captions and designing the newsletter's layout. Learning communication skills that I hoped to use to empower myself was so fulfilling.

Ms. Hoffman exemplified wanting to know everything about whatever you are involved in and leaving nothing to chance. When things didn't go right, she didn't simply dismiss it as a coincidence; she wanted to understand why they happened.

Once when I was asking her questions and soaking her brain, she turned

The Green Sheet

on me and asked, "What do you want from me?" I thought that meant for me to back off; she was feeling job insecurity.

"I just want to learn."

I was enjoying every moment of learning from both work and college. Imagine learning at work that reinforces what I was learning at school and vice versa; I was in heaven.

My first written assignment at work came in November 1977. As opportunity would have it, Hoffman became ill and had to take a leave of absence before the scheduled dedication of the HEW headquarters building to honor the late Sen. Hubert H. Humphrey, the then cancer-stricken, former vice president, and 1968 presidential candidate, and champion of liberal causes.

By default, I covered the historical event. There was no way I would have gotten the assignment if Helen was not sick. This was a national event. The office trusted me to attend and capture the Who, What, When, Where, Why, and How of the event in my hand-scribbled notes, return, regurgitate them, and write the official historical article that would grace the *HEW Now* newsletter's front page, read by tens of thousands of employees. It was a daunting responsibility for me. But I would aim to write the story of my life.

I witnessed the dedication from the privileged press section amid television news anchors and other journalists from around the country. These were my colleagues, I pondered.

They looked rich and in control. We were reporters. It sounded a lot

To Be Loved

better than "ex-convict."

My report, "South Portal Renamed Humphrey; Senator Honored at Dedication Ceremony," led the next issue of the *HEW Now* newsletter, which included a photograph of Sen. Humphrey unveiling the commemorative plaque that would be mounted in the Great Hall of the building. My editor, Ms. Hoffman, included as my byline: "*This article was written by Ronald Steele, who is a Project Start intern recently assigned to the Office of the Assistant Secretary for Public Affairs,*" alerting everyone who cared to look up Project Start that I was an ex-convict. I guess she wanted to let everyone know how generous our government was that they would give a black ex-convict another chance, which was true, and I was grateful, so the publicity was a small price to pay, just so unnecessary.

I had learned to resolve a calculated reply that benefited me quietly.

Further, in the corporate environment, "attitude," which some famously confuse with power, is viewed as inappropriate, beneath corporate culture; it's a convenient way for white folks to dismiss Blacks and justify their discrimination with: He's got an attitude problem!

I was grateful that HEW gave me a chance, exemplifying its mission as the nation's most prominent social services agency. I felt redeemed for all the crap I had to endure in trying to get a job in the government when I first got out of prison. Things happen for a reason, usually a good reason, even though, at the time, you can't tell. But this act reminded me that, like in prison, a little paranoia around whites was healthy.

The Green Sheet

The Civil Rights Movement ushered African Americans into the mainstream in unprecedented numbers. But white supremacy kept us at the door; so much for "integration." Indeed, I would have to fight for everything I wanted at HEW, things that the white boys took for granted, including the job. I had always been a fighter, always able to handle rejection that would surely await me. The primary point was not the price that I had to pay to have what I wanted in life but having the tenaciousness to obtain what I wanted despite the price; I wasn't gonna be denied.

Chapter IX

Love of Self: Ain't Gonna Be Denied

What mattered most during my college years was the invaluable and transformative experience FCC offered. It was a place that offered me an exceptional education, full of challenges and rewards, and I fell in love with FCC instantly. I studied Philosophy, Public Speaking, Radio, TV-Film, Journalism, and more, fueled my passion for communications and satisfied my thirst for knowledge. College was not only an academic endeavor; it was my personal laboratory, where I could put into practice all the self-determination and positive thinking methodologies, I had studied to rebuild my self-esteem. It was a platform where I could not only acquire knowledge but also learn vital life skills and effective time management.

I realized the profound impact of words in shaping our thoughts and actions. I learned that committing to a task and following through with action generated a surge of self-confidence, like an endorphin charge. On the other hand, failing to act upon commitments only reinforced self-doubt and undermined my self-esteem. I discovered that sometimes our inner selves subtly guide us toward what we truly desire or need, and it is crucial to trust those instincts and follow through with action. By doing what I said I would, I freed up mental space, allowing me to fully concentrate on resolving challenges. Neglected tasks, on the

Love of Self: Ain't Gonna Be Denied

other hand, accumulated and cluttered my mind, making it difficult to handle even the simplest matters.

Developing effective study habits became a cornerstone of my college experience. I took thorough notes, diligently; asked as many questions as was necessary to grasp the subject matter, and reviewed my notes before bedtime. Whenever possible, I would read the upcoming chapter before class, fighting drowsiness driven by my academic and job workload. As a result of my dedication and enthusiasm, I consistently achieved top grades, aiming not only for As s but also aiming for my personal best in everything.

What made the difference between my college success, marked by As and Bs, and my struggles in grade school, where Cs and Ds prevailed, was a shift in attitude, purpose, and self-confidence. It took adversity and maturity for me to grasp this realization. I couldn't help but think about my fellow Brothers and Sisters, who possessed immense potential and talent, but due to societal pressures and their own acquiescence, never recognized their true worth. Society had played a defining role in their lives, suppressing their abilities and self-esteem. I had turned an unjust prison sentence into a catalyst for my self-discovery and unwavering self-determination. It was in those challenging circumstances that I became the captain of my ship and the master of my destiny.

I firmly believed that if I dedicated myself to juggling full-time work and full-time college, it would prepare me for even greater responsibilities in the real world after graduation. College reinforced a notion that I had learned in

To Be Loved

childhood: when I applied myself and strived for excellence, it was transformative: it attracted the positive attention I craved. This principle applied just as vigorously to academics as it did to all other aspect of my life. Eventually, my unwavering belief in and pursuit of excellence propelled me to a higher level of both achievement and self-confidence.

***

In my English class, I had the privilege of immersing myself in the works of many great Black authors, including Chester Higgins, James Baldwin, Richard Wright, and more. Their immense talent as writers inspired me, but I couldn't help but feel a sense of despair from their stories. When we were assigned to write a paper, I chose the provocative thesis: "Why Black Literature Depresses Me."

While these literary works were masterfully written, I found that the protagonists, often hesitant to confront white supremacy directly, would self-destruct under the weight of racism. In the end, the hero would either perish or end up in a pitiful state. I used the assigned books to substantiate my thesis, highlighting the recurring pattern of defeat and despair.

Upon examining literature by and about white individuals, I noticed a stark contrast. In these stories, the hero consistently triumphed, sometimes unrealistically so, and a positive out was expected. If literature is meant to inspire rather than depress, I strongly believed that the protagonist, the hero, must overcome seemingly insurmountable adversity.

Love of Self: Ain't Gonna Be Denied

Furthermore, I had reservations about the language used by some Black writers. I felt that even when attempting to convey positivity, they often expressed a negative self-image. For instance, in one of James Baldwin's essays, he referred to himself as "a fly in milk," metaphorically portraying his Black identity as something distasteful. but the author viewed his metaphor from the perspective of racists, rather than from Baldwin's Black viewpoint. It seemed to perpetuate a negative portrayal of his character's courageous pursuit of a quality education, while overlooking the hostile environment created by white individuals. If the metaphor were reversed, portraying Black as positive and white as unfavorable, it could have presented a more empowering perspective to Black readers, like a plant emerging through a frigid, desolate carpet of snow, where Blacks represented by a plant that is supposed to be there and against the persistence of snow, which may melt away soon. My paper received an "A."

The announcement of FCC becoming a university and the relocation of the Washington Technical Institute (WTI) to the main campus stirred strong emotions among students. We vehemently demanded that the new university maintain its downtown anchor at the former D.C. Public Library on Mt. Vernon Place, ensuring accessibility for inner-city D.C. students. There was a genuine fear that the merger would lead to a majority-white institution, and the relocation of the campus away from the inner city only intensified these concerns. In true '60s style, the Student Government Association organized a rally where hundreds

To Be Loved

of students marched from the hopeful main campus site at Mt. Vernon to FCC's location at 2nd and D Streets, N.W., voicing our demands.

Ultimately, FCC, WTI, and the District of Columbia Teachers College merged to form the University of the District of Columbia (UDC). The most modern campus of the three, WTI, became the university's main campus in upper Northwest Washington, consolidating future classes in a single location. Little did we know that D.C. and its university would later be gentrified.

During my time at college, I learned the art of reporting an event by capturing the essential "who, what, when, where, how, and sometimes why" details while embracing brevity and conciseness. I also honed my skills in interviewing and writing in the pyramid style of journalism, where the most significant facts are reported first, gradually descending to less essential details. This methodology extended to crafting each sentence and paragraph, prioritizing words or sentences based on their weight and relevance.

As a news editor, reporter, and photographer for the student newspaper, Free Voice, I had the opportunity to explore the power of shaping narratives. I traded the title of news editor for features editor in the following semester, further expanding my editorial responsibilities.

The president's office became my beat, the pinnacle assignment at the paper, during the historical transition from FCC and DCTC to UDC. In October 1978, I wrote an article titled "President Jimmy Carter Hails UDC." President Carter tipped his hat to incoming leadership of Lyle C. Carter, president of the

Love of Self: Ain't Gonna Be Denied

nation's first land-grant university. He addressed the challenges and his vision of consolidating the three institutions. It was a privilege to witness and report on this transformative period, reminding me how far I had come from my aim less days as a juvenile delinquent to a professional on the rise.

I also had the opportunity to interview the outgoing presidents of FCC and DCTC, including Wendell P. Russell, for the Free Voice. In December 1978, I wrote an article titled "Russell Now Without Top Position," where President Russell discussed the significance of compensatory education and emphasized the importance of maintaining open admissions at UDC. He reflected on his years as president and the tremendous challenges he faced. Uncertainty loomed over his future, as he contemplated an UDC offer to become an "advanced professor." His ambivalence regarding the job offer shed light on the university's treatment of someone who had dedicated many years to leading its predecessor colleges.

A few weeks later, the Washington Post published an article titled "Courtesy Job Pays $43,950, Ex-College Head Reported 'Doing Nothing'," quoting my article from the Free Voice, which I had written. A UPI reporter, covering HHS, noticed me reproducing the article, at work, and remarked, "It shows that the Washington Post reads your school's newspaper." However, this incident exposed the racially discriminatory nature of white newspapers, more interested in exploiting controversies than recognizing Black talent. To my dismay, when I saw Dr. Russell, again, he directed a disapproving gaze at me, as if I was responsible for the Post's angle.

To Be Loved

This experience led me to a crucial realization: as a reporter, I lacked the power to effect the changes I sought through reporting alone. It is the editors who hold the final say in shaping the scope, angle, length, and prominence of an article. I did not want to become just another Black reporter for the white media. It reminded me that white racists do not abandon their discriminatory behaviors when they enter the professional fields; instead, they employ their talents to express their racism.

For far too long, we have entrusted ourselves to white individuals who may secretly harbor white supremacist views. The consequences of our naiveté and reliance on others over ourselves cannot be fully measured.

***

Daphne Northington, our journalism instructor, passionately encouraged us not to wait until graduation to seek job opportunities or gain experience. Her words resonated with me, and I embraced the idea that my internship could serve as valuable job experience.

During my internship, I delved into the multifaceted aspects of newspaper production. It became evident to me that the media wielded immense power and influence, although it could also be deceptive. I realized that the purpose of information dissemination was not solely to inform but rather to shape thoughts and actions. Reporters played a crucial role in influencing how people perceived events and issues. Beliefs, in turn, often shaped behavior.

Love of Self: Ain't Gonna Be Denied

In the white-controlled media, the image of Black people predominantly reflected a narrow and hostile perception held by another group. Daily images in the media perpetuated poisonous stereotypes, further distorting the public's perception of Black people and their treatment in society. The concept of white supremacy ran deep, rooted in the fear that the black color gene could sexually obliterate the white gene. Consequently, within white culture, black symbolized death, negativity, and inferiority. This belief was reinforced through slogans, cultural symbols, and societal associations, permeating various aspects of daily life.

However, it was essential to recognize that the culture associated with Black identity carried its own deep significance. Black represented Africa, oil, the beginning, the Black Madonna, the original Jews, the first people, the first highly developed civilization, and power centers. These positive connotations clashed with the negative associations imposed by white culture.

Americans have a biased cultural proclivity to negate Black people, no matter what good we do.

The image of Black people in white controlled news media reflects that proclivity. Blacks are portrayed largely as insignificant, negative or both. Editors use typeface, size, and placement of the article on a page above the fold, below it, the right side of page or left, number of page, and section to reflect relative news value, and thus, shape how it's perceived. Other considerations include the size of photo (usually head shot for Blacks), whether it's a head shot, bust shot, or full

To Be Loved

shot, whether Blacks are identified in the photo, whether posture and facial expression photographed match the story or editor's attitude towards the subject, length of story, what the article or broadcasters say and don't say --- all contribute to how an event is both presented and consequently, how it is perceived. The American culture, steeped in white supremacy, systematically stacked the deck against black people and it would likely take a miracle to level it.

***

In 1975, my family relocated once again, this time to a larger brick house. Since 1974, I had been living on my own, and I would never live with my siblings again. Nonetheless, visiting my mother's home provided a sanctuary for me. It was a place where I could connect with my family, engage in conversations, and bond with my nieces and nephews, whom I took great pleasure in mentoring. Paula, the daughter of Paulette, Kenny, the son of Yvonne, and Ngina were around the same age. Similarly, Paul, the son of Paulette, Stacy, the son of Audrey, and Kwanza, were of similar age. My children now had cousins to play with whenever I visited. As they grew older, I often took Kwanza out and included my nieces and nephews, creating meaningful memories and providing them with a fatherly love that I had longed for in my own childhood. These interactions allowed me to make a positive impact on their lives.

During the Christmas season of 1979, I eagerly visited my mother's house. I still held onto the hope of earning my mother's and siblings' love, which eluded us during our childhood. Although my attempts to persuade them to

Love of Self: Ain't Gonna Be Denied

modify their old ways and values were met with ridicule, I had learned to accept them for who they were. That Christmas, I arrived with my arms full of gifts for my nieces, nephews, and mother.

Ngina, who was eight years old at the time, had always been assumed to be my daughter by my family, despite my occasional doubts. As I observed Ngina playing her cousins, I couldn't help but notice a striking resemblance between her and myself. What if Ngina truly was my daughter? Regret washed over me for the pain my doubt had caused, and I made a decision to take responsibility for her, just as I had done for Kwanza. When it was time for Ngina to go home, on Christmas, I offered her a ride.

During the car ride, I mustered the words to express what I felt inside. With a hint of uncertainty, I asked Ngina if she thought we looked alike. She replied affirmatively. Then, cautiously, I asked her if she believed I was her father. Once again, she answered with a resounding "yes." Taking a deep breath, I began to share my thoughts. After all the years of uncertainty, I confessed that I was starting to believe she was indeed my daughter. I apologized for the pain caused by our misunderstanding and made a heartfelt commitment to be involved in her life from that point forward. Ngina responded with a genuine smile, expressing her happiness that we were finally going to be a family.

I took Ngina to her home and shared spoke with her mother. It was a beautiful Christmas, filled with newfound connection and a shared sense of love and belonging.

To Be Loved

Ngina, My Daughter

When I informed my four-year-old daughter, Kwanza, that she had a big sister and that they would be spending weekends together, she was filled with joy. She didn't question the details or reasons behind it; she simply embraced the idea wholeheartedly.

"When will I get to meet her?" Kwanza asked, brimming with excitement at the thought of having a "big sister." Ngina, on the other hand, was already aware of Kwanza. However, after their meeting, Ngina didn't initiate any interactions with either Kwanza or myself. She remained reserved, perhaps feeling challenged by the emotional bond between Kwanza and me, which mirrored her own emotional distance.

I contemplated the dynamics of sibling rivalry and believed that with time, Ngina would come to accept Kwanza. To encourage their bond, I would take them both to work with me on Sundays, providing an opportunity for them to play and connect. However, after around six months, Ngina was unavailable whenever I called to pick her up. Even group activities failed to draw her out of her reserved cocoon. It was as if she existed in her own world, and I had no knowledge of the experiences she had gone through during my absence. I was willing to do whatever it took to help Ngina heal from any pain caused by my absence. Friends told me that she might have blamed me for many things during those years, as influenced by her mother and other relatives.

Ngina, My Daughter

In an attempt to initiate the healing process, I asked Ngina about her feelings regarding the years when I didn't believe she was my child. She responded with a perplexed expression, saying she felt "nothing." I thought she might have been too young to delve into such introspection, but I wanted to begin the process of healing and open communication.

"Did it hurt you or cause you any pain that I wasn't there?" I inquired, hoping to encourage her to express her emotions.

Her response was a simple "no."

Realizing that she wasn't quite ready to discuss the matter, I assured her, "Well, if you ever want to talk about it with me, I will always be here, ready to listen and talk, okay?"

Ngina, seemingly uncomfortable with the subject, replied with a hesitant "okay."

***

The workplace served as the arena where Black individuals faced their white conquerors in a highly competitive setting where the latter held control. White individuals often entered the workplace equipped with superior education, experiences, and the reinforcement of racist ideologies, while we, as Black people, had often faced a nightmare of challenges or had been caught up in naivety, playing and getting into trouble. In the workplace, we had to compete and interact as if we were equally prepared, all the while striving to catch up during the intense race for success.

To Be Loved

Racism at Work

In the early mornings before most other employees arrived, there existed a network of white male public affairs officials who gathered for breakfast. During these gatherings, they exchanged office notes that solidified their power dynamics. I stumbled upon this knowledge because I would join breakfast as soon as the Green Sheet was distributed. As I arrived early, the only Black person at the table, the conversation would conveniently shift to sports.

Working in the Office of the Assistant Secretary for Public Affairs was considered a prestigious assignment within the department. To reach the Secretary's office, a writer had to work their way up. The other professional writers had spent as many years working for newspapers as I had lived, a total of 26 years, before securing a position there.

However, it became apparent that not much had changed despite the promise of progress from the Civil Rights Movement. Many Black workers had been conditioned to accept powerless and dead-end positions, making it difficult, if not impossible, to effectively fight back against discrimination. The oppressed Black community had been conditioned over generations to prioritize potential loss over potential gain when challenging discrimination.

The prevailing attitude often settled on thoughts like, "What if I lose the fight? They'll always harass me. I could lose my job; I can't afford that." In turn, they resigned themselves to the belief that things could be much worse, perpetuating a mindset that eroded the soul's defences and led to further

Racism at Work

compromises. The discrimination, coupled with the failure to confront it head-on, resulted in ramped alcoholism, mediocre careers, lifestyles, and various forms of self-depreciation.

Black and white people constantly clashed, driven by conflicting values and expectations, particularly due to the arrogant imposition of power by the latter over every Black person. To find some semblance of contentment in a hostile homeland, many Black people adjusted their aims and expectations, having been repeatedly reminded by America that even if they desired more, they were unlikely to attain it.

My generation of Black Americans, while they certainly had the desire, they had not had the experience to seize the unprecedented opportunities presented by desegregation in the 1970s. Society at large continued to resist desegregation, perceiving us as a threat, people to be used, and discarded, despite the Civil Rights Movement which outlawed discrimination.

In a surprising turn of events, Vincent, a demoralized employee who suffered from high blood pressure and other illnesses, dared to sue the office for racial discrimination. He demanded early retirement on disability, which would guarantee him 80 percent of his then income for life. It would have been embarrassing for the Administration to be sued on an issue they claimed as a symbolic achievement. An effective lawsuit could ignite a rebellion or, at the very least, shed light on other instances of discrimination throughout the department, reaching even the Immediate Office of the Secretary. Consequently, it was in their

To Be Loved

best interest to prevent potential discrimination lawsuits. Vincent warned them that he had established media contacts and would send a copy of his complaint to all of them. Negotiations ensued, and he ultimately retired on a disability pension.

Vincent's employment dispute highlighted the need for Black people to take a stand and be willing to fight, armed with knowledge of the rules of the game, including personnel rules and regulations.

***

Gary Parker, the new individual appointed to supervise the Green Sheet production, began each morning by editorializing about what he read in the white media regarding Black people. He ridiculed Andrew Young, the UN Ambassador at the time and the highest-ranking Black official in the Carter Administration. Parker criticized the Civil Rights Movement, and Rudy, the Howard University student intern, would often acquiesce'. Observing this, I questioned whether Howard University taught its students to conform rather than equipping them with the skills and the will to fight for their beliefs.

Not only did I defend both Andrew Young and the Civil Rights Movement, but I also took an offensive stance, going for the jugular. I argued that white liberals, like Parker, believed it was possible to integrate millions of African Americans into the mainstream while maintaining the status quo. This belief is impossible, I argued, pointing out that white individuals had benefited from a racist form of affirmative action. Their current wealth stemmed from exploiting African Americans and through discrimination, subjecting them to

Racism at Work

intergenerational poverty. I made it clear that Black people were still disenfranchised, a century after Emancipation, due to the continued oppression, discrimination, and exploitation perpetuated by white America. And, that in order for African Americans to have more of the pie, whites would have to have less. Parker labelled me a troublemaker, and as a result, I was reassigned from the Green Sheet staff, without a hearing. The newsletter was winding down, heading towards abolishment, which left me with limited options within the office. The office reassigned me to the Resource Center, an office media library room. The echoes of my previous work experience in the government and being pulled from the Comptroller's Office at the GAO and sent back to the. I refused to acquiesce to Parker's daily diatribes against progressive Black people.

I told Parker that it didn't matter what my duties were at the Department of Health, Education, and Welfare (HEW), considering the impending abolishment of the HEW Now newsletter. The experience gained from working on the Green Sheet didn't exactly lead to a higher paying job. However, I warned Gary that if the office interfered with my work schedule, I would file a discrimination suit. They didn't alter my schedule, but something more challenging would soon follow.

***

That December, I received a call from Jerry Williams, one of the coordinators of Project Start at HEW, regarding my eligibility to continue in the program. A six-month leave of absence without pay within 18 months of

To Be Loved

graduating from the program, to my surprise, one of the program requirements. This was potentially devastating new, as I couldn't afford to be without income for six months. It seemed like a deliberate attempt to push me out of the program.

I approached Melinda Blain, the administrative officer, hoping to find a solution. I suspected that Gary Parker had influenced her perception of me, as I often saw him in her office before my reassignment. I knew he had likely complained about dealing with a young Black ex-convict militant like myself. However, I had done nothing wrong. I knew more than he assumed, and I wasn't afraid to express my knowledge.

I asked Melinda if it was possible for the office to appoint me to a temporary job within the department while I was on leave from the program. She initially said no, and her demeanor seemed subdued, she seemed intrigued by the prospects of how I would manage without income. Perhaps she wondered if I would resort to criminal activities, again to survive.

The short notice and suspicious circumstances made me question who was behind this decision. I had come too far to quit now. I was aiming for permanent status and a promotion, and they were trying to deny me.

I went to the cooperative education program coordinator in personnel and demanded to see the regulation or rule that prevented me from being appointed to a temporary position in the vast department while on leave from one of its programs. Personnel sent me on a fruitless search from one office and person

Racism at Work

to another, consuming days of my time. Eventually, I ran out of time and had to pack up for my leave starting on December 28, 1978.

While on leave, I maintained daily contact with program officials, demanding written evidence of the supposed rule that prohibited me from being appointed to a temporary position. I received a call from Ms. Blain.

She informed me that personnel couldn't find the prohibitive rule and offered me a temporary six-month appointment while on leave from the cooperative education program. I was elated to have an income and not have to quit the program. It seemed that my conscientiousness of history had helped me thwart their scheme. I was in control of my destiny, rejecting racism.

Upon my return to work, Deputy Assistant Secretary Dupree and others in the old boy network congratulated me, though their reasons remained unclear. It was a recognition of my stand against the office's attempt to force me out of the program into a permanent position without the program's protections and benefits. By challenging the system, I had emerged victorious. However, it was evident that I had been labeled as the troublemaker at work for expressing my opinion, which didn't align with others. They wanted to control my thoughts.

Back in the Resource Center, where I had been assigned, I imagined that people wondered why I wasn't working on the Green Sheet. The reassignment felt like a public reprimand. Nevertheless, what mattered to me was my impending graduation and staying on track with my goals.

To Be Loved

In the Resource Center, I worked with Brandy Hall, a white woman who was a friend of Blain's. Brandy was friendly but disorganized, with papers scattered everywhere. I took the opportunity to reorganize the office during her absence, brightening up the space and bringing order to it. Officials and co-workers noticed the transformation and spent time engaging with me, countering the negative image that had been associated with me.

New Style Best Friends

Robert Harris, my friend who resided in Mt. Vernon, Virginia, had recently separated from his partner and moved into a new apartment. Whenever I spent time with Robert, I felt empowered. We shared a similar background, although he was fortunate to have both parents present. Despite his exceptional talents, he often felt alienated within his own family, never receiving the attention he deserved. However, we both had a shared belief that nothing could impede our progress toward achieving our goals.

Robert, being more sophisticated and experienced, always seemed to be a few steps ahead of me. He became a symbol of what I aspired to be—a person capable of effortlessly navigating any environment and accomplishing anything goal.

His apartment was a testament to his dedication and passion for excellence. Adorned with handmade wool rugs, antique furniture, and captivating pop art on the walls, it showcased his commitment to doing things exceptionally well. Robert's state-of-the-art stereo component system filled the room with mesmerizing jazz music, which we often enjoyed together. His culinary skills were unparalleled, and he had an uncanny ability to repair almost anything electrical. However, he wasn't interested in the typical partying, dancing, or indulging in substances. Our conversations would often revolve around various topics, accompanied by the smooth sounds of jazz resonating in the background.

To Be Loved

One day, while relaxing at Robert's apartment, we received a phone call. He informed me that a girl he had met in the apartment complex was coming over and bringing a friend.

The two ladies arrived shortly after. Robert's acquaintance was tall and friendly, but not particularly attractive. On the other hand, her friend, Tracy, caught my attention. Tracy exuded a soft, caring demeanor and possessed a freckled-faced, innocent charm. Her simplicity and a hint of a southern accent added to her allure. We spent the evening together in the living room while Robert and his companion retreated to the bedroom. With each passing minute, I found myself growing more infatuated with her. The ambiance set the stage, and I couldn't resist kissing her, a tender moment interrupted by her gentle words, "Not here. Let's go to my place."

We ventured to her apartment complex. The night unfolded with passionate lovemaking, but as dawn approached, I realized I didn't want to leave her side. Tracy had captivated me with her softness, gentleness, and pure innocence. I yearned to know her better and establish a deeper connection. She possessed a remarkable ability to engage in meaningful conversations, displaying intelligence and a refreshingly plain and simple nature. I genuinely liked her, and from that moment on, we began dating, embarking on a journey filled with joy and shared experiences.

One of the highlights of our relationship was our trips to West Virginia, where Tracy's parents and family resided. They embodied a typical traditional

New Style Best Friends

southern country family, living on farmland, with their children aspiring to pursue urban life and employment in the north. It felt like I had found the genuine country girl that Mitchell and I had written to each other about while I was in Hagerstown. Through these experiences, I realized that getting what you want, primarily revolves around understanding your desires and actively pursuing them.

To Be Loved

Controlling Destiny

Meanwhile, I enrolled in a required advertising course for my communications degree. One of our assignments was to research an advertising agency and prepare a report on its structure and business practices.

In March 1980, I selected First Georgetown Advertising from the Yellow Pages and scheduled an interview with the owner, Hank Crawford. To my pleasant surprise, Hank turned out to be an African American brother. With a deep, resonant voice and a down-to-earth demeanor, Hank exuded confidence and charm. He effortlessly presented himself, leaving a lasting impression. During the interview, he unexpectedly shifted the dynamic and began asking me questions about my major, my studies, and future plans after graduation. As the conversation concluded, he offered, "How would you like to come work for me after you graduate?"

Eager to seize the opportunity and gain exposure in the advertising industry, I enthusiastically responded, "Part-time?" to which Hank replied, "Sure." I couldn't contain my excitement as this presented a potential career path in advertising. Graduating from college opened up broader options in the mainstream for me. I had no desire to work for white newspapers, and Black newspapers didn't offer the desired level of financial compensation.

In another aspect of my life, I unexpectedly ran into Robert Massey, an old acquaintance from the neighborhood. He embodied the type of friendships I wanted to foster—successful individuals from our community. Robert and I had

Controlling Destiny

lived around the corner from each other on Sheriff Road and even took a few classes together at Spingarn High School.

Reflecting on the past, I reminded Robert of his memorable appearance during our graduation year in 1970, of him wearing a dashiki, a large Afro, stylish sunglasses, beige Levi flair jeans, sandals, and a red, black, and green bracelet—a stark contrast to the conservative, starched-shirt interviews he pursued. We shared a laugh, reminiscing about the audacity of our youth and the job market's response to our culture.

Curious about his post-graduation experiences, I inquired, "Did you get a job?" Robert responded with a resounding "Hell, no!" We laughed together, recognizing that our paths had been challenging. Just like me, Robert grappled with the same demands and possessed an unwavering determination to conquer any obstacles in our way. Unlike the valley boy jocks living nearby, Robert had never succumbed to a drug habit or faced criminal convictions. Throughout his journey, he had worked as a U.S. postal letter carrier, been involved with the Black Panther movement, and embraced the Nation of Islam. In fact, he had legally changed his name to Kashaka O. Keita, severing ties with his "slave" name.

Robert, or rather Kashaka, and I were a natural pair. We hailed from the same neighborhood and shared similar family backgrounds, having been propelled outward by the absence of parental guidance in our lives. Despite the challenges, Kashaka had overcome, proudly raising a beautiful daughter named Imani from a previous relationship. Like Kwanza, my daughter, Kashaka spent

To Be Loved

every other weekend with his child. His residence in Fairmont Heights, just a few blocks from my own on Eastern Avenue, made it convenient for us to spend time together.

Kashaka possessed excellent communication skills and was an entrepreneur at heart. He passionately extolled the virtues of self-employment, often emphasizing the significance of land ownership as a requirement for revolution. He enjoyed playing tennis and shared my passion for photography. In fact, he had set up a darkroom in the basement of his house, where he pursued a home correspondence course in photography. Intrigued by his endeavor, Kashaka invited me to join him, knowing I was also taking a photography course at school. While Kashaka displayed immense potential and an innate understanding of what it took to succeed, he sometimes lacked the motivation to see his endeavors through to completion. This is where I came in—I thrived on taking immediate action and getting things done right away.

Together, we explored the photography world, refining our skills and nurturing our shared interest. We spent countless hours developing our tennis game, capturing images of nature, celebrities, and aspiring models, and immersing ourselves in the darkroom, witnessing our black and white prints materialize under the red photo development light. Kashaka, ever animated and full of laughter, taught me various darkroom techniques.

This marked the beginning of our budding photography business, reminiscent of my previous partnership with Rufus a few years ago. However, this

Controlling Destiny

time, we approached it with a heightened sense of seriousness and professionalism. We photographed weddings, ceremonies, and parties, immersing ourselves in this endeavor with renewed dedication and determination.

To Be Loved

Relationships' Emotional Challenges

My experiences with relationships with women continued to be challenging even as I entered adulthood, despite improvements in other areas of my life.

Roberta Hall and I were both scheduled to graduate in May 1980, but her decision to have a baby caused a setback in her graduation date. However, she discovered that by going on welfare, she could graduate on time. So, that's what she did. It struck me that females are conditioned and socialized from a young age to aspire to motherhood, just as boys are encouraged to focus on cars and guns through the toys they are given. It's no wonder that as teenagers, boys become infatuated with cars and guns, while girls start yearning for babies, wanting to fulfil what they have been conditioned for—the real thing—now that they have reached adulthood.

But, the liberation movement of the 60s also saw a liberation of young teens electing to have a child to have someone to love, to have someone to love them, and or to avoid entering the mainstream.

At that time, I was burdened with two court-arranged child support bills that I struggled to manage. While the court showed no concern for my predicament, Tracy, my girlfriend at the time, offered to help me pay one of the bills until I could manage both. Although I appreciated her support, I wasn't entirely comfortable with someone else paying my child support. Eventually, I found a way to continue making the payments

Relationships' Emotional Challenges

myself. However, Tracy's gesture highlighted her kindness and willingness to assist me during a difficult time.

I was aware that Tracy was deeply infatuated with me. Coming from a rural background, she had never been involved with someone like me before. I couldn't imagine ever having to fight or argue with her; she had never done anything wrong to me. Tracy possessed a clean, caring, and responsible nature, and I believed she would have made a wonderful wife.

One evening, Tracy revealed that she was pregnant. Having a baby held immense significance for her, especially considering that her sister was unable to conceive and had resorted to adoption. I knew our relationship was about to end, and I urged Tracy to consider having an abortion. Although the idea pained her, she reluctantly agreed. At that time, it didn't occur to me that I should accompany her to provide support and comfort. She didn't ask me to go, nor did she ask me for financial assistance. Naively, I believed that abortion, like birth control, was a simple and private procedure for women. It would take years for me to realize the potential trauma associated with abortion. On the way home from the clinic, during a heavy rainstorm, Tracy called me to inform me that the procedure been completed and while driving home she had been in a car accident.

Filled with concern, I anxiously asked, "Are you hurt?"

She responded, "No, I'm just shaken up pretty badly."

To Be Loved

"I'm sorry," I offered.

Not long after that eventful episode, I ended my relationship with Tracy. I knew it would deeply affect her for some time, and it hurt me as well. I was becoming bored with a relationship that didn't align with my dreams, so I had to let it go to prepare myself for the kind of relationship I believed I truly wanted. Surprisingly, Tracy didn't hold it against me, and over the years, we managed to stay in touch. Eventually, it became evident that we would not reconcile. Tracy went on to marry and have children, and I was genuinely happy for her.

I often boasted about my mastery of photo composition, while Kashaka excelled in the technical aspects of photography. Kashaka would diligently follow the instructions in books and videos before adapting the process to suit his needs. Together, we participated in numerous civil rights marches and demonstrations, capturing images of celebrities such as Muhammad Ali, Sugar Ray Leonard, Muhammad Ali, Stevie Wonder, Bill Cosby, Dizzy Gillespie, Jesse Jackson's presidential campaigns, Shirley Chisolm, Minister Farrakhan, and many more.

On a different occasion in 1980, Kashaka, and I, along with our girlfriends, attended an Ebony Fashion Fair at the Kennedy Center for the Performing Arts. A Washington Post photographer singled out my girlfriend and I. The photo was featured in the Post's article covering the

Relationships' Emotional Challenges

event on October 20, 1980. For a brief moment, I experienced a taste of local celebrity, with everyone congratulating my girlfriend and I.

Kashaka and I continued to develop tennis. As we played together, our skills improved in parallel until Kashaka, being meticulous in his approach, had progressed beyond me. He diligently studied books and videos to refine his game, which led him to complain during our matches, saying things like, "I don't know why I even play you! You don't read any tennis books or watch the videotapes. Playing you messes up my game!" Realizing he was right; I began watching Vic Braden's "How to Play Tennis" tapes and delving into tennis books. As I studied the game more seriously, Kashaka soon found himself unable to defeat me again.

During another photography outing, Kashaka and I photographed models, and one of them stood out as exceptionally attractive. She had an alluring presence, standing at five feet four inches tall with an enticing figure. Laura, a charming and cheerful Southern belle, quickly captivated me. Her demeanor, walk, and way of talking were incredibly appealing. She embodied the ideal of the women sung about in those Temptations songs; she was "my girl." We started our relationship as lovers, and she became a source of inspiration for some of my best work photographing models. We explored downtown areas, monuments, and pursued our crafts together. I adored that woman, and my family shared the sentiment.

To Be Loved

The Green Sheet: Managing Editor

At HEW (Department of Health, Education, and Welfare), my former supervisor Gary Parker and Rudy were soon offered more significant positions within the department. In November 1979, management approached me with an opportunity to return to the Green Sheet, this time as the managing editor. Everything seemed to be falling into place for me, a testament to the idea that opportunity comes to those who are prepared. My previous performance on the Green Sheet had never been an issue, and they clearly recognized that. Otherwise, they wouldn't have extended the offer.

However, the office abruptly removed me from the Green Sheet for reasons that seemed insignificant. So, when they finally realized they needed me to manage it, I decided to play hardball. At first, I told them I needed time to consider their offer. The best time to negotiate for what I wanted was when they needed something from me. A couple of days later, I approached Parker and informed him that I would only accept the job if they guaranteed me a raise. I expressed my dissatisfaction, stating, "I'm supposed to be excited that they want to use me again? They would have to guarantee me more money and job security if I were to accept the position."

Meanwhile, I sought advice from Robert and a friend in personnel. They agreed that I should accept the job and use it as leverage to secure a

The Green Sheet: Managing Editor

permanent position after graduating from college. Gary conveyed my message to the office management, and we scheduled a meeting.

During the meeting, the supervisor said to me, "We made a good faith offer, but we're not certain how you will work out in the long term." the official hinted, in other words, at the possibility of terminating my employment after I graduated.

"Here's how I see it," I responded, "Secretary Califano loves news, and you need someone who can step in for Gary and Rudy and seamlessly produce the Green Sheet. That person is me. If we're talking about grudges, I have as much reason as anyone else. But I believe we should all let bygones be bygones, don't you?" In that moment, I abandoned my demand for a higher salary. I opted for job security.

"Okay," she reluctantly agreed. "That's what we aim to do here— match employees with jobs they enjoy."

And so, on a Monday in November 1979, six months before my scheduled college graduation, I became the managing editor of the Green Sheet. It seemed like a cool path that could lead me to many of the things I desired, including a permanent position in the office, a parking permit in the garage, increased compensation, visibility among senior staff, minimal supervision, and an assistant.

Having worked as an assistant for several years and having studied composition, printing, and worked on the "HEW Now" newsletter

To Be Loved

and the Free Voice student newspaper, I had numerous ideas on how to improve the efficiency and legibility of the Green Sheet. I wasted no time in implementing them. As the editor of the Green Sheet, I had substantial discretion to determine which news items made the cut and which did not—an opportunity I likely would not have had on a newspaper unless I was editor or assistant editor. I began to reap the rewards of my philosophy: know yourself, know what you want, make your desires known, and act accordingly to achieve them.

Secretary Califano, Jr. was known for his deep interest in news, kept HEW buzzing with activity. The Office of the Secretary's Speakers Bureau provided opportunities for employee enlightenment, featuring notable figures such as Ralph Nader, Reverend Jesse L. Jackson, Katherine Graham (then Chairman of the Board of the Washington Post Group), Civil Rights Activist James Farmer, and many others.

Califano had an insatiable appetite for news. Even when he traveled to China, he wanted the Chinese press clippings included in the Green Sheet, despite few people in the department being able to read Chinese. He was a bold character, frequently calling our office for fast-breaking wire stories and occasionally venting his impatience towards the Press Office, demanding swift action. Califano was a tireless worker, arriving early and leaving late. He had quit smoking cigarettes and became a staunch anti-smoking advocate, taking on the powerful tobacco lobby and

The Green Sheet: Managing Editor

causing friction with the Carolina delegation in Congress. Rumor had it that when the White House attempted to rein him in, he would sometimes disregard their calls and act independently, much to their chagrin.

On August 3, 1979, Califano resigned amidst controversy. I recalled attending a speaking bureau event where Katherine Graham was featured, and I had a burning question about racism in the media. Despite being ignored by the moderator, Califano ultimately called on me, allowing me to ask my question. Later, when I passed him in his office corridor, he said, "Hey, you got that question in, didn't you? It was a good one."

As we left Califano's resignation press conference, escorted by a couple of bodyguards, he stood in the elevator, clutching his wife and children, struggling to hold back his emotions. The doors closed, and he was gone. HEW would never be the same.

The esteemed Patricia Harris, Secretary of Housing and Urban Development and former diplomat and dean of Howard University Law School, was nominated as Califano's successor. Her nomination achieved notoriety when during her Senate confirmation hearing, Senator William Proxmire questioned whether, despite her distinguished career, she still understood and cared about the concerns of the poor. In response, Harris answered: "You do not understand who I am. I am a black woman, the daughter of a Pullman car waiter. I did not start out as a member of a prestigious law firm but as a woman who needed a scholarship to go to school. If you think I have forgotten that, you are wrong." Her impassioned response highlighted her commitment, toughness, and assertiveness to the predominantly white power structure; she was confirmed as the first Black Secretary of HEW.

It was my hope that as the first African American HEW Secretary, Harris would address the glaring racial discrimination within the department's personnel hierarchy. While she did hire more Black individuals in upper-level positions compared to her predecessors, she largely ignored the systemic racial employment discrimination within the department.

By May 4, 1980, Education would be separated from HEW, forming an independent department. Patricia Harris would become the first Secretary of what would become the U.S. Department of Health and Human Services. Despite these changes, business continued as usual within the bureaucracy, perpetuating the existing disparities and limitations placed upon Black employees, who were often confined to clerical roles without significant professional power.

Who's Who Among Students

While awaiting the decision on whether my internship would be converted into a permanent position, I focused on strengthening the Green Sheet, determined to create my own opportunities rather than relying on others to recognize my worth.

As college graduation approached, it was unbelievable how much joy, and fulfilment, and personal growth that I had experienced during college. At the age of 28, six years after being released from prison, I had made tremendous strides and had surpassed my previous self. I was on the verge of becoming a public affairs specialist—a professional role that had once seemed impossible. This achievement would enable me to pursue other professional opportunities.

My dedication and commitment to both work and school led UDC to nominate me to receive the Danforth Scholarship. The nomination was based on my full-time schedules, GPA, and my involvement in extracurricular activities such as managing the Free Voice student newspaper and volunteering. During the selection process, the panel scrutinized my transcript and expressed concern about the random sequencing of my courses. I explained that the decentralized structure of the college led to the non-sequential course arrangement.

To Be Loved

When asked about my interests in graduate school, I hadn't given it much thought initially. My main focus was on earning a Bachelor of Arts degree. However, UDC wanted to honor me by nominating me for a scholarship to graduate school. I considered studying law if I were to pursue advanced education. Unfortunately, I discovered that the Danforth Scholarship did not sponsor law degrees.

Despite this, UDC nominated me as one of only 13 inductees into Who's Who Among Students at American Universities and Colleges 1979-1980. I hadn't aimed for this recognition; I was simply doing my best, and it was heart-warming to know that others had noticed and wanted to encourage me. This honor solidified the fact that I had completely transformed my life. It symbolized my transition from a troubled past—filled with fights, neglect, crime, fear, and self-doubt—to a future where I knew myself, pursued my goals with determination, and achieved significant gains with minimal risks.

UDC hosted a reception for the inductees, and Roberta Hall accompanied me to the ceremony. However, none of my family members attended, although my mother purchased the Who's Who book to commemorate the occasion. The LPCP (Lorton Prison College Program) held a separate ceremony during the workday for its three graduates, where I gave remarks. On my behalf, only my mother, who worked at a downtown beauty salon, was present.

Who's Who Among Students

On May 10, 1980, I woke up, prepared myself, dressed in a suit and tie, packed my cap and gown, and drove to the D.C. Armory. It was the gathering place for UDC faculty, students, their families, and friends, who came together for the university's first convocation. The D.C. Armory was a familiar venue for me, having attended many concerts there during my teenage years. I remembered a James Brown concert where gunshots rang out and chaos ensued. Back then, I could never have imagined that I would be standing here on this day, amid this graduating class, about to receive a Bachelor of Arts degree with honors. My induction into Who's Who Among Students at American Universities and Colleges further affirmed my journey of personal growth and achievement. The degree represented my transition from adolescence to adulthood, from the ghetto to downtown and the suburbs, from failure to redemption, and from irresponsibility to empowerment.

Amidst the sea of happy faces in the crowd, I reflected on a range of emotions. I was both happy and sad—happy that I had turned my life around and rescued it from the cycle of poverty, neglect, and abuse, and sad for those who remained trapped in either of those cycles of. I also realized that the most exciting and promising period of my life was coming to an end, and now I would have to deliver on the opportunities that lay ahead. Each goal achieved would bring new growth and new challenges.

To Be Loved

Kashaka, my friend, photographed my graduation, and the Washington Informer newspaper ran a photo and caption featuring me and two other LPCP graduates. It was a milestone for all of us.

As our row of graduates stood to march to the stage, I thought about my intention to give a Black Power salute during the ceremony, but I was taken aback by the ceremonial pomp and the presence of dignitaries on the dais. Mayor Marion S. Barry Jr., Lyle C. Carter (the university's first president), and Board Chairman Ronald H. Brown (future Secretary of Commerce) were among those seated, symbolizing a new level of achievement for me.

My whole family did not attend. Perhaps, it was like gathering everyone to visit Mitchell; everybody didn't care to attend. I was thankful that my mother, my sister, Yvonne, and her daughter, Kim, and Milton, my younger brother attended. Mitchell, well, he was away, again.

I received my degree with a feeling of triumph and applause, raising my fist in the air in celebration. I walked off the stage, ready to embark on my future—the first member of my family to enroll and to graduate from college.

My family chose not the customary lunch to commemorate this momentous occasion.

Following the graduation, Michael Harris, accompanied by his new white girlfriend, invited me to hang out with them and her parents in

Who's Who Among Students

Old Town, Alexandria, Virginia. It felt like an ironic and perhaps foreshadowing end to one phase of my life and the beginning of another. I was on the verge of propelling myself into the mainstream, ready to embrace new experiences and opportunities.

After the graduation ceremony, the Office of the Assistant Secretary for Public Affairs threw a congratulatory party in my honor. I expressed my gratitude to UDC, HHS, and Project Start for providing me with the opportunity to demonstrate that a past mistake does not define one's entire life.

To Be Loved

Chapter X

The African American Writers Guild

My co-worker Jim Ivery gave me a profound gift—a flyer that would alter the course of my career. This flyer heralded the inaugural gathering of a groundbreaking organization, the African American Writers Guild.

The meeting took place on April 25, 1987 at the residence of one of the co-founders, Dr. Cuthbert "Tuffy" Simpkins, situated on Arkansas Road, N.W., just across from the magnificent Rock Creek Park. Their abode was a grand, brick townhouse boasting a spacious living room adorned with vibrant Haitian and African American artwork. Approximately 30 individuals had assembled, gracefully depositing their jackets before ascending to the second level of the house—a spacious family room that became the backdrop for the guild's inaugural gathering. As the meeting unfolded, it became evident that the attendees were erudite, well-read, articulate, and profoundly committed to establishing a distinguished writer's guild.

Regrettably, my writing aspirations had not received the fervent pursuit they deserved. My time had been consumed mainly by assisting Kwanza throughout her journey in grade school, pursuing a photography career, and working as an account executive at an advertising firm. Consequently, when the AAWG convened, I eagerly seized the opportunity to join the steering committee, the planning committee, and any other committee where I believed my

The African American Writers Guild

contributions could be meaningful. Immersing myself among poets, novelists, journalists, bibliophiles, aspiring writers, avid readers, and more promised to shape and invigorate my nascent writing skills while allowing me to contribute something valuable to our community.

Dr. Simpkins, a neurosurgeon and jazz enthusiast, had penned a captivating biography of the jazz luminary, John Coltrane, aptly titled "Coltrane." Despite his remarkable achievements, "Tuffy," as he was affectionately known, remained approachable and down-to-earth. He played a pivotal role as a co-founder and the first vice president of the guild.

Marita Golden, the esteemed author of "Migrations of the Heart," served as the president and co-founder of the AAWG. While embarking on her journey as a novelist, she sought a supportive writers' group but found none. Consequently, she rallied with Tuffy and other writers and hosted a book party at Union Temple Baptist Church in October 1986. The overwhelming response to the event fueled Marita, Tuffy, the poet and Howard University instructor Calvin Forbes, and other like-minded individuals to establish the African American Writers Guild.

Our weekly gatherings primarily took place at Tuffy's and his wife Diane's residence, although occasionally, we would convene at a Black-owned restaurant such as French's on H Street, N.W. When presiding over these meetings, Marita Golden exuded a calm and laid-back demeanor, skillfully orchestrating the proceedings while offering ample opportunities for everyone to

To Be Loved

contribute. Her leadership style embraced consensus, and our productivity knew no bounds.

During one of these meetings, which Tuffy chaired, a heated exchange occurred when Clyde McElvene, a former record seller, bibliophile, and ardent supporter, made a suggestion. Viper, a fellow member, and poet, accused Clyde of pilfering his idea, and tempers flared, resulting in a physical altercation. Members swiftly intervened, diffused the situation, pacified Clyde, sent Viper on his way, and relocated to another venue to convene the meeting. It was astonishing to witness such an erudite and principled gathering of individuals from the middle class degenerate into conflict so rapidly. Seeking solace, I confided in Tuffy, who reassured me by likening it to the familial infighting that occurred even within the Civil Rights Movement during the 1960s.

During other meetings, we forged bylaws and devised plans for future meetings to include conflict resolution protocols. At the subsequent board meeting, with a security guard standing watch, the AAWG collectively voted to exclude Viper from all future board meetings. Eventually, I joined the marketing committee headed by the energetic and visionary Clyde McElevene. His drive and ambition resonated with me, and I was eager to contribute.

The AAWG's first major public event, the "Conference on Publishing and The Black Writer," occurred in October 1987 at Howard University's School of Business. Distinguished panelists included South African poet Dennis Brutus, esteemed poet, author, and publisher Haki Madhubuti, and other luminaries. The

The African American Writers Guild

conference attracted over 200 attendees, and the accompanying book sales appeared to be an overwhelming success.

At a subsequent meeting held at Calvin Forbes' apartment, where we discussed the creation of a newsletter, Clyde expressed frustration as his suggestions were dismissed. Certain board members deemed him a capitalist due to his persistent focus on finding ways for the guild to generate funds to support its mission. However, through consensus, the guild collectively proclaimed that our primary objective was promoting literature and literacy within our community. These two principals were to remain sacrosanct and never compromised by financial pursuits. Nonetheless, a professional business consultant, Clyde understood that principles required resources to thrive. On our way out of the meeting, I encouraged him not to be disheartened and proposed a daring idea—let's strive to have one of us elected as president during the next election and implement our ideas, ensuring they receive the consideration they deserve.

Unbeknownst to us at the time, that seemingly innocuous remark would foreshadow a future we had scarcely imagined.

To Be Loved

Public Affairs Specialist

During my tenure at the U.S. Department of Health and Human Services, I had the privilege of working in the administration of several Cabinet secretaries. Upon graduation, I was fortunate enough to be offered a permanent position as a public affairs specialist, starting at the GS-7 level. In this role, I assumed various responsibilities, including managing the production of the Green Sheet and handling a range of press office duties. These tasks involved supporting HHS press conferences, engaging with the media, drafting press releases, conducting interviews, and writing staff profiles, among other public relations responsibilities.

While I was grateful for the opportunities for professional growth, it was disheartening to witness the deep-rooted presence of white supremacy within the department, a reflection of the broader societal challenges faced by America. This reality evoked anger, and I resolved to confront it head-on whenever it reared its ugly head.

In the face of such challenges, my resolve to fight against white supremacy remained unyielding. I recognized the importance of speaking out and taking action to counteract these harmful forces within the department and society.

In November 1980, Republican Presidential Candidate Ronald W. Reagan emerged victorious, defeating President Jimmy Carter. Ordinarily, the HHS Secretary did not involve themselves in "The Green Sheet" content unless

Public Affairs Specialist

something specific was missing or needed attention. However, the outgoing Secretary Harris, who had naturally campaigned for President Carter's re-election, took an unusual step. During the presidential campaign, Secretary Harris repeatedly associated the presidential candidate Reagan and the GOP with Ku Klux Klan.

However, when Reagan won, she ordered that the front page of "The Green Sheet" feature a photograph from the "New York Daily News" capturing President-elect Reagan laughing joyously, like the devil.

To Be Loved

MPD Brutality Suit Won

After a grueling week-long trial in December 1980, characterized by police blatant lies and tampering with records to support their falsehoods, Rufus, Rich, Cain, and I emerged victorious in our civil suit, against the Metropolitan Police Department, with a judgment award of $125,000. The division of the award corresponded to the injuries we had sustained: Rufus received $75,000, Rich $25,000, Cain, who set us on this path, received $10,000, and I was awarded $15,000. It was a hard-fought win, and I cherished it.

Following Reagan's election as president, the former Pennsylvania Senator Richard Schweiker became Secretary of Health and Human Services on January 22, 1981. As I interacted with Audrey Jones, the Reagan Administration appointee overseeing the Press Office, it became apparent that she was generally pleased with my work performance. However, a particular incident involving my girlfriend led to a tense encounter. Audrey had witnessed us sharing a goodbye kiss in the parking garage, and she summoned me to her office after my lunch break.

I couldn't fathom what she wanted to discuss. As I entered her office, she declared her intention to remove "Jet" magazine from the reading list of "The Green Sheet" reading list. I respectfully voiced my opinion, highlighting that "Jet" was the most popular news magazine among African Americans, the country's most significant minority.

Audrey's response was dismissive, exclaiming, "Get out of here, that's bullshit."

"No, seriously," I persisted.

"Get out of here," she shrugged and laughed.

I shrugged off the incident and continued to subscribe to "Jet." Audrey never raised the issue again. A friend who knew her intimately later informed me that she had a crush on me. It seemed unbelievable, and I laughed it off.

Over time, I implemented several changes that significantly enhanced "The Green Sheet," transforming it into the most comprehensive, legible, and efficiently run news digest within the federal government. Armed with this achievement, I believed I deserved promotion to a GS-9, having inherited the position of a GS-5 from a white male at the GS-13 level. I wanted recognition for my contributions.

Audrey Jones and her deputy, Peter, listened to my pitch for a promotion. However, the response I received reflected the grim financial state of the government at the time. Audrey remarked, "You know, the government is almost broke. We're happy to just pay salaries." Her words were not false. The Reagan Administration had pledged to reduce the government's size and had implemented severe workforce reductions, which disproportionately affected marginalized communities while safeguarding the interests of the white male establishment.

To Be Loved

Though I understood the financial constraints, I also recognized that paying me a GS-7 salary was unjust without allowing me to earn the same compensation as my predecessor at the GS-13 level.

Subsequently, during the next round of performance evaluations, Audrey Jones delivered the harshest evaluation I had ever received, further intensifying the situation. As a relatively new government employee without veteran status or strong job protections, I lacked the right to resist a reduction in force. Nevertheless, determined to fight back, I was shocked by the evaluation and resolved to challenge it.

The Carter Administration, with its commitment to equal employment opportunities, had given way to the Reagan Administration, which arrived with a set of slogans that concealed sinister motives. Phrases such as "No entitlements and no hand-outs," "reverse discrimination," "states' rights," and "trickle-down economics" hid the underlying intentions of dismantling bureaucracy and perpetuating an infrastructure that favored white males, in particular.

I filed a grievance against the evaluation, which was met with skepticism from my co-workers, who believed I couldn't win or feared that I would be fired in the battle. However, I firmly believed that remaining passive was not an option. Even in the face of potential defeat, fighting on principles gave me the best chance of winning.

Through the cooperative education program, I developed a relationship with a personnel classification officer who taught me personnel rules. It became

MPD Brutality Suit Won

clear that job position descriptions not only defined roles but also determined salary levels. Recognizing that my position description was outdated and inaccurately represented my responsibilities, I approached my friend in personnel for assistance. He reviewed my position description, revealing that my position had been classified as a "crew leader" rather than a manager or supervisor, which was the work I was performing.

Armed with this knowledge, I requested a Personnel classification appeal, an audit of my duties to assess whether I was appropriately compensated for my work level. However, if personnel agreed to audit one person in the office, it would have to audit all positions, potentially exposing the office's bank of outdated position descriptions and potentially affecting others' salaries.

Additionally, I filed a grievance against my supervisor for the unfair evaluation. This step required representation from a union official and further strained my relationship with my immediate superiors, who resented the complaint's challenge to their authority.

While the office celebrated Christmas with a party, I remained at my desk, outlining my grievance. Unexpectedly, the office secretary, Sharon Holmes, approached me.

"Ron! I didn't know you were still here. You're supposed to leave at 2:30, and you're not at the Christmas party. I thought you had left," she remarked.

"No, I had some work to finish," I replied.

"Well, Secretary Schweiker is there, and he wants to meet you."

To Be Loved

"Really?"

"Yeah, hurry over because he won't be there for long."

Excitedly, I quickly gathered my papers, put on my jacket, and rushed to the Christmas party. Claudia Brown, the Assistant Secretary for Public Affairs, introduced me to Secretary Schweiker, and he warmly greeted me as "Mr. Green Sheet," eliciting laughter from the celebrants.

He expressed his admiration for my work, emphasizing that not a night went by without him reflecting on something I had featured in "The Green Sheet." The room erupted in laughter once more. Overwhelmed, I thanked him, unable to articulate more before he moved on to greet others. Left in the crowd, I suddenly felt like a stranger among colleagues, as nobody patted me on the back or acknowledged the Secretary's compliment. The Secretary's words spoke for themselves, and I returned to my desk to resume writing my grievance, concluding it with Secretary Schweiker's compliment.

Officially contacting personnel prompted the matter to come back to my superiors. Ms. Bain, the administrative officer, approached me in response to my query.

"Ronald, I'm sorry you felt you had to go outside the office to seek promotion. You're going to be promoted; I just don't know when."

"This isn't about being promoted," I lied. I understood that management would label me undeserving if I asked for more money. "This is about an inaccurate position description that downplays my work performance and denies me fair compensation. That's illegal."

Perplexed, she asked for my position description to review it.

"What's a 'crew leader'? Was Gary Parker, my predecessor, a crew leader?" I inquired.

She hesitated before responding, "Well, Ronald, let me take a look at your position description. I'll see what I can do."

"What are you going to do?" I asked.

"I'll rewrite it. I can't promise it will result in a promotion, but if you withdraw the classification appeal, I'll do my best to correct it for you."

"Okay," I agreed. My goal was not to provoke a fight but to secure what was right and just. It seemed I was on the path to achieving that.

Completing the stages of the grievance process involved attempting mediation first, where Audrey Jones maintained her position without wavering. The next stage required serving notice of intent to grieve the evaluation and providing reasons for overturning the performance evaluation. Undeterred, I submitted my appeal to the assistant secretary, with ample documentation and evidence countering each rating in my supervisor's evaluation.

The process was tense, lasting several weeks, during which I had to continue working under a supervisor whose authority I was openly challenging. Finally, Claudia Brown, the Assistant Secretary for Public Affairs, upgraded my

To Be Loved

evaluation to "excellent," marking another victory in my ongoing battles with the office. Soon after, Audrey Jones was reassigned.

A couple of weeks later, my position description, rewritten by Blain, was submitted to personnel and approved, resulting in my promotion to a GS-9. The fight had been worth it. I refused to be denied. Fighting intelligently, armed with research and clear, concise writing, had led to my success, and I was overwhelmed with joy at the outcome.

Oakcrest Towers: Tennis Community Meetup

I bought my first home in Capital Heights, Maryland, a 15-minute commute from work. It was a small cape cod, two-bedroom house with a detached garage. Kashaka, my best friend and realtor, urged me to purchase. Homeownership was lovely; my space. I could see my neighbors or not. Most of all, it was living in my investment vehicle and earning equity that I could use to reduce taxes and purchase my next home. I was the first member of my family to buy a home.

Nearby was Oakcrest Towers Apartments, which had three tennis courts, and three caged backboards for practice, and it attracted over 30, primarily men in their 30s and older.

It was said that a former tenant named "Pops" ran a tennis program, including tournaments. He had since been recruited to another apartment complex. So, his tennis center was gone, but the tennis hub he had started still buzzed with players rotating in and out from other nearby courts. It was like old times again, hanging out on the corner and socializing. But, this time, it was for fitness and stress release. And, like the rest of the guys, I was a tennis jock. I would cut my tennis teeth at Oakcrest. Every day, after work, we would gather while waiting on the sidelines for our turn; we'd socialize about the day's issues as we were young and settling into careers, family, business, and more. Once on the court, it was all testosterone. We were all developing our game. I would pick

To Be Loved

challenge levels in players, and when successful, I would gradually work my way up the competition ladder.

The big hitters were David Barnes and Brickhouse, who occasionally graced the courts. Sometimes, Phil Lucas would come by and socialize. No regular players at Oakcrest, but when they came by, there was a buzz.

My primary hitting partner was Pernell Williams.

His game was like mind, all heart and hustle. He has a serving motion that gyrated and nearly hypnotized you before exploding for a winner. As importantly, he ran down every ball. So, when we played, it would be a marathon match. What distinguished Pernell's play was that he was as competitive as the best players, but it never compromised his court etiquette or character.

Over the years, court etiquette had declined, replaced by grinding competition, from players calling an out ball and specifying how the ball was out, whether long or wide, to simply saying fault; from announcing "Ball" before throwing it to you, to simply throwing it to your side of the court, often to your inconvenience, or simply dropping the balls on the serving side of the court. And even worse, with more than seven linesmen officiating professional tennis matches, they still can't get it right. But, players, in the heat of competition, would argue ad infinitum over a line call.

Pernell and I would run, run, run after each other's good shots while laughing at each other's attempt to outwit the other. We never argued or had line call issues, not ever.

Oakcrest Towers: Tennis Community Meetup

And, for those reasons, nearly 35 years later, Pernell and I still meet to play. Over the years, Pernell had resolved that his time for tennis dwindled, and he would only make time to play me. Soon, he would quit the game entirely for a year or two. But, missing the fun of the competition we used to have, I persuaded him to return to the game. And, still, only hitting with me, he has thanked me for getting him back into the game we both love to play.

However, Pernell, a small businessman, married, had two sons and got deeper involved in his church and growing his business and family life, which curtailed his tennis activity while my game continued to evolve.

We still have marathon matches, he's an awesome foe, but I usually prevail.

***

Occasionally, I would venture to Hillcrest Heights Tennis facility on Alabama Ave., S.E., DC.

Hillcrest was distinguished with four courts and a backcourt grassy hill from which we had to retrieve our errant balls, and at the opposite end of the court, if your ball went over the 10-foot fence, was a deep incline of brush, from which you had to retrieve your errant ball. Hillcrest was also highly cliquish. If you didn't know members of the clique, they wouldn't play you. The clique played on only the first two courts.

Players would have the most hellacious arguments while they played with abandon. Harold Coan was the loudest, most raucous voice; Cornelius

To Be Loved

Green, the most dramatic and humorous. All manner of drama would spill off the bench into the courts and vice versa. There was only one woman player, in her 50s, Ruby, who played and whipped some of the guys.

There was also only one white guy who played tennis at Hillcrest. He was also old enough to be my father. He would sit on the bench behind Court 3 and not say anything to anyone. He'd waited patiently until someone asked him to play.

He was very agile and capable of getting the ball back. I would play with him until I learned to play better and would begin to challenge the clique.

I soon learned that if I turned my racquet upon contact with the ball, I could hit it as hard as possible, and it would come down toward the court.

I would learn to hit every ball with topspin. I also committed myself to running down every ball, and I would note how my opponents responded to specific shots, whether with a backhand, lob, drop shot, etc. I would attack their weakness until they fixed it or lost the game. By 1993, I competed against the best players at Oakcrest and often won.

Aminata

In February 1983, I began to launch my career and desired someone to share it with. Enter Roberta, a young woman who had briefly worked at the former HEW as an intern and with whom we became acquainted. We began dating passionately, and by March, I had asked her to move in with me into my newly purchased two-bedroom cape cod-style house. At 23 years old, Roberta fit the bill, bringing fun and youthful energy to the relationship. She had no children and had never been married, focusing primarily on her appearance and fashion sense.

In September 1983, we decided to get married at a Justice of the Peace ceremony. Roberta's friends and my daughters, Ngina and Kwanza, served as witnesses, and we celebrated with a reception for family and friends at my house the following Friday. The age gap between us, 10 years, became apparent as the responsibilities of maintaining a home weighed on her. It often challenged her commitment to sharing the burdens, leading to irreconcilable differences that ultimately resulted in our separation two and a half years later. However, before parting ways, we welcomed a beautiful baby daughter named Aminata on December 19, 1984.

I cherished my time with Aminata, even from her early months. I would pick her up from daycare after work, lay her on my bed, and read and talk to her. As she grew older, we enjoyed playful moments together, like zooming through

To Be Loved

the house in her little red wagon, watching recorded TV video shows from the previous night, and capturing her dance routines with my camcorder. I taught her various activities, from roller skating to riding a bicycle and driving a car. One of my proudest accomplishments was developing a system to teach her how to read at age four. Our relationship was filled with joy and fruitful experiences.

However, the challenge of finding a woman who would genuinely commit to keeping our home and sharing financial responsibilities left me dissatisfied. I questioned why I grew bored with relationships and why I thought women would not equally sacrifice or commit wholeheartedly to me. They argued that they could never please me. This led me to reflect on my relationship with my mother and family and the lessons I learned about love during my upbringing. I desired understanding and self-awareness rather than placing blame on anyone.

I acknowledged that my mother had worked hard to provide for our family and had instilled in me the value of striving for excellence. I aspired to find a partner who embodied those high standards.

Family tensions were put aside when we began having annual cookouts at a local park. Milton or I would spend the night under the park's only gazebo to preserve it for the day's family outing. Each family member came together to ensure that our 100 guests of family and friends ate well and had a good time. The annual gathering convened for about 15 years, bringing families together from New York, North Carolina, and the DMV. The children could feel a sense of their extended family. My friend Raheem and his TUMOM Jazz Band performed jazz on occasion.

I would invite Pernell or Kashaka to play tennis. It was a good time. Then, my family would close summer in the fall with a Fish Fry at my mother's house.

She and her sisters would eat, talk, and mostly laugh throughout. These were wonderful times with my family.

Also, on Memorial Day, annually, George, my best friend, and his wife, Meilani, coordinated a week-long vacation in Hilton Head, S.C., at the Sea Pines Plantation.

It would be a week of daily tennis on clay, putt-golf, movies, dinner rotating at each villa, or dining out.

We'd drive in a caravan of 6 automobiles and have a tennis blast for a week.

***

Still seeking understanding, in 1984, I asked my mother why she whipped me so much as a child. I needed to know.

She cried. My sisters and brothers felt a need to defend my mother, and someone screamed,

"You were the worst child – that's why!" An opportunity for meaningful dialogue with my mother was lost.

To Be Loved

But, twelve years later, on March 23, 1996, on the way home from work, I stopped by my mother's and asked her again about my upbringing.

Momma sat at her favorite place, at the head of the table. She had aged very well, except for her ailing health. Momma is beautiful, as ever, softened by time. She has raised eight children, nine grandchildren, and four great-grandchildren.

She's had a nearly 30-year career as a self-employed hair stylist, although she's semi-retired. She owns her brick, four-bedroom cape cod home in Seat Pleasant, Md. She's cooking now but doesn't cook much anymore.

I said, "I got more whippings than the whole family combined."

"You think so? I don't think so," she said, somewhat taken aback by the subject she thought had long been forgotten.

"Yes, I do," I said.

"And Mitchell got away with murder; he never got whipped for anything."

"You don't think Mitchell got whipped?" She asked.

"He didn't. I don't recall him ever getting whipped," I said.

"He got whipped," she said.

"I don't remember," I said, trying to recall.

Yvonne never got whipped.

Paulette never got whipped.

Aminata

Carleen never got whipped. Milton never got whipped. Audrey never got whipped. Wayne never got whipped. I got all the whippings!

Momma said, "If you did get whipped more than anybody else it was because you were doing more than anybody else."

"I know I wasn't easy," I said, "I wanted positive attention. All I was getting was whippings from you."

"You were a mean child!" she shot back. "You were as mean as a snake. And, you must have gotten it from your father. You couldn't have gotten it from me!"

"So, you were getting back at Daddy through me?" I asked.

"What do you mean? No, you were just a mean child," she said.

"Children are innocent," I replied.

She said, "They are born innocent, but they learn to do devilish things."

"How mean was I?" I asked.

"When I had Wayne," she said, "You sat around the house whispering about me."

"What did I say?"

"Look at her; she's pregnant," she mocked how I must have looked to her back then.

"I was disturbed by that," I said.

"What do you mean?" Momma asked.

To Be Loved

"You were always getting on me about doing what was right," I said, "That wasn't right.

"I am an adult!"

"I understand now; that's why I don't hold it against you now," I replied. "But, as a kid, I didn't understand you doing that."

"Then, I would send ya'll out to get switches," Momma began to recall. "Carlean would bring the smallest switch she could find. You'd bring back a little tree."

"Couldn't it have been that I was bringing back what I thought you wanted, not trying get you angrier for bringing back a little switch?"

"No," she snapped, "you thought I was so mean; that I would whip you with something like that, but I didn't."

"But, there was no love," I interjected.

"There was no touching, holding embracing, no saying 'I love you.'"

"All that stuff makes people weak," Momma said.

"I wanted ya'll to grow up strong.

Not weak. My parents didn't love me like that. Whenever I made a mistake, I got whipped."

"So, you passed it down?" I asked.

"Maybe so," she said, "I hear Kenny complaining to Yvonne that she's never talked to him."

Aminata

"Right, we've created generations upon generations where there's no love," I reasoned.

"We love each other," she said.

"Right, we just express it differently," I said.

"But, that's why I talk to my children," I said, "hold their hands, try to understand them."

"You whip your children; does that mean you don't love them?"

"I didn't whip them all the time. I've just whipped Aminata, but she's 11. I've only whipped her once before, and I hope this was the last time.

I also balance the butt whippings with love and sacrifice."

"You can do more for your children than I could."

"I agree. You did the best you could with what you had."

I may never know why my mother whipped me so much without giving me any praise as a kid. I suspect it was partly because of the way she was raised; partly because, as a child, I messed up so frequently; and partly because I reminded her of my dad. Reflecting on my journey, I recognized the importance of seeking understanding and self-awareness. While I may never have all the answers, I strived to break the cycle and provide a different upbringing for my children, offering them the love and nurture I yearned to receive.

***

1986 another opportunity arose for me at HHS when a higher-graded coworker retired. I was also asked to assume her duties, even though I was a GS-

To Be Loved

9 and she was a GS-13. This was the second time I had been asked to take on the responsibilities of a GS-13 position without receiving the corresponding pay. Martinez, my new supervisor, was very kind to me, and I suspect she may have had former Secretary Schweiker intervene on my behalf during my difficult times with Ms. Jones. I wasn't sure if I was assigned to fill in for Sally because of Martinez or Virginia, or perhaps both.

Suing Employer for Discrimination

In addition to my regular duties as editor of the Green Sheet, I was assigned an agency mole reporter at HHS. I would attend fast-breaking press conferences on Capitol Hill or at the National Press Club, quickly return to the office, and provide an oral and written report, which would then be passed on to the chief of staff and/or the secretary. I enjoyed the challenges and experiences with this role, but despite my increasing responsibilities, I was still being paid at the GS-11 level, not quite reaching the GS-13 level.

Frustrated with the lack of promotion, I decided to take action and wrote a memo to my supervisor, David Goldstein, threatening further measures if I wasn't promoted. Knowing that he was close to Virginia, I anticipated some resistance. To my surprise, Virginia called me into her office and advised me to hold off on being confrontational, stating that it wasn't necessary.

A few weeks later, I was promoted to a GS-12. It had been seven years since I graduated from college and had become a permanent professional, but it would be almost another decade before I would receive another promotion. It seemed that I was being held back by an invisible barrier they called a "glass ceiling," which I perceived as white racism. Despite assuming the duties of higher-graded officials and receiving excellent or outstanding evaluations, I remained stagnant in terms of advancement.

To Be Loved

Furthermore, the office had sent a secretary to attend writing courses, and she was subsequently promoted to a GS-12 or GS-13, while my efforts seemed to go unnoticed. Feeling the need to address the unfair treatment, I filed a formal EEO complaint on October 1, 1996, alleging sexual discrimination as the cause of my non-promotion.

I delved into learning about the EEO process and realized that the EEO counselor was working for the government, not for me. They captured my complaint, ensured it met their requirements, and guided me through the process. I understood that the battle would be fought on paper, and effective communication was crucial. I also understood that I would be suing the agency and my supervisor, with the agency having the Chief Counsel's Office at their disposal. Hiring a lawyer became necessary once the complaint reached the formal stage, as the agency's lawyers would likely advise them to reject my claims, and I had to be prepared to take the claims to the next level. Making those in power uncomfortable and pushing them to take me seriously became paramount.

For the next phase of the EEO process, I hired a K Street lawyer and submitted a formal complaint. Little did I know then how long the process would drag on. However, regardless of the costs involved, I was determined to go the distance.

Meanwhile, in the political landscape, riding on the two-term legacy of Reagan, George Bush was elected as the successor with the help of figures like

Suing Employer for Discrimination

Willie Horton, Jesse Jackson, and Michael Dukakis. Louis Sullivan, an award-winning hematologist, and president of Morehouse Medical School, was appointed as the Secretary of Health and Human Services. Sullivan, a distinguished Black college alumnus, had impressed Barbara Bush during fundraisers for his school, and now, as the first lady, she remembered him.

Sullivan tried to maintain a "man of the people" image, given the constraints of being part of a right-wing administration. The primary tool of the Secretary of HHS is the bully pulpit, and Sullivan used it to give speeches before various professional, medical, and social organizations, spreading the administration's message and awarding grants. As the CEO overseeing institutions like the National Institutes of Health, Social Security Administration, Office of Human Development Services, and Health Care Financing Administration, Sullivan faced the challenge of addressing disparities in health between African American and white populations.

Everywhere Sullivan spoke, he highlighted the significant health gaps and disparities, particularly among minority communities. He tirelessly advocated for improving health status and addressing preventable causes of mortality such as homicide, tobacco use, and substance abuse. While acknowledging the impact of poverty and racism, Sullivan emphasized personal responsibility and a culture of character in addressing health issues within minority populations.

To Be Loved

During his tenure, Sullivan assigned a special assistant to review all of HHS' 300 programs and recommend ways to make them more responsive to African Americans. He also increased the representation of Black individuals in upper management positions. Additionally, Sullivan engaged with the Black press, although their hopes of influencing the department to place more public service announcements in Black media were not realized. He even led a delegation on a seven-nation tour of Africa, including health experts and AID officials. He occasionally wore a Kente bow and cummerbund set at White House events.

***

When a new secretary was named, they first came aboard the department as a consultant, for on-the-job training, in preparation for a senate confirmation hearing.

During a newspaper interview before he was sworn in as secretary, Dr. Sullivan got into a flap over abortion, in which he expressed his personal view without considering the Bush Administration's view. The right-wing leaped on him with everything. It became a Senate confirmation issue. Sullivan won the job as secretary of health and human services. Still, for peace, he had to agree to, among other things, that the Right to Life movement would have to influence his selection of his spokesperson, the assistant secretary for public affairs. And so it was. With Sullivan came Kay Cole James, another African American, to replace Virginia.

Suing Employer for Discrimination

She was the former spokesperson for the Right-to-Life movement. She showed no particular affinity for black people. She was no Virginia. She would only last a year in that position.

Virginia left HHS on March 31, 1989, to work for another federal agency. The level of responsibility that she had exposed me to was curtailed. The office had a going away party, where she and Secretary Bowen presented selected employees with certificates of appreciation. She autographed my photo: "My favorite OASPA professional! Hang in there!"

I did an enlarged faux front page of "The Green Sheet," with her official photograph and my article, chronicling her tenure, the longest of any HHS assistant secretary for public affairs. They usually come and go with the secretary, if not before. Her tenure was for five years. Her companion went to the party, Mr. Hughes, a vice president for Newsweek who also taught at Hampton University. They eventually married. I knew Virginia could have the best. I photographed her going-away party for her.

To Be Loved

Writers' Guild President

By June 1989, AAWG activities were coming to a slow halt. We had not met for what seemed like a month or two. Marita was spending a lot of time on her first book. She tried to coordinate an election for a second generation of AAWG leaders to take over the guild. I decided that I would run for president. It would be an opportunity to test my leadership skills and challenge me to use all the skills I had learned in college and by working in public affairs at HHS. However, apathy had set in, and the election committee didn't organize an election.

It had been so long since AAWG had done anything public that it had lost much of its momentum among the membership.

Forbes, the second vice president, went to teach at the University in Maryland. When Tuffy, the first vice president, announced that he would resign to dedicate more time to his first love, scientific research, McElevene recommended me as first vice president. The board unanimously agreed.

By then, I had seen the potential of an active Guild and witnessed its fade. I had some ideas about how we could put life back into the organization.

In September, Golden announced that her first novel, *Long Distance Life*, would be released. By October, she announced at a steering committee meeting before only a handful of attendees at Watha T. Daniel Public Library in the Shaw area of D.C. that it would be her last meeting as president of AAWG. She was about to embark on a tour promoting her book.

Writers' Guild President

I succeeded Golden as AAWG's president.

Oh, what an honor. Tuffy took me to an Ethiopian restaurant for dinner after the announcement. He told me I had his complete confidence and support in running the guild and that he thought I was the best person to succeed Marita.

At the first meeting after Golden's departure, on his behalf, Tuffy's wife, Diane, became active in AAWG's Steering Committee.

The first thing that I would incorporate into the meetings was structured discussions. Further, as chair and secretary of the meetings, I would record the minutes, including assignments the board members agreed to work on. At subsequent meetings, we would review the minutes for continuity and assignments. These two measures encouraged accountability and progress.

I told the board we had a long list of agenda items to take action on quickly. I set up a structure for debates/discussions. I wanted us to stick by our agenda of progress and not be distracted by deep, intellectual discussions. So, fellow member James McBride's proposal that AAWG merge with his private organization became a model for the new debate structure.

I told the board that we would not discuss his proposal ad infinitum. Instead, we would go around the table two or three times, listening to each board member's pros and cons of McBride's proposal. Then we would vote on whether to adopt it. After the discussions, we voted against the proposal. It was too impractical to absorb another's agenda before we had gained control of our own.

To Be Loved

I knew I risked turning people off by being so blunt. Debates had to have limits if we were to progress.

McBride would never attend another board meeting.

But, he would continue to come to the general meetings. Occasionally, inspired by our efforts, McBride would donate money on the spot or come to AAWG's need whenever he was called.

AAWG had no money in its bank accounts and owed $169 for its untimely telephone answering service.

I asked the board to meet weekly until we got control of the organization. I told them AAWG needed to live, and whether it lived or died would be up to us. My strategy for revamping the guild and helping it to live out its potential included raising its visibility, increasing services to our members, and raising its revenue.

To accomplish this, I said we would revamp and expand the two-page newsletter; make the Meet the Author Series a monthly event featuring a reputed author and an AAWG aspiring member writer. We would also form a public relations committee, whose mission would be to sell AAWG member literary triumphs to TV, radio, and newspapers.

The PR committee hyped it to the media whenever an AAWG member's work was published. Also, we would periodically sponsor seminars to enhance our member's skills. By doing all of this, we would raise visibility, membership, and revenue.

Writers' Guild President

A handful of committee members supported my vision. People were giving up these thankless volunteer assignments after three to six months. Sometimes, I had to wear several hats. For the first six months to a year of my tenure as president, I served as chairman of the steering committee, membership director, and treasurer. When those who stayed saw my determination, they redoubled their efforts. Soon, the board grew from four to 10 active volunteers.

Over the three years of my leadership, the newsletter would reach as many as 10 pages of current events in the guild and industry, featuring writers' tips on contests and how and where to get published, highlighting member accomplishments, a message from the president, and samples of other members' literary or journalistic efforts.

Diane headed both the Book Discussion Group and the Writers' Workshop. Under her leadership and guidance, the Writers Workshop met regularly and grew from a handful to about 12 members. We had general meetings quarterly in which, after accounting for the guild's activities for the previous quarter, we would have performers entertain with live music from my friend Raheem (Brian Coleman) Rasta's jazz band, TUMOM.

We had food and refreshments, which Diane or fellow member Margaret Levacy purchased and prepared. The business meeting's activities included an open mic session in which attendees were welcome to read their work or make other literary-related announcements. At every meeting, I would have a membership recruitment table, which displayed membership applications, the

To Be Loved

membership's published works, leaflets representing AAWG events, and other AAWG paraphernalia.

AAWG soon grew to attract writers and aspiring writers from across the country, including the Caribbean Islands of Barbados.

The Schomburg Library of New York and Enoch Pratt Libraries of Baltimore subscribers to our newsletter.

We would have some of our best receptions in the Simpkins' home. We hosted Gwendolyn Brooks, the first African American Pulitzer Prize-winning poet and first African American Consultant in Poetry, to the U.S. Library of Congress, a position now called the Poet Laureate. As president, I was honored to welcome and present to her.

We also honored Octavia Butler, the most prominent African American female science fiction writer. Additionally, the guild hosted the 25th Anniversary of the publishing of The Choice by Samuel Yette at Sumner School. At Tuffy's suggestion, we planned a tributed Marita Golden, which included a plaque presented to her at a reception as "mother of the African American Writers Guild." I was proud to honor Golden, an accomplished writer. She left the guild reluctantly. It was her baby, and she had to let it go. It was growing, and I wanted her to know that no matter what became of the guild, it had one "mother."

It was a time that saw a rebirth of Afrocentricity in Washington. On WHUT TV, a weekly series called "For the People" featured African American scholars such as Asa Hilliard and Leonard Jefferies. Tony Browder ran the

Writers' Guild President

Kemetic Institute locally, which featured speeches by prominent Afrocentric scholars, like Dr. Francis Crest Welsing, family psychologist and author of the "Isis Papers." AAWG's attorney was member Nkechie Taifa, a rising community attorney-activist and author of "Shinning Legacy." There were Jeanette Carson's Black Memorabilia Exhibits, and we were all connected with Watoto, Roots and Ujuma Shule Afrocentric Independent Schools, and Hodari Ali's Pyramid Books Store. It seemed like a rebirth of the 70's Negritude or Black Arts movement. Being a part of that movement, and contributing to my community, made me feel worthy and redeemed from when I worked in the struggle to integrate the GAO and was fired for stealing.

***

I held AAWG meetings at Edna's Restaurant, a black-owned gourmet seafood restaurant in China Town. We'd greet, eat, and conduct AAWG's business.

By 1992, when I stepped down from the guild, it was a robust emerging organization with over 260 members, a structure, and coffers of $5,000 in its checking account and $1,000 in its endowment account.

***

I began to freelance articles regularly in newspapers and magazines nationwide, covering current events but from an Afrocentric perspective.

This was taking writing to a new level, requiring that I study a magazine's or newspaper's style and subjects for at least six issues, write a piece

To Be Loved

and query the magazine's editors to sell it to them or to otherwise arrange for them to publish it.

Throughout my tenure as AAWG president, I would write about 30 articles which were published in either "Players" magazine or "Upscale" magazine or published in other magazines and newspapers from the local Afro-American Newspaper, of which I distributed as a kid, and the Washington Informer, to the "Chicago Defender" and "Palm Beach Gazette."

I sent a query for "African Americans Know Thyself (about the need to know our empowering history)" to several publications, including "Players," a magazine for Blacks similar to "Playboy." The editor responded with an informal note asking that I send the article. He subsequently followed with a contract to buy the piece. So, began a two-year relationship with the publication. Granted, folks may have come to "Players" for other intentions, but through my articles, they would be enlightened with cultural and historical information.

My other such essays and articles included "Don't Call Me Nigga, Brother!", "Don't Believe the Hype!! (how the white media eschew statistics that prop up whites and beat down Blacks' public image)", "Who Are the Boys N the Hood (about the movie, 'Boyz N the Hood)," Black Male Schools," "Fugitive Fathers: Are Black Men Deserting Their Kids? (about paternity and child support issues)", "The Black Stereotypes Whites Love to Hate," "Unlocking the Power of the African American Mind," "No Justice, War!!! (the Rodney King verdict)", "Ollie North, Pete Rose, Why the Inner City? (about white ex-cons doing community service in the Black community)", and "Africentricity: Attaining Our Own Identity (about the reemergence of cultural identification)."

Either the subject of one of my articles or a social event would lead to my appearance on radio or television. On one such occasion, Nkechi Taifa was tapped to appear and recommend another panelist to appear on Black Entertainment Television's Our Voices with host Bev Smith. Nkechi recommended me as the other panelist. That appearance was one of the proudest moments in my career. It manifested my desire to influence public discussion of social issues that affected my community. The panel included noted author and publisher Haki Madhubuti. The subject was the Sentence Project report about the high instance of black males being absorbed through mass incarceration.

The AAWG had achieved a measure of stability and visibility in the city, and so had I.

I had not told anyone at AAWG that I was an ex-convict; it never seemed relevant to anything.

***

In 1992, Geraldine Davis, the new assistant secretary for public affairs, recommended me to be honored as the employee of the month for March. Along with 12 other employees from different offices within the department, I received a plaque and a cup with the department's seal. At the luncheon with the secretary, I wore my Kente bow and cummerbund set, which caught Secretary Sullivan's attention.

To Be Loved

He admired my Kente set and asked, "Where did you get it from?"

"Thank you, Mr. Secretary. I got it from Timbuktu," I responded.

"Oh, you've been to Timbuktu."

"Yeah, Timbuktu, the clothing store in Northeast, D.C."

He and everyone else broke out in laughter.

"Mine was a material gift from the Ivory Coast," the secretary said. "I had it fashioned into a bow and cummerbund set."

While Secretary Sullivan made efforts to bring about change, he, like his predecessor Harris, largely overlooked the hierarchical structure within HHS personnel. Towards the end of his administration, he gained greater control over the bureaucracy and appointed senior Black professionals to key positions. However, it was a bit late to have a significant impact. Sullivan returned to the presidency of Morehouse Medical School when Bill Clinton took office in 1992, and Donna E. Shalala succeeded Sullivan as secretary of health and human services.

Tennis Alchemy

1993 I sold my first home and moved to Clinton, Md., nearer to Rt. 301, where my journey into adulthood began. I purchased a four-bedroom colonial with a family room, a two-car garage, and a large deck and basement. The house was also Near Padgett's Corner tennis facility in Oxon Hill. Padgett's Corner, with six tennis courts, would prove to be the PG County' tennis academy' for me.

These guys and ladies were not only more competitive than at Oakcrest Towers; there were more of them. They were more organized. They had organized a tennis ladder, helping to rank players. They also played USTA League Tennis and won local, regional, and national tournaments. I played league tennis for a couple of years and didn't like it.

Too many moving parts to keep up with.

Varying levels of commitment, favoritism, and racist judges in Va. at the sectionals. Besides, I was getting all the tennis competition I needed at Padgett's Corner.

Padgett's Corner was not as cliquish as Hillcrest but not nearly as cozy as Oakcrest. At Oakcrest, everybody knew everybody. At Padgett's, you didn't. You learned a particular crew within the larger group.

To Be Loved

I preferred hitting with Rufus Lassiter at Padgett's Corner, one of the best players.

He used me like a human backboard while he surgically delivered the ball across the court, with me running furiously to get it and return it with authority and precision. He demonstrated that you hit the ball with authority to a place on the court where it was most challenging for the opponent to return. The opponent would have to go and fetch your ball, notwithstanding return it in kind. I would have to learn to get and return the ball well, or Rufus, with a sneaky grin, would run me into the ground chasing his balls. It lifted my game. In April 1996, I reached number 4 on the tennis ladder at Padgett's Corner, a milestone in my emerging tennis prowess.

After two years of hitting with Rufus, I asked another friend, Ben Mills, who could teach me to serve fundamentally. Just on sheer grit, I would serve the ball in a windmill fashion. With no consistency, I gave away many double-fault points. I would give away approximately three games in faults and still win; that's how strong my ground strokes game had become. Ben referred me to George Sledge, another tennis player I met at Oakcrest. He was a former USTA League regional and national competitor, with stories about his wins and tennis travels.

He had taken courses. He had the tennis fundamentals down. I had never even taken one tennis course; my game comprised determination and drive. George spent his club membership and his time teaching me the fundamentals of

Tennis Alchemy

the serve, in particular, but we would also drill me on the fundamentals of the topspin backhand and volleying the short court. We became best friends. Three years later, while watching Tennis Great Agassi's service motion, it finally clicked, and I began serving more effectively and not giving away so many points through double faults.

Padgett's Corner was a robust social center, attracting hundreds of players, locally and from across the country. Whenever players across the country came to Maryland, they seemed to know they could find ample competition at Padgett's Corner. We would have cookouts on Memorial Day and July 4th, with me serving as a player-DJ. I dedicated my first year of retirement to converting my collection of over 300 albums and cassettes into Mp3, which enabled me to store the soundtrack of my life on my phone and to DJ get-togethers, with a portable Bluetooth speaker, at will.

The most competitive tennis players at Padgett's Corner were Jimmy Clayton, Dave Barnes, and Nick Nyack. Nyack had Roger Federer's finesse, but he didn't compete in league tennis or many tournaments. However, Jimmy Clayton and Barnes did. They were among the most decorated and accomplished players in Southern Maryland. Clayton, unassuming personally, was a cagey player with an excellent suite of strokes and a moderate pace. Still, he played the court tirelessly and would wear his opponents down chasing shots, preferring to make his opponents run to get his balls rather than running after his opponents'

To Be Loved

balls. He would enroll in the American Tennis Association National Annual Tournaments, and for decades, he would daringly play three events, which was unheard of for any player, and Clayton would win all three events, year after year.

However, due to wear and tear on his body, at age 75, he played the ATA 2023 and lost all three events. It was unprecedented. It was a sign of a passing of the guard. And it mirrors the dying will of Padgett's Corner. Age, injury, COVID-19, illness, and others moving to year-round tennis climate states have conspired to decimate competitive tennis at Padgett's Corner. Only a few of the players remain from its heyday. And, we play doubles mostly, rise and fly. Young people, raised by pressing the buttons of computer games, did not follow in their parents' quest for physical exercise. In the 12 years that have passed, no other group has returned to the MNCPPC annual budget meetings to maintain the momentum we started and advocate on behalf of Padgett's Corner.

Another great tennis social gathering was at Bradbury Heights Tennis Courts, off Suitland Road, a two-court park tucked in the woods.

There, a small group gathered, like at Oakcrest, and they played with reckless abandon and, afterward, talking big bravado. Some would "pass the hat" for beer, chips, and more smack-talking or talking about politics, history, and culture.

Tennis Alchemy

They had short memories, particularly concerning their lost tennis matches. But, they would not let you live down their victory over you; you would never hear the end of it. Each time the yarn is told, it grows.

I developed a reliable serve, 2-story lob, drop shot, and backhand chip slice shot. But what my opponents always seemed to remember was my laser-like forehand shots, which allowed me to place a ball with torque anywhere on the court. That, combined with my ability to run down almost any ball, forced my opponent to have to hit the ball one more time.

Almost nothing gives me more pleasure than what I derive from playing tennis.

I think it has to do with swinging that racquet, not to mention the exhilaration of deep breathing, figuring out how to win, returning unbelievable shots, and fighting to defend your side of the court while waging an attack.

I would also serve as the Prince Georges County Tennis Association newsletter editor for our tennis club at Padgett's Corner, in which I interviewed and wrote the profile on James "Pops" Robinson that was part of our posthumous tribute to him for the service he provided to the local area tennis community.

Years later, in 2011, a group of fellow tennis players gathered and attended a Maryland National Capital Parks and Planning Commission annual budget meeting to get needed support for maintaining the Padgett's Corner

To Be Loved

"historic" tennis facility. In my testimony, I highlighted that people from all ethnic groups and all walks of life came to Padgett's Corner for their love of playing tennis. We didn't need an administration and staff; we only needed the MNCPPC to do their part and maintain our facility in good working condition. I determined that I would learn the structure of MNCPPC and where to advocate to preserve the Padgett's Corner tennis facility.

However, the MNCPPC Director, Ronnie Gathers, asked for a copy of my remarks. My relationship with the director ultimately resulted in the MNCPPC granting $500,000 to renovate the "Padgett's

Corner Tennis Facility" to a then state-of-the-art facility, including renaming the park the Allentown Splash, Tennis and Fitness Park" to officially include "tennis" in its title and installing a landmark, which tributed the history of Padgett's Corner and its importance to the Southern Maryland tennis community. That meant the facility is a budget line item that can be replenished or increased with the MNPPC annual budget. Since I had researched and written that historic tribute for the landmark, I required that MNCPPC attribute the byline accordingly.

In 2018, I moved to Bowie, Md., near Watkins Regional Park's 4-court tennis facility and Prince Georges' Community College's 8-court facility. The now seniors who played tennis at PGCC regularly call themselves "The Breakfast Club." They mainly were school administrators and teachers who played tennis during summer school breaks; many have played tennis together year round for

Tennis Alchemy

over 50 years. Kevin Woodruff, 59, is the best player among these approximately 40 men and women players who routinely play at Watkins.

A self-taught tennis player and an MNCPPC tennis instructor, Kevin hits like a pro with a full suite of strokes and exceptional efficiency. Dan Barnes is the so-called "Dean" of the group. At age 81, a mild-mannered gentleman who's as clever as a fox on the court. And, the effervescent Bruce Hill, at 73, has more energy than most players half his age as he explodes shots with his entire body; otherwise, he and Dan handle facility logistics. The competition is fierce but friendly. The group also includes Bruce Sellers, 72, whom I call "Frosty" because his game generally comprises moderate pace, but he uses the gentleness of his strokes as slick as ice. I knew him as a teen when I lived on Sheriff Road. The Breakfast Club welcomes all comers and includes lady ballers, too. Led by La Wade Garris, 68, the Queen of the Breakfast Club, is a forceful player, tennis fashionista and a fierce opponent. She will routinely warm up with a few players who only hit tennis balls for a couple of hours as a workout, then she joins the rotation with the rest of the players.

After COVID-19, the Breakfast Club was relocated to Watkins Regional Park. The Breakfast Club plays rotational doubles, i.e., a player joins a doubles team after every game, starting at the deuce court, and another player comes out leaving on the adv. court. After each game, each player rotates their position on the court counterclockwise. Each player plays four games, win or lose, and sits

To Be Loved

out until their next turn. With this play protocol, with 12-16 players aged 50s-80s, no one has to wait to play for more than four games (15-20 mins.)

I began to play with The Breakfast Club during the pandemic as Padgett's Corner Tennis Facility began to thin. And we have a regular tennis jamboree now because I provide the music that is the soundtrack of many of our lives.

HHS Discrimination Complaint Settled

Five years had passed before my discrimination suit against HHS was settled, and in 1999, I was finally promoted to a GS-13. Throughout that time, I went to work every day, maintaining professionalism and performing my duties as if nothing was happening behind the scenes. However, I constantly collected and processed data, attended meetings with a tape recorder in my pocket, and filed retaliation complaints.

Three years later, I discovered that I had developed hypertension, possibly due to the stress I had endured. Eventually, my then-girlfriend convinced me to leave HHS. Despite winning the battle against discrimination, the war was ongoing, as they continued to retaliate until I went. I had filed four subsequent retaliation complaints when the suit was settled.

I don't recommend anyone stay in the same office for as long as I did. Changing jobs, minimally every two years, is advisable, leveraging the additional experience gained from each role to advance further. Staying in one place for too long can lead to career stagnation.

To Be Loved

U.S. Mint: Internet Project Manager

I applied for an Information Technology Specialist job at the US Mint, GS-14, parlaying my budding technological wherewithal.

I brought my hand-held video recorder and taped my supervisor's response as he read my surprise letter of resignation. The office gave me a graduation party, saying nice things about me and giving me gifts.

I grew up at HHS. And, now, I had to leave after 23 years. You win the battle but not the war. Ultimately, they will retaliate until you leave.

***

When my work day ended at around 2:30 p.m., I would take the elevator to Garage Level 3-B and drive my Lexus automobile home to semi-rural Clinton, Md., out Branch Avenue, near 301 South, coincidentally, near to where my journey in adulthood began.

***

At the U.S. Mint, I was an Internet Project Manager. I served as the federal technical liaison with IBM, overseeing the upgrade of the US numismatists' online catalog and contributing to the significant, state-of-the-art redesign of the US Mint's Online Catalog home page.

After the online catalog launched, I was assigned to provide Web Catalog technical support to the Mint's customer call center and to customer support directly when the call center could not service them. A customer's letter of commendation about my support garnered me a $300 office cash award.

U.S. Mint: Internet Project Manager

But, my boss used to harass me and make biased comments, for which I began recording. I requested a meeting with the Chief Information Officer to address his remarks and smothering supervision. At the meeting, I revealed a comprehensive record of his comments. To her shock and amazement, the officer stopped and asked that her deputy join the discussion to hear my complaint. The supervisor thought it would be a meeting addressing his complaints, but I was better prepared and turned the tables on him.

The officer said she was appalled if my allegations were true and asked my supervisor to address my complaints in the following weeks. The supervisor decided to take early retirement, which suited me just fine.

I retired from federal service in 2007, paid at the rate of a GS-14 on a scale that goes up to a GS-15, starting my service as a GS-2 clerk. To my astonishment, after 15 years of retirement, my pension has paid me more than I had earned in my 30 years of service, a career perk that most people do not get to enjoy.

***

However, in 1993, a co-worker, Jim Ivery, gave me a flyer advertising a trip to Senegal, Africa. I convinced my childhood friend, Robert, my best friend on Sheriff Road, to join me on the trip. Robert, Raheem, and Carl Bennett used to gather together to watch pro boxing fights on TV. Robert was doing well working for a CPA firm but seemed uneasy during the trip. Little did I know that this would be our last time hanging out together.

To Be Loved

Tragically, upon our return home, Robert had a heroin relapse and overdosed. He was left in front of DC General Hospital as John Doe and remained in a coma. Raheem and I visited him at the hospital, reminiscing about our shared experiences from our youth. Raheem, being Muslim, prayed for Robert. Sadly, Robert never responded, and we left hoping he would recover. However, he did not.

In November 1996, I attended Robert's funeral with my 12-year-old daughter, Aminata. On the way to the funeral, I cried several times. This occasion marked our Sheriff Road crew's first reunion since our wild adolescence 25 years prior. Unfortunately, only Sly Squirrel and David Williams from the old crew attended. Carl Bennett and Kashaka, my other friends, were also present. I introduced them to my daughter, and we chatted cordially. Sly, who had aged considerably, appeared around age 70 despite being only 41. His involvement with drugs had taken its toll, leaving a permanent scowl on his face. Squirrel, who seemed to never let go of an adolescent grudge, looked like he had experienced the horrors of war, with reddened eyes and a dazed appearance. The last I heard about Tyson, my former hustling buddy, was that he had been in and out of prison and drug rehabilitation. Gilbert worked hard at the 7-Up bottling plant but sadly died from a heroin overdose in 1982, and Smooth, who had converted to Islam and disappeared, was also absent. Nutbush, known for his big heart and cool style, was last seen stumbling in an alcohol stupor in Southeast DC. Jake, our nemesis, had passed away from HIV. David Williams, whom I narrowly escaped a car

U.S. Mint: Internet Project Manager

accident with as a kid, had become a self-employed auto mechanic and motorbike racer. Sadly, he would later have a relapse into heroin abuse and pass away from complications of HIV.

I had come to terms with the painful life choices many of us had made. Some had never taken control of their lives, continuing to live as we did in our teenage years, engaging in self-destructive behaviors. Others never saw themselves beyond their roles in the neighborhood during adolescence. These reasons for "staying true to the hood and not changing" are detrimental in adulthood. We were systematically programmed and conditioned to self-destruct rather than prosper and were largely unaware of it. Reunions for others, such as high school or college reunions, often celebrate their prosperity and allow them to build networks. I no longer felt a strong connection with my old buddies. Instead, I preferred to remember how we were, wounded yet full of youthful energy, turning from home to the streets.

Robert was buried in the Grand Bubba we had purchased during our trip to Africa. It was hard to imagine that my teenage best friend would ever die. I spoke at his funeral, reminiscing about our bond and the brave act he had performed when he saved my life by running while a guy started shooting after us. Attendees laughed as I shared anecdotes, but I also spoke seriously, acknowledging that Robert had fought a tough battle in life. Although he had fallen, many of us brother warriors would continue to rise. I pledged to stand and

To Be Loved

continue the struggle for a life of dignity on his behalf. As they lowered his casket into the grave, I placed a Kente Cloth ribbon as a final tribute.

The Trauma

By God's grace, I have overcome a great deal of trauma born of racism, poverty, neglect and abuse. I have long revamped my self-worth and self-esteem, underscoring their importance to my well-being. I determined my destiny and realized most of my dreams. A self-made man, and one of my role models.

To overcome a life born in adversity I developed a steely resolve in childhood that I would have what life had to offer; I wasn't gonna be denied.

I own my home in a gated community in the Washington, D.C. suburbs. I have traveled a couple continents, several countries, and many U.S. landmarks and hotspots. I am an avid tennis player, having played in local, regional and national tennis tournaments in cities across the country. Despite my past, I have learned to navigate life's challenges and my trauma with finesse; I make a difference in almost every scenario that I am involved. I often exceed expectations. However, I couldn't repair that soft stuff: the emotional trauma. You may fix almost everything, but you can't go back in childhood and redo your emotional motherboard.

Therefore, emotional love challenges me in all relationships.

To Be Loved

I learned self-love working hard at achieving and warranting positive attention; and by loving my children, nieces, and nephews. I aimed to love them like I thought I have been loved as a child.

Despite my efforts to avoid passing on intergenerational trauma, it is a burden I carry. Over the years, Pat, Ngina's mother, would contact me through social media. On one occasion, I suggested resolving the lingering paternity question, once and for all, with a DNA test. Initially, she agreed, but then waivered, claiming we had already done a blood test (which we hadn't). Next, she blocked me from messaging her. The issue of paternity reigned unresolved for 50 years.

Several years had passed since I last saw Ngina, again, when I invited her along with other adult daughters to my home for a dinner. We had a great time. Despite my uncertainty about parenting Ngina, I have never rejected her. However, Ngina admitted that she never bonded with me. While years later, Ngina and I lost touch again, her daughter, Brea, mother of two daughters, Charli Amor and Blu, remained connected with me on social media. I shared her grandmother's text with her and pleaded with her to urge her grandmother to participate in a DNA test. After six weeks, the test results returned, indicating a 99% likelihood of me being Brea's biological grandfather.

I was stunned and overwhelmed by the revelation; relieved to finally know that I am Ngina's father. How could I have been so wrong all those

The Trauma

years? I felt shock, anger, and deep sorrow for the pain my suspicions had caused. We had lost precious time to doubt and uncertainty that may never be recovered. I apologized to Brea, and Ngina by text and expressed my desire to meet with them and apologize and make amends for my terrible mistake. I just needed to know the truth. However, my appeals to Pat and Ngina have gone unanswered.

Instead, Ngina, despite having lived with me on two separate occasions, each time after 6 months to a year, she would leave, without complaint, except she felt that she needed to be with her mother. I had treated her with the same love and attention that I bestowed on Kwanza and Aminata, as much as Ngina would allow. Regardless of my overtures to Ngina, always seemed emotionally inaccessible to me.

Following Ngina's lead, when Kwanza and Aminata became young adults, they behaved similarly, making me feel they had outgrown me in their lives. It seemed that independence from their weekend Dad had become a badge of maturity. I had become an asterisk; someone they would rather not have to explain to their friends.

And, after giving their growth and development all I had, my daughters have rarely shown gratitude for my sacrifice to maintain a fruitful presence in their life against their resentful mothers' resistance, and when they were children and needed me most.

To Be Loved

Instead they have shown mostly increasing angst, with arguments, and periods of not speaking; treating me like I imagine they would treat an errant boyfriend, rather than their father.

Today, I protect my happiness at all costs. I have invested in my happiness and in those around me; not only because I love being positive-centric and enriching others but also because it is the lack of love and appreciation, especially among adults, who haven't learned better, which triggers my history of pain and rejection: the trauma.

I am still overly sensitive to people, including family and friends, who fail to appreciate my positive nature. I have witnessed nieces and nephews whom I had helped to care for growing up, and instead of showing me gratitude for the positive role I have played in their lives, they have chosen to disrespect me, including a couple of nephews even wanted to fight me. I refuse to go down my rabbit hole of trauma. Respect is not negotiated; it is earned; it is deserved and granted. And I refuse to tolerate disrespect.

I will challenge people, but I will not disrespect them, unless they are deliberately offensive. If one continues disrespecting me, whether family, friend, or foe, I will likely quietly withdraw my interactions; I lack the emotional soft tissue or energy necessary to negotiate mutual respect.

The Trauma

Good Timber

The man who never had to toil

To Gain and farm his patch of soil,

Who never had to win his share

Of sun and sky and light and air,

Never became a manly man

But lived and died as he began.

Good timber does not grow with ease,

The stronger the wind, the stronger the trees..."

Excerpt from, "Good Timber," by Douglas Malloch.

***

Tennis friends introduced me to a budding tennis player who I could work with in more ways than one. She is Beverly Taylor, a vivacious, 5 foot 4, muscular, "forever athlete" and unassuming matriarch of her family.

Mother of a daughter and two sons in their 30s-40s, 7 grandchildren, and one great-grandson, Beverly, at age 65. She is the second oldest of 8 sisters, widowed and grieving for two years when a mutual friend thought

To Be Loved

I could be just the spark she needed. I was reluctant for fear that old habits from long marriages. Our friend persisted. I was introduced to Beverly on the tennis courts and was struck by her green eyes, brownish-blonde natural locks (that changes shades of brown to blonde depending on the season); she would be the missing piece in my life's puzzle.

An alpha woman, Beverly has many friends. She is a hand dancer, a former dance teacher, and a tax preparer. A USTA League coach for two tennis teams, and a board member of the Prince Georg's Tennis Education Foundation, Beverly is a walker, (a former marathon walker) who shops only organic food, is a great cook who is famous for her catered seafood pasta salad. We both tested negative for Covid-19 and have since been inseparable for nearly three years. Her family calls me "Mr. Ron" or "Poppa Ron." Beverly is very loving family matriarch; her family has get-togethers periodically like my family did when we were younger. I asked Beverly to live with me a year ago. Yep, we are planning our wedding and our happily ever after.

The End

About the Author

I am a writer, photographer, traveler, and avid tennis player. I worked from 1977 to 2000 as a public affairs specialist for the federal government. In 2000, I became an information technology specialist with another federal agency and in 2007, I retired. I also freelanced journalism for five years, with articles published in local media from across the country, leading to appearances on several television and radio stations. I served as president of the African American Writers Guild,1989-1992.

Born in Manhattan, N.Y., I grew up as the third child in a family of eight children in Washington, D.C. I am the father of three daughters, and two grandchildren, and two great-grandchildren. Since graduating from the University of the District of Columbia in 1980, I have lived in Prince Georges County, Maryland.

www.ingramcontent.com/pod-product-compliance
Lightning Source LLC
Chambersburg PA
CBHW050333010526
44119CB00004B/134